John Collinsworth Simmons

The kingdom and comings of Christ, wherein is explained the prophecies of Daniel

John Collinsworth Simmons

The kingdom and comings of Christ, wherein is explained the prophecies of Daniel

ISBN/EAN: 9783337274900

Printed in Europe, USA, Canada, Australia, Japan

Cover: Foto ©Lupo / pixelio.de

More available books at **www.hansebooks.com**

THE KINGDOM

AND

COMINGS OF CHRIST,

WHEREIN IS EXPLAINED

THE PROPHECIES OF DANIEL, THE PREDICTIONS OF
JESUS WITH REFERENCE TO THE DESTRUCTION OF JERUSALEM.
AND THE BOOK OF REVELATION.

BY REV. J. C. SIMMONS, D.D.,
Of the Pacific Conference.

"Whoso readeth, let him understand."

PRINTED FOR THE AUTHOR.
PUBLISHING HOUSE OF THE M. E. CHURCH, SOUTH.
BARBEE & SMITH, AGENTS, NASHVILLE, TENN.
1891.

DEDICATION.

To My Only Living Brother,

REV. W. A. SIMMONS.
Of the North Georgia Conference,

With Whom I Have Kept Up a Weekly Correspondence for More Than a Quarter of a Century,

THIS BOOK IS AFFECTIONATELY DEDICATED.

The Author.

PREFACE.

God established the Church of Jesus Christ in Eden immediately after the fall. Man showed his sorrow for sin by making aprons and hiding from God. When called to account, he confessed his sin, and God at once provided a Saviour—"the seed of the woman." And however brief the account given in Genesis, yet full and explicit explanations of the plan of salvation were doubtless given at once; and man was instructed as to how he was to become reconciled to God. And now, lest he should come direct to the tree of life without the mediation of Christ, and eat and live forever as he was, God "drove out the man; and he placed at the east of the garden of Eden cherubim, and a flaming sword which turned every way, to keep the way of the tree of life." Here man was to worship God through Christ, and through him and him alone he was to "have right to the tree of life." The cherubim here are identical with those found in the tabernacle and temple with their wings shadowing the mercy-seat; and what is called a "flaming sword" here was the "shekinah," as it was called in the temple worship. And all this was not to keep man from the tree of life, but to *preserve* the way of the tree of life. There were symbols of Divinity perpetually present to man before the flood. In Hebrews ix. Paul speaks of these symbols, and shows that they were ordained of God until "Christ being come a high priest of good things to come, by a greater and more perfect tabernacle, not made with hands, that is to say, not of this building; neither by the blood of goats and calves, but by his own blood he entered in once into the holy place, having obtained eternal redemption for us." And again: "For Christ is not entered into the holy places made with hands, which are the figures of the true; but into heaven itself, now to appear in the presence of God for us." Evidently there was at the east of the garden of Eden a mercy-seat, with cherubim on either end of it, whose wings shadowed this mercy-seat, and over which was the shekinah. Here man was to bring the blood of his sacrifice and sprinkle it on the mercy-seat, in faith of the blood of Jesus Christ, who, in the fullness of time, should enter into the "true tabernacle which the Lord pitched, and not man," and sprinkle the mercy-seat in the presence of God with his own blood.

Hence we see that the Church of Jesus Christ has been the same in all ages, but there have been different dispensations; and, while the worship of God through Christ has been identical in all ages, yet God has adapted this worship to man's surroundings and condition. From the fall to the flood, men worshiped God here at the east of the garden of Eden. From the flood to Moses, men erected altars and worshiped God where it was most convenient for them; for we read that Noah, Abraham, Isaac, Jacob, and others built altars, and worshiped God. When God gave the law by the hand of Moses, then the tabernacle was erected, and men came unto that. When they reached the promised land, God chose Jerusalem as the place of worship; and here it was observed until Christ came, was crucified, rose from the dead, and ascended on high "to appear in the presence of God for us." From that time to the present, men "worship him in spirit and in truth," "for God is a Spirit: and they that worship him must worship him in spirit and in truth."

All along through the ages the coming of Christ was promised: first, as the "seed of the woman;" then as "the seed of Abraham;" then as the "Star of Jacob;" then as the "Son of David," etc. As the time of his coming approached, the prophecies concerning him became more and more explicit, and revelations of him more abundant. His *first coming* was in the flesh; his *second coming* was after his ascension, when he came to judge and overthrow the Jewish nation; his *third coming* will be at the end of time, to judge the quick and the dead.

There has been much confusion in the minds of many with reference to the prophecies concerning these several comings of Christ, and we propose to try and present these comings in their regular order, pointing out the prophecies connected with each one. It is not our purpose so much to combat the errors that have arisen in the minds of many as it is to present the truth. If the views we shall present be correct, then all others opposed to them must be false. We do not profess to be wiser than others, nor are we so vain as to think we are infallible.

In our researches we have availed ourselves of every help in our reach. We have adopted no man's theory as a whole; but after studying the subject, first in the Bible itself and then with the help of others, we have formulated our own views, and shall ask the reader to examine them as carefully and prayerfully while reading as we have done before writing.

We shall not burden our work with quotation marks; but, here and now, acknowledge our indebtedness to Rev. T. O. Summers, Rev. Henry Cowles, and Canon Farrar. When we make any extended quotations from these or other authors, we will make due acknowledgment, but do not feel it necessary to mark every thought suggested by them.

In all our work we have labored to make the Scripture its own interpreter. Often symbols in the New Testament can be explained and understood only by referring to the same symbols as used in the Old Testament.

CONTENTS.

CHAPTER I.

First Coming of Christ to Set Up a Kingdom—Second Coming to Judge the Jews—Four Parallel Visions of Daniel—Nebuchadnezzar's Dream 13

CHAPTER II.

Vision of the Four Beasts—The Ten Kings—The Little Horn Antiochus Epiphanes—The Ancient of Days—Christ's Kingdom—An Angel Explains the Vision 20

CHAPTER III.

The Third Parallel Vision—The Medo-Persian Empire—The Grecian Empire—The Four Kingdoms—Syria and Egypt—Antiochus Epiphanes—A Day Not a Year in Prophecy—Cleansing the Sanctuary—The Vision Explained—Death of Antiochus—The Little Horn Not Papal Rome 37

CHAPTER IV.

Daniel's Confession and Prayer—Gabriel Comes to Explain—When Christ Is to Suffer and Die—His Kingdom Established.. 62

CHAPTER V.

The Fourth Parallel Vision—The Angel Comes to Explain What Should Befall the Jews—Michael the Archangel.. 76

CHAPTER VI.

The King of Persia—Xerxes—Alexander—Egypt and Syria, Their Wars and Intrigues—Antiochus Epiphanes; His Vileness—His Punishment of the Jews—He Profanes the Temple—The Daily Sacrifice Taken Away—Persecution of the Jews—Judas Maccabeus—Death of Antiochus Epiphanes............................. 83

Chapter VII.

Trials and Persecutions of the Jews—The Seven Brethren and Their Mother Martyred—The Resurrection to Joy and Shame—The Thousand Two Hundred and Ninety Days—The Sanctuary Cleansed—The Kingdom of Christ. 108

Chapter VIII.

The Prophecies of the Old Testament Center in Israel—False Interpretations—The Triumphal Entry of Jesus into Jerusalem—Its Object—The Fig-tree Cursed—The Two Sons—Parable of the Vineyard—Marriage of the King's Son—Scribes, Pharisees, and Herodians Assail Jesus—Their Hypocrisy Unveiled—Prophecy Concerning the Destruction of Jerusalem.................. 121

Chapter IX.

The Book of Revelation—Letters to the Seven Churches—The Book Sealed with Seven Seals—Sealing of the Saints—The Seven Trumpets............................ 160

Chapter X.

The Angel with the Little Book—The Temple and Altar Measured—The Two Witnesses—The Third Woe....... 207

Chapter XI.

The Second Great Persecuting Power, Pagan Rome—The Messiah Born—The Dragon—The Beast from the Sea—The Beast from the Earth—The Lamb on Mount Sion—The Fall of Babylon, or Rome...................... 223

Chapter XII.

The Seven Golden Vials—Unclean Spirits Like Frogs—Preparations for the Great Battle—Judgment of the Great Whore, and Who She Is—The Joy Over the Fall of Babylon—The King of Kings and His Armies—The Fowls Summoned to the Great Supper—The Beast and the False Prophet Cast into the Lake of Fire—The Dragon Cast Into the Pit—The Millennium—The Judgment-day..... 249

Contents.

CHAPTER XIII.

The New Heaven and the New Earth—The New Jerusalem
The General Invitation.................................. 292

CHAPTER XIV.

The Folly of Modern Adventism—Christ to Remain in
Heaven to the Judgment—Mistakes of Modern Adventists.. 313

THE KINGDOM AND COMINGS OF CHRIST.

CHAPTER I.

First Coming of Christ to Set Up a Kingdom—Second Coming to Judge the Jews—Four Parallel Visions of Daniel—Nebuchadnezzar's Dream.

THE coming of Jesus Christ in the flesh is one of the great events in the history of our race. Then he, as Christ the anointed King, was to set up a kingdom. John the Baptist began preaching, "Repent ye, for the kingdom of heaven is at hand;" and Jesus uses the same language. Matthew says: "From that time Jesus began to preach, and to say, Repent: for the kingdom of heaven is at hand." Mark says: "Jesus came into Galilee, preaching the gospel of the kingdom of God, and saying, The time is fulfilled, and the kingdom of God is at hand." In Luke we find this language: "And he said unto them, I must preach the kingdom of God to other cities also."

He came, then, to set up a kingdom. As he had committed the work of his Church to the hands of the Jews, they were looking forward to this coming with the deepest interest; and God, from time to time, revealed facts in connection with it. Nearly all the prophets spoke more or less of it. But to Daniel especially are we indebted for the terms so

(13)

freely used by the evangelists: the "kingdom of heaven," "the kingdom of God."

There was another coming of Christ in which the Jews were specially interested. They were to prove themselves unworthy of the trust God had committed to their hands; and shortly after the ascension of Christ he was to come in judgment upon them, destroy their city and nation, take from them the Church and its work and give it to others, who, as he expresses it, should "bring forth the fruit thereof."

These two comings of Christ are predicted faithfully and explicitly in Daniel. Some portions of these predictions have been misapplied and wrenched out of their meaning. We therefore desire to present these prophecies in their order with their meaning.

In the prophecy of Daniel we have four great parallel visions, all bearing on the same subject, all embracing the same facts and personages. The first of these visions is brought out in the dream of Nebuchadnezzar, as found in the second chapter. There the great empires and nations immediately preceding the "kingdom of God" are brought to view. The second is found in the seventh chapter, where symbols are used to represent these same empires and nations, with an addition of a king, who was to "make war with the saints, and prevail against them." The third is in the eighth chapter, where the explanation is a little more full and explicit.

And the fourth is in the tenth, eleventh, and twelfth chapters, where, toward the latter part, all symbols are dropped and a full explanation of them is given in plain language.

Bearing these things in mind, we will now proceed to give these several parallel visions in their order, and try to show their meaning. Without burdening the reader with the preliminaries which lead to this dream, we give it at once:

"Thou, O king, sawest, and behold a great image. This great image, whose brightness was excellent, stood before thee; and the form thereof was terrible. This image's head was of fine gold, his breast and his arms of silver, his belly and his thighs of brass, his legs of iron, his feet part of iron and part of clay. Thou sawest till that a stone was cut out without hands, which smote the image upon his feet that were of iron and clay, and brake them to pieces. Then was the iron, the clay, the brass, the silver, and the gold, broken to pieces together, and became like the chaff of the summer threshing-floors; and the wind carried them away, that no place was found for them: and the stone that smote the image became a great mountain, and filled the whole earth."

Daniel tells King Nebuchadnezzar: "Thou art this head of gold. And after thee shall arise another kingdom inferior to thee, and another third kingdom of brass, which shall bear rule over all the earth. And the fourth kingdom shall be strong as iron: forasmuch as iron breaketh in pieces and subdueth all things: and as iron that breaketh all these, shall it break in pieces and bruise. And whereas thou sawest the feet and toes, part of potter's clay, and part of iron, the kingdom shall be divided; but there shall be in it of the strength of iron, forasmuch as thou sawest the iron mixed with the miry clay. And as the toes of the feet were part of iron and part of clay, so the kingdom shall be partly strong and partly broken. And whereas thou sawest iron mixed with miry clay, they shall mingle themselves with the seed of men: but they shall not cleave one to another, even as iron is not mixed with clay. And in the days of these kings shall the God of heaven set up a kingdom, which shall never be destroyed: and the kingdom shall not be left to other people, but it shall break in pieces and consume all these kingdoms, and it shall stand forever. Forasmuch as thou sawest that the stone was cut out of the mountain without hands, and that it brake in pieces the iron, the brass, the clay, the silver, and the gold; the great God hath made known to the king what shall come to pass hereafter: and the dream is certain, and the interpretation thereof sure."

These kingdoms were: First, the Chaldean, then in existence and in the height of its glory; second, the Medo-Persian, represented by the silver; third, the Grecian, whose sole representative was Alexander. For, as we shall see, Daniel makes no account of his father, Philip, or of that portion of the Grecian empire found in Europe. He deals only with that part which comes in contact with his people and affects the kingdom of Jesus Christ, as seen in this vision. The image seen in this dream is a compact, consistent image, occupying the same ground, and composed of the same people, as we shall see in our further investigations. The Grecians, under Alexander, overthrew the Medo-Persian empire. The fourth was that which immediately succeeded the Grecian empire in Asia—the field on which the others had existed.

Alexander died in Babylon in the height of his glory, leaving no definite instructions as to his successor. It is said that upon being asked to whom he bequeathed his empire he replied, "To the strongest," or, as otherwise reported, "To the worthiest," adding the very natural prediction that he foresaw a bloody competition at his funeral games. He left no born legitimate offspring, but his wife, Roxana, was at the time of his death about to become a mother. Both she and the child to whom she gave birth fell victims to the jealousy of one of the competitors for his throne. After a struggle of more than twenty years between contending parties, his vast dominions were divided into four great kingdoms by four of his principal generals. Cassander took Macedon, with part of Greece; Lysimachus established himself upon the throne of Thrace; Seleucus became master of Syria and nearly all the countries which had composed the Persian monarchy, founding the dynasty of the Seleucidæ; and Ptolemy became King of Egypt, commencing the line of the Ptolemies.

Now the portion with which the Jews came specially in contact were the Syrian kingdom and the Egyptian. In point of time these two kingdoms fill the two or three centuries immediately following the death of Alexander, B.C. 323. This divided state of the image is represented by the iron and clay mixed. There was the strength of iron in some parts of it, and the weakness of clay in others. During the existence of these kingdoms, or, as Daniel expresses it, "in the days of these kings shall the God of heaven set up a kingdom, which shall never be destroyed," and this is the fifth kingdom. Four of these kingdoms are earthly, one is heavenly.

We have this to guide us in this view of this vision. A clear beginning, a distinct end, and all the rest must lie within these extremes. The beginning is Nebuchadnezzar as representing the Chaldean kingdom; the end is Jesus Christ, representing the kingdom of heaven as set up by him in person during his incarnation.

The feet of this image have been placed by many interpreters of this prophecy from seven hundred to a thousand years after Christ. Rome has been looked upon as the iron kingdom. But mark you this does not fit Rome, but does fit the divided kingdom of Alexander in every particular —time, place, and policy. God was revealing to

Daniel what should befall his people "in the latter days" all along down to the coming of their Messiah. "These prophecies touch the political history of the kingdoms of this world *only* because these particular kingdoms sustained very special relations to the great kingdom that is not of this world, which lay in embryo in the Jewish state, yet nursed and guarded there under the perfect eye of God till the time was fulfilled and the kingdom of God truly come—*i. e.*, came forth visibly before all the world."

Daniel did not aim to teach universal history, or to point out the course of empires for their sakes; but he held to the fixed purpose of dealing only with those nations that affected his people, and had their bearing on the kingdom of Jesus Christ. Neither pagan nor papal Rome has any place whatever in these prophecies.

CHAPTER II.

Vision of the Four Beasts—The Ten Kings—The Little Horn Antiochus Epiphanes—The Ancient of Days—Christ's Kingdom—An Angel Explains the Vision.

DANIEL retained his high position during the rest of the reign of Nebuchadnezzar, and was continued in office throughout the reign of Darius and into the reign of Cyrus. His last recorded vision was in the third year of the reign of Cyrus. This vision is found in the seventh chapter of his prophecy. He says: "I saw in my vision by night, and, behold, the four winds of the heaven strove upon the great sea. And four great beasts came up from the sea, diverse one from another." These beasts did not come up all at once, but in succession. They symbolized different kingdoms. "The first was like a lion, and had eagle's wings; I beheld till the wings thereof were plucked, and it was lifted up from the earth, and made stand upon the feet as a man, and a man's heart was given to it."

There is no diversity of opinion, we believe, as to what this beast symbolizes. It is thoroughly Chaldean in every respect. Winged lions, winged bulls, and even winged men have been exhumed by the indefatigable Layard in his researches amid the ruins of Nineveh.

While Daniel is looking at this powerful beast

a change comes over it. Its wings are plucked; it is lifted from all fours and made to stand like a man, and a man's heart is given it, an evidence of its waning strength. Daniel had been connected with this empire in the days of its lion-like power. He now saw it waning to its fall, plucked of its swift moving-armies, and despoiled of its lion-like strength. And here we see the first point of parallel between this vision and Nebuchadnezzar's dream as interpreted by Daniel.

The beasts came in succession: "And behold another beast, a second, like to a bear, and it raised up itself on one side, and it had three ribs in the mouth of it between the teeth of it: and they said thus unto it, Arise, devour much flesh."

This was the Medo-Persian empire, and answers well to its character and movements. The side on which it raised up itself was Chaldea. This power, when it began to assume strength as a nation, made its first grand movement against Chaldea. The capture of Babylon by Cyrus is predicted in Isaiah (chapter xlv.), and is a well-known fact in history. The lion went down under the bear. The "three ribs in its mouth" may refer to the destruction of other nations, not now clearly known for want of an accurate history of this period. It and the "devouring of much flesh" denotes the subjugation of other nationalities, and the absorbing them into its own.

"After this I beheld, and lo another, like a leopard, which had upon the back of it four wings of a fowl; the beast had also four heads; and dominion was given to it."

This was the Grecian empire of Alexander. Perhaps no conqueror ever moved his armies with more celerity, nor won conquests more rapidly than did he. Hence he is symbolized by one of the most lithe and active of ravenous beasts, the leopard; and wings are added, an additional emblem of his swiftness. "Dominion given him" indicates his success in enlarging his empire. In the parallel vision (chapter ii. 39) the record is: "Another third kingdom of brass, which shall bear rule over all the earth." The "four heads" may or may not refer to the four successors of Alexander that precede the "little horn" king. Some think it refers to the intellectuality of the Grecians. We incline to the former opinion as more natural, and as coming in its proper place.

"After this I saw in the night visions, and behold a fourth beast, dreadful and terrible, and strong exceedingly; and it had great iron teeth: it devoured and brake in pieces, and stamped the residue with the feet of it: and it was diverse from all the beasts that were before it; and it had ten horns. I considered the horns, and, behold, there came up among them another little horn, before whom there were three of the first horns plucked up by the roots: and, behold, in this horn were eyes like the eyes of man, and a mouth speaking great things."

This fourth kingdom is that which immediately

followed the Grecian, existing first under Alexander's four generals, then under ten kings, and finally under Antiochus Epiphanes, who is symbolized by the "little horn." But let us look to the development of this kingdom as seen in this vision. The history of this kingdom is symbolized in this beast. It was "dreadful and terrible," especially to the Jews, Daniel's people. Never in their history did they pass through such dreadful scenes, and were encompassed by such terrors, as we shall see in the further development of this prophecy. It was "strong exceedingly, and it had great iron teeth." The Jews had no power to resist the armies brought against them, and they were crushed in the jaws of this monster as between great teeth of iron. "It devoured and brake in pieces, and stamped the residue with the feet of it." Antiochus Epiphanes robbed them of their treasure, despoiled their temple, stamped upon their most sacred rites, hurled their beloved priests from their places, and defied God and man. "It was diverse from all the beasts that were before it." All other conquerors had, if they did not respect the religion of the Jews, at least left them in the enjoyment of it. Not so this. Every appliance of power was brought to bear to break up the customs of the nation and introduce the worship of strange gods. "And it had ten horns." Now where and when are we naturally to look for these ten horns. Surely not in Europe; surely not hundreds of years after the coming of Christ in the flesh—but right here on the ground occupied by their kingdom, and during its existence. *They must exist* between the death of Alexander and the rise of Antiochus Epiphanes, and we hold that they must have some relationship to the Jews. And here we see no difficulty, inasmuch as Daniel himself (chapter xi. 5-27), in the last of the four great parallel visions, has pointed them out so clearly that nearly all commentators agree in naming them. But best of all the revealing spirit in this eleventh chapter has mapped out the movement of the powers of this period so distinctly that we can without difficulty find in the track of their contending armies all ten of these kings.

Of the four kingdoms into which the great Grecian empire was dissolved, two—Syria and Egypt—affect the Jewish nation especially. Five of these kings are from the North, or Syria; and five from the South, or Egypt. The five from the Greek-Syrian dynasty are: 1. Seleucus Nicator. 2. Antiochus Theos. 3. Seleucus Callinicus. 4. Antiochus the Great. 5. Seleucus Philopator. The five from the Græco-Egyptian dynasty are: 1. Ptolemy Lagus. 2. Ptolemy Philadelphus. 3. Ptolemy Euergetes. 4. Ptolemy Philopator. 5. Ptolemy Philometer.

These were not kings of separate and distinct kingdoms, into which the one great kingdom was divided, but five of them in succession sat on the throne of Syria, and five on the throne of Egypt. And, mark you, only those who came in special

The Kingdom and Comings of Christ. 25

contact with the Jews are reckoned. For instance, there was Ptolemy Epiphanes, who was put upon the throne of Egypt at the age of five years, and whose history amounts to nothing. Then there were two that reigned in the Syrian throne, covering a period of thirty-two years, that are intentionally omitted; but the revealing spirit points this fact out in chapter xi. 6, by saying: "In the end of years," etc. Thus this hiatus is indicated that there may be no mistake.

"I considered the horns, and, behold, there came up among them another little horn, before whom there were three of the first horns plucked up by the roots: and, behold, in this horn were eyes like the eyes of man, and a mouth speaking great things."

This "little horn" was Antiochus Epiphanes, every feature of the symbol answering to him. Three of the first horns were plucked up by the roots. He was the son of Antiochus the Great; his elder brother was Seleucus Philopator; and while there is a conflict among historians as to the cause of the death of these two, one on the throne and the other next entitled to it, yet it is asserted that Antiochus effected the death both of his father and his brother, thus "plucking up by the roots" these two horns that stood in his way to the throne. One of his first acts on coming to the throne was to turn his attention to the possession of Egypt, which was then enjoyed by Ptolemy Philometor, his nephew, son to his sister Cleopatra, whom Antiochus the Great had married to Ptolemy Epiphanes, King of Egypt. He subdued this kingdom, thus "plucking up another horn that stood in his way." In this horn were eyes like the eyes of a man, indicating the keen intelligence and far-seeing policy that characterized his every movement, "and a mouth speaking great things." His command was to change the religion of every nation subdued by him. On this point he was inexorable, as we shall see in the subsequent visions.

"I beheld till the thrones were cast down and the Ancient of days did sit, whose garment was white as snow, and the hair of his head like the pure wool: his throne was like the fiery flame, and his wheels as burning fire. A fiery stream issued and came forth from before him; thousand thousands ministered unto him, and ten thousand times ten thousand stood before him; the judgment was set, and the books were opened. I beheld then, because of the voice of the great words which the horn spake: I beheld even till the beast was slain and his body destroyed and given to the burning flame."

This refers not to the great judgment-day; but it, like the other, is symbolic language to express the providential judgment in time for the destruction of the fourth beast and his horns. Nations, as such, can only be judged in this life, or in time. We find that the final outcome of this judgment is in the fourth beast. This fixes it unmistakably to the period of which the prophet writes: "I beheld

The Kingdom and Comings of Christ. 27

till the thrones were cast down and the Ancient of days did sit." "Cast down" here does not mean overthrown or demolished, but it means *firmly set*. God is about to sit in judgment upon a guilty nation, and he plants his throne and seats himself ("the Ancient of days") upon it. The destruction of this nation must be done in righteousness after careful judicial inquiry into the crimes for which it is to suffer. Isaiah speaks of a time when he "saw the Lord sitting upon a throne, high and lifted up." And this was preparatory to judging his people. He had come unto his own, and his own received him not, and John says: "But though he had done so many miracles before them, yet they believed not on him: that the saying of Esaias the prophet might be fulfilled, which he spake, Lord, who hath believed our report? and to whom hath the arm of the Lord been revealed? Therefore they could not believe, because that Esaias said again, He hath blinded their eyes, and hardened their heart; that they should not see with their eyes, nor understand with their heart, and be converted, and I should heal them. These things said Esaias, when he saw his glory, and spake of him." Here the Lord was "upon his throne," that he might providentially judge his people when he took the kingdom from them and gave it to a nation bringing forth fruits of righteousness. Again Micaiah (1 Kings xxii. 19) says: "I saw the Lord sitting on his throne, and all the host of heaven standing by him on his right hand and on his left."

Ahab had filled up the cup of his iniquity, and was to be led to Ramoth-gilead to be slain, and God sits to judge him and prove the righteousness of the penalty inflicted.

"Whose garment was white as snow," a symbol of the purity of his character. He could not do wrong. "The hair of his head like the pure wool." Age is venerable. "The hoary head is a crown of glory if it be found in the way of righteousness." "His throne was like the fiery flame, and his wheels as burning fire." See a similar representation of God's throne as seen by Ezekiel in the first chapter of his prophecy. God moves to fiery judgments. His knowledge is not confined to a single spot; as a flash of lightning his messengers, that bear up the sapphire pavement upon which rests his throne, go wherever the Spirit bids. "A fiery stream issued and came forth from before him." His judgments are to be destructive: "Upon the wicked he will rain fire and brimstone, and a horrible tempest." It was with fire that he destroyed the guilty cities of the plain.

"Thousand thousands ministered, etc." His resources are illimitable; his attendants numberless. "The judgment was set, and the books were opened." No arbitrary proceeding; every thing done must be done for cause. A record has been kept, and now it is revealed to satisfy the world that all is done in justice.

"I beheld then because of the voice of the great words which the horn spake: I beheld even till the beast was slain, and his body destroyed, and given to the burning flame."

Hear the blasphemy of Antiochus Epiphanes, in which he speaks against the Most High, and proposes to change the religion of the Jews, ranking it on a par with the idolatrous worship of heathen nations. These are the sins for which he and his kingdom are to be destroyed by this righteous Judge. If the awful scenes described in these three verses (9, 10, 11) referred to the final judgment of the world, then that judgment precedes the first advent or coming of Christ instead of following his second advent, as we are taught in the New Testament. But they are scenes that transpired when the judgments of God fell upon this last of the four great kingdoms, with their last and blasphemous king, Antiochus Epiphanes, and when the God of heaven sets up the kingdom of our Lord Jesus Christ.

"As concerning the rest of the beasts, they had their dominion taken away: yet their lives were prolonged for a season and time."

"The rest of the beasts"—the first three. The judgments of God do not fall upon them so suddenly nor so terribly as they fall upon this fourth kingdom. These three, and their slower destruction, is contrasted with the swift and awful doom that falls on this fourth one.

"I saw in the night visions, and, behold, one like the Son of man came with the clouds of heaven, and came to the Ancient of days, and they brought him near before him. And there was given him dominion, and glory, and a kingdom, that all people, nations, and languages, should serve him: his dominion is an everlasting dominion, which shall not pass away, and his kingdom that which shall not be destroyed."

This passage graphically describes the setting up of the kingdom of Jesus Christ at his ascension. This is precisely the same event described in the first vision (chapter ii. 44): "And in the days of these kings shall the God of heaven set up a kingdom, which shall never be destroyed: and the kingdom shall not be left to other people, but it shall break in pieces, and consume all these kingdoms, and it shall stand forever." After the ascension of Christ the apostles with one voice testified to the fact that God had made him "both Lord and Christ." Hear them on the day of Pentecost when the Holy Ghost revealed the fact: "This Jesus hath God raised up, whereof we all are witnesses. Therefore being by the right hand of God exalted." And again: "Let all the house of Israel know assuredly that God hath made that same Jesus, whom ye have crucified, both Lord and Christ."

"Him hath God exalted with his right hand to be a Prince and a Saviour." Peter, at the house of Cornelius, when opening his commission to the Gentiles, said: "He is Lord of all."

Paul says (Eph. i. 20–22): "When he raised him from the dead, and set him at his own right

The Kingdom and Comings of Christ. 31

hand in the heavenly places, far above all principality, and power, and might, and dominion, and every name that is named, not only in this world, but also in that which is to come: and hath put all things under his feet, and gave him to be the head over all things to the Church," etc. And Peter says (1 Pet. iii. 22): "Who is gone into heaven, and is on the right hand of God; angels and authorities and powers being made subject unto him." We might fill pages with such quotations, but these are enough.

The disciples followed their Lord out to Olivet, and when they asked him, "Wilt thou at this time restore the kingdom to Israel?" he replied: "It is not for you to know the times, or the seasons, which the Father hath put in his own power. But ye shall receive power, after that the Holy Ghost is come upon you," etc. He bestowed his blessing upon them, and then "was taken up; and a cloud received him out of their sight." They saw him enter the cloud, and saw no more. But Daniel, in a vision, witnessed the full scene. He saw him "come with the clouds of heaven to the Ancient of days," and saw the dominion and glory spoken of by Paul and Peter given him. It was a grand sight—this inauguration of the Son of man. Now for the first time, as God-man, is he crowned Lord of all. Because of his entering the flesh and suffering the death of the cross "God highly exalted him, and gave him a name above every name: that at the name of Jesus every knee should bow, of things in heaven, and things in earth, and things under the earth; and that every tongue should confess that Jesus Christ is Lord, to the glory of God the Father." He was to enter upon that reign and conquest that should continue until all the kingdoms of earth should become the kingdoms of our Lord and of his Christ; and he shall reign forever and ever.

"I Daniel was grieved in my spirit in the midst of my body, and the visions of my head troubled me. I came near unto one of them that stood by, and asked him the truth of all this. So he told me, and made me know the interpretation of the things."

He wanted an explanation of the symbols and wonders he had seen, and he seeks light from "one that stood by," and he graciously explains: "These great beasts, which are four, are four kings, which shall arise out of the earth. But the saints of the Most High shall take the kingdom, and possess the kingdom forever, even forever and ever."

This explanation of the angel does not fully satisfy Daniel, for we find him saying immediately: "Then I would know the truth of the fourth beast, which was diverse from all the others, exceeding dreadful, whose teeth were of iron, and his nails of brass; which devoured, brake in pieces, and stamped the residue with his feet; and of the ten horns that were in his head, and of the other which came up, and before whom three fell; even of that horn that had eyes, and a mouth that spake very great things, whose look was more stout than his fellows. I beheld, and the same horn made war with the saints, and prevailed against them; until the Ancient of days came, . . . and the time came that the saints possessed the kingdom."

He seems to be satisfied with the knowledge he has of the first three. But the fourth troubles him, and he would know all about him, and he points out the things he would know of the angel. Daniel saw the consecutive order of the events unfolded in his vision. He saw the persecutions of the saints by this "little horn" until the Ancient of days took from him the kingdom and gave it to the saints. This gift follows immediately upon the overthrow of this "little horn," and not hundreds of years after, as must be the case if this "little horn" be papal Rome. The evidence in favor of Antiochus Epiphanes being this "little horn" will accumulate as we advance in this investigation; and if it be Antiochus, it cannot be papal Rome, and all theories based upon this fact must fall to the ground.

"Thus he said, The fourth beast shall be the fourth kingdom upon earth, which shall be diverse from all kingdoms, and shall devour the whole earth, and shall tread it down, and break it in pieces. And the ten horns out of this kingdom are ten kings that shall arise: and another shall rise after them; and he shall be diverse from the first, and he shall subdue three kings. And he shall speak great words against the Most High, and shall wear out the saints of the Most High, and think to change times and laws: and they shall be given into his hand until a time and times and the dividing of time."

This explanation is of vital importance in understanding this vision. The beasts are kingdoms. The fourth in consecutive order was different from the others, and the difference is pointed out. It is his hostility to God and his saints, as we shall see. The ten horns are ten kings. The little horn is yet another king arising after the ten diverse from them. So the "little horn" cannot be the papal Church, as many suppose; and all such applications of this symbol are wild and fanciful, unsupported by the prophecy, as explained by this heavenly teacher of Daniel.

We have shown that Antiochus Epiphanes, in pushing his way to the throne of this fourth kingdom, uprooted or subdued three kings: his father, Antiochus the Great; his brother, Seleucus Philopater, who took the throne on the death of his father; and Ptolemy. That he "spake great words against the Most High, and shall wear out the saints of the Most High, and think to change times and laws," is beyond a question.

Rawlinson says: "Antiochus, having not only plundered and desecrated the temple, but having set himself to eradicate utterly the Jewish religion, and completely Hellenize the people, was met with the most determined resistance on the part of a moiety of the nation." Again the same author says, when speaking of his death: "In the popular belief his death was a judgment upon him for his attempted sacrilege."

"And they [the saints] shall be given into his hand until a time and times and the dividing of time." On account of the wickedness of the Jewish nation, notwithstanding the few saints that still held firmly to the religion of their fathers, they were given into the hand of this vile king, and for three years and a half the daily sacrifice was suspended. "Time" here means a year, as we learn from its use in chapter iv. 16, 23, 29, 32. There the "seven times" means seven years, and the "time" here means one year; "times," the plural, two more; and the "dividing of time" a part of a year, which was in this case, according to the history of this event, six months—altogether making three years and six months. Thus we have the cumulative evidence that "the little horn" is Antiochus Epiphanes.

"But the judgment shall sit, and they shall take away his dominion, to consume and to destroy it unto the end. And the kingdom and dominion, and the greatness of the kingdom under the whole heaven, shall be given to the people of the saints of the Most High, whose kingdom is an everlasting kingdom, and all dominions shall serve and obey him."

This we have already explained (verses 9–11). History shows us that this vast empire went to pieces about this time, and that its fall was followed by the setting up of the Messiah's kingdom, which was "given to the people of the saints of the Most High." And it was but a little time until, as Paul tells us, the gospel "was preached to every creature which is under heaven." And again: "Their sound went into all the earth, and their words unto the ends of the world."

"Hitherto is the end of the matter. As for me Daniel, my cogitations much troubled me, and my countenance changed in me: but I kept the matter in my heart." The calamities that he foresaw coming upon his people greatly troubled this good man, and he laid the whole matter up in his heart.

CHAPTER III.

The Third Parallel Vision—The Medo-Persian Empire—The Grecian Empire—The Four Kingdoms—Syria and Egypt—Antiochus Epiphanes—A Day not a Year in Prophecy—Cleansing the Sanctuary—The Vision Explained—Death of Antiochus—The Little Horn not Papal Róme.

WE now come to the third of the great parallel visions of Daniel, contained in the eighth chapter. It was seen about two years subsequent to the one recorded in chapter vii. He says: "In the third year of the reign of King Belshazzar a vision appeared unto me, even unto me Daniel, after that which appeared unto me at the first. And I saw in a vision; and it came to pass, when I saw, that I was at Shushan in the palace, which is in the province of Elam; and I saw in a vision, and I was by the river of Ulai."

He was actually in Shushan when he had the vision, but in vision he was by the river of Ulai, as one in a dream conceives himself to be where he is not.

"Then I lifted up mine eyes, and saw, and, behold, there stood before the river a ram which had two horns: and the two horns were high; but one was higher than the other, and the higher came up last. I saw the ram pushing westward, and northward, and southward; so that no beast might stand before him, neither was there any that could de-

(37)

liver out of his hand; but he did according to his will, and became great."

The Chaldean empire lasted only a period of 88 years, from B.C. 625 to 538. At the time of this vision there remained only about 15 years of its existence; and hence it is dropped out of this vision. The prophet's stand-point is Persia, and here his vision begins. But the leaving out of Chaldea does not in any degree prevent this from being a parallel vision to the former two.

Gabriel tells Daniel (verse 20) that "The ram which thou sawest having two horns are the kings of Media and Persia." These are Darius and Cyrus. The kingdom itself is a united kingdom, and draws its king from either. The higher of these two is Cyrus, for he came up last in point of time. This kingdom pushes its conquests west, north, and south; never to the east. This is perfectly in accordance with history. There was no power that could stand before him. None "could deliver out of his hand."

"And as I was considering, behold, a he goat came from the west on the face of the whole earth, and touched not the ground: and the goat had a notable horn between his eyes."

This is a correct portrait of Alexander and of his movements, and so says Gabriel (verse 21). He comes from the west (Greece), sweeping over the "face of the whole earth," bearing all before him, "and touched not the ground," so rapid were his movements, so swift his marches. The "notable horn" was Alexander, Gabriel says, the "first king." So far as this kingdom affected the Jews, Daniel's people, he was the *first king*, and so far as his conquests embraced the territory of the two former kingdoms, he was the first. These visions have nothing to do with European kings or empires. They must agree chronologically, geographically, politically, and in respect of the Jews.

"And he came to the ram that had two horns, which I had seen standing by the river, and ran unto him in the fury of his power. And I saw him come close unto the ram, and he was moved with choler against him, and smote the ram, and brake his two horns: and there was no power in the ram to stand before him, but he cast him down to the ground, and stamped upon him, and there was none that could deliver the ram out of his hand."

With one dash of his pen Daniel pictures the overthrow of the Medo-Persian Empire by Alexander. Every touch is to life, every point verified by profane history. Years before, Xerxes, the King of Persia, had invaded Greece with his millions, and, although beaten back disgraced, yet these haughty Greeks were not satisfied, but nursed their hate and waited for their revenge. And now, as their daring leader gave them the opportunity, they "ran upon him in the fury of their power," and "cast him down to the ground, and stamped upon him." When we read the history of the wars waged by Cyrus with the Persian armies, when he "pushed westward, and northward, and southward" with a power that none could resist, we are struck with wonder at the amazing rapidity with which Alexander uses up these armies. "Twelve years sufficed him to master not Persia alone, but Tyre, Egypt, and all the east, even deeper into India itself than the ancient powers of Western Asia or Europe ever went before or after." No wonder he "touched not the ground" as he moved from west to east.

"Therefore the he goat waxed very great: and when he was strong, the great horn was broken; and for it came up four notable ones toward the four winds of heaven."

This mighty conqueror, who knew no defeat, but whose swelling empire bid fair to cover the known world, when in the zenith of his power and success was "broken." He died suddenly at Babylon—fell a victim to strong drink. "He died on the eleventh or twelfth day of his illness, about midsummer B. C. 323, being in the thirty-third year of his age and the thirteenth of his reign." He was surrounded by his victorious army, with plans for other wars; "when he was strong, the great horn was broken."

"And for it came up four notable ones toward the four winds of heaven." His kingdom was divided after some twenty years of conflict and bloodshed among his four generals. Of these four, the Jews stood in close relation only to Egypt on the south and Syria on the north. Hence the others are dropped from the visions.

"And out of one of them came forth a little horn, which waxed exceeding great, toward the south, and toward the east, and toward the pleasant land. And it waxed great, even to the hosts of heaven; and it cast down some of the host and of the stars to the ground, and stamped upon them. Yea, he magnified himself even to the prince of the host, and by him the daily sacrifice was taken away, and the place of his sanctuary was cast down."

Antiochus Epiphanes came from the Syrian kingdom, one of the four. And although he was but "a little horn" at the beginning, he became very powerful by dint of personal effort and energy. He pushed his conquests toward the south (Egypt), toward the east (Babylonia and Persia), and toward the pleasant land (Palestine). This always in Daniel and Ezekiel means Palestine. It was regarded by them as "the glory of all lands," not only because it was the inheritance of their fathers —the land "flowing with milk and honey"—but because God's sanctuary was there, and there he had recorded his name. These were the very directions in which Antiochus made his conquests. And here we will say to those who hold that this "little horn" is the papal Church, although the revealing angel makes no sort of mention or hint that it is, that Church never did push its conquests in these directions, and has never held possession for any length of time of "the pleasant land," Palestine. "And it waxed great, even to the host of heaven." It is a well-recognized fact that God's people are called his host. God said to Joshua: "Nay; but as the captain of the host of the Lord am I now come." Antiochus assailed God's people, and did all in his power to crush them out. He succeeded in destroying many of them. "And it cast down some of the host and of the stars to the ground, and stamped upon them." The stars here are symbols of the leaders, high priest, and elders of Israel. Onias, a high priest, was slain. Three noble Jewish deputies who went to meet the king at Tyre and obtain his interposition against Menelaus, who had offered a greater price even than the vile Jason, who had been made high priest in room of Ananias, were killed by his order. These are but a few of the many "stars" that were cast down by him.

"He magnified himself even to the prince of the host." He even dared to make war against the God of the Jews, making an effort to destroy his religion from the earth. "And by him the daily sacrifice was taken away, and the place of his sanctuary was cast down."

While he was in Egypt a false report of his death was spread among the Jews in Palestine, at which there was great rejoicing in Jerusalem. Antiochus, when he returned from Egypt, entered the city by force, treated the Jews as rebels, and commanded his troops to slay all they met. Eighty thousand were killed, made captives, or sold on this occasion. Antiochus, conducted by the corrupt high priest, Menelaus, entered into the holy

The Kingdom and Comings of Christ. 43

of holies, where he took and carried off the most precious vessels of that holy place to the value of one thousand eight hundred talents. He afterward sent Apollonius into Judea with an army of twenty-two thousand men, and commanded him to kill all the Jews who were of full age, and to sell the women and young men. (2 Macc. v. 25.) These orders were too punctually executed. These misfortunes were only preludes to what they were to suffer; for Antiochus, apprehending that the Jews would never be content in their obedience to him unless he obliged them to change their religion and to embrace that of the Greeks, issued an edict enjoining them to conform to the laws of other nations, and forbidding their usual sacrifices in the temple, their festivals, and Sabbaths. The statue of Jupiter Olympus was placed upon the altar of the temple, and thus "the abomination of desolation was seen in the temple of God." Who can doubt, when this prophecy and the history of this man agrees so perfectly and wonderfully, that the "little horn" is Antiochus Epiphanes?

"And a host was given him against the daily sacrifice by reason of transgression, and it cast down the truth to the ground; and it practiced, and prospered."

The Israelites had become very corrupt. In the first book of Maccabees we are told: "Whereupon they built a place of exercise at Jerusalem according to the customs of the heathen: and made themselves uncircumcised, and forsook the holy covenant, and joined themselves to the heathen, and were sold to do mischief." " By reason of transgressions" God gave this wicked king power over his people, and over his daily sacrifice to take it away. These judgments were looked upon by the righteous as sent upon the nation on account of sin and transgression.

Again we find in Maccabees: " Now I beseech those that read this book, that they be not discouraged for these calamities, but that they judge those punishments not to be for destruction, but for a chastening of our nation." God made use of this " little horn " to scourge his people for their sins, and hence " it practiced and prospered." It seemed to have every thing its own way.

" Then I heard one saint speaking, and another saint said unto that certain saint which spake, How long shall be the vision concerning the daily sacrifice, and the transgression of desolation, to give both the sanctuary and the host to be trodden under foot? And he said unto me, Unto two thousand and three hundred days; then shall the sanctuary be cleansed."

While one of the saints in the hearing of Daniel was speaking, another saint interrupted him with the question as to the duration of these calamities, including the " daily sacrifice, and the transgression of desolation, to give both the sanctuary and the host to be trodden under foot." This question was not to be answered for his satisfaction, but to be given to Daniel for his information. For Dan-

The Kingdom and Comings of Christ. 45

iel said: "And he said unto me, Unto two thousand and three hundred days; then shall the sanctuary be cleansed."

· As this is the first time we have come to a period indicated by days in this prophecy, and as the world has almost with one consent accepted the theory that a day in prophecy stands for a year, and all calculations of time in prophecy are based upon this theory, we will pause to examine into the correctness of it.

The great question is: Does the word "day" in prophecy mean a year? and are we to be governed by this principle in reckoning all other times, as months, years, etc.? We are indebted to Rev. Henry Cowles for valuable arguments and demonstrations on this subject. His dissertation at the close of his commentary on Ezekiel and Daniel is clear and exhaustive. He says: "So the broad principle is that prophetic notations of time must be multiplied by three hundred and sixty to get the real historic duration. I am compelled to discard this theory as utterly baseless, false, and of course mischievous and delusive."

But let us weigh this theory in the scale of God's word, and see if it will stand the test. Take a passage that is looked upon as strongly in favor of this theory (Num. xiv. 33, 34): "Your children shall wander in the wilderness forty years. . . . After the number of the days in which ye searched the land, even forty days, each day for a year, shall ye bear your iniquities, even forty years." Here a day means a day, and a year means a year—nothing more. God tells them they shall wander a *year* for each *day* of their search—nothing more. No one could misunderstand this language. If he had said, "Your children shall wander in the wilderness forty days," and the history had shown that they wandered forty years, then the case would have been in point. If, upon the other hand, this theory be true when God tells them they shall "wander forty years," he meant they should wander *fourteen thousand and four hundred years*, for that is forty years multiplied by three hundred and sixty. When God says, "Each day for a year," he means just what he says, and nothing more. He wanted their punishment to remind them of their sin.

Another proof text very analogous to the preceding is Ezekiel iv. 4–6. Ezekiel is commanded to lie on his right side forty days, and on his left three hundred and ninety days, before all Israel, to indicate that he bears (in symbol) the iniquity of Judah forty years, and of Israel three hundred and ninety. The language is: "For I have laid upon thee the years of their iniquity, according to the number of the days, three hundred and ninety days: so shalt thou bear the iniquity of the house of Israel. . . . Lie again on thy right side, and thou shalt bear the iniquity of the house of Judah forty days: I have appointed thee each day for a year." But observe throughout this passage that in every instance the word "day" is used for a common day, never in the sense of a year; and the word "year" means only one year, never three hundred and sixty years. A day here is used as the symbol of a year, and God plainly told the prophet so—nothing more, nothing less.

Again (2 Pet. iii. 8): "One day is with the Lord as a thousand years, and a thousand years as one day." But this is a two-edged sword in the hands of "a-day-for-a-year" theorist. Where "day" is spoken of it means a thousand years instead of one, and a thousand years becomes *one day*. So when it is said, "And they lived and reigned with Christ a thousand years," it meant but *one day*. And the devil's imprisonment of a thousand years is also shortened to a day. But the passage is not "One day is with the Lord *a* thousand years," but *as* a thousand.

But the passage most relied on, and the one, doubtless, that has given the clew to this theory, is Daniel ix. 24–27, the celebrated prophecy of the "seventy weeks." Mr. Cowles says of this: "The original word means, in its singular number, a seven, a heptad; and this may be a seven of days or a seven of years. The feminine plural is currently used for heptads, or sevens, of days; the masculine plural (which we have here) never by itself for the common week of days, but when a week of days is meant the word *days* is appended, as in Daniel x. 2, 3; and finally after a word, and a special form of a word, which simply suggests the idea of a seven (a seven of something), we must ask, A seven of what? and must look for our answer in the context, in the thought already before the mind. In the present case there can be no doubt that this thought is the seventy *years* of captivity. Then seventy sevens of *years* must be the sense of this phrase, and it involves no usage of the word day to mean a year; no usage of any current notations of time in a way to need multiplying by three hundred and sixty to get the actual time."

But to see the folly and weakness of this day-for-a-year theory it is only necessary to strike a few offensive blows at it. When fixing the time of the flood the Lord said: "Yet his days shall be a hundred and twenty years." Did he mean that in plain language? or did he mean forty-three thousand two hundred years? Again: "Yet seven days and I will cause it to rain forty days and forty nights." Was the flood to commence that day week, and continue a month and ten days? or was it to commence in seven years, and then keep it up for forty years? "Your children shall wander forty years in the wilderness." Surely fourteen thousand four hundred years would be a long time to wander, and yet this would be the time according to this theory. The captivity of Israel, about which Daniel had read, and of whose end he was so solicitous, would have left him in despair, for it was to be for seventy years, or twenty-five thousand two hundred years.

But let us come to Daniel's prophecy. He

The Kingdom and Comings of Christ. 49

prophesies of Nebuchadnezzar's insanity, and says: "Let his heart be changed from man's, and let a beast's heart be given unto him, and let seven times pass over him." And again: "Let his portion be with the beasts of the field, till seven times pass over him;" and "they shall wet thee with the dew of heaven, and seven times shall pass over thee;" and "they shall make thee to eat grass as oxen, and seven times shall pass over thee." All agree that Daniel's use of *time* in this way means *year*. Then seven times means seven years. Was Nebuchadnezzar to be with the beasts of the field, be wet with the dews of heaven, and eat grass like oxen for seven years, or for two thousand five hundred and twenty years? It will not do to have a theory to serve you only when it suits. Daniel's "time and times and the dividing of time" is built by the use of the same word; and it means, as all the advocates of this theory contend, twelve hundred and sixty. Then Nebuchadnezzar was among the beasts two thousand five hundred and twenty years. But is not this enough to satisfy any reasonable mind that the usage of the Bible is wholly against it; and that it is one of those strange errors into which, when some one falls, others follow without a thought?

We now return to the consideration of the time during which the daily sacrifice was to be taken away, the sanctuary and the host to be trodden under foot. The angel announces it at "two thousand and three hundred days; then shall the sanctuary be cleansed." The fixing of this time in the history of this period will do much to establish the truth of the position we have taken: That the "little horn" is Antiochus Epiphanes, and not the Pope of Rome or the papal Church. One grand reason why the day-for-a-year theorists hold so tenaciously to that theory is because only with it can they stretch Daniel's times to the period of this Church and its persecutions. Hold it to the common computation, and it falls far too short; but it does exactly fill out the time of oppression under Antiochus. The question is with Daniel, how long? How long are these oppressions to last? How long before the sanctuary shall be cleansed? These are of vital interest to him.

In fixing these two thousand three hundred days (six years, three months, and twenty days) we must begin at the end and follow the history back, as we can fix almost definitely the end or the cleansing of the sanctuary. This, according to the best authority, occurred December 25, 164 B.C., and an annual feast was to be kept in commemoration of it. 2 Maccabees x. 8 says: "They ordained also by a common statute and decree, That every year those days should be kept of the whole nation of the Jews." John tells us that this feast of dedication was kept in our Lord's time, and that it was in the winter. At this point, then, the two thousand three hundred days must close. Going back from this period three years and six months, we reach June 25, 167 B.C. For this period the daily sacrifices were taken away. No altar fires burned; "the transgression of desolation" reigned. Just two years before this, June, 169 B.C., Antiochus Epiphanes returned from his second military expedition to Egypt, greatly enraged against the Jews because he had heard that they had been making great demonstrations of joy over a report of his death. He fell upon the city with the sword, making a terrific slaughter of "the hosts of the Lord's people." These things we find fully recorded in the book of Maccabees. "He thought that Judea had revolted: whereupon removing out of Egypt in a furious mind, he took the city by force of arms, and commanded his men of war not to spare such as they met, and to slay such as went up upon the houses. Thus there was killing of young and old, making away of men, women, and children, slaying of virgins and infants. And there were destroyed within three whole days fourscore thousand, whereof forty thousand were slain in the conflict; and no fewer sold than slain." But the full period of twenty-three hundred days runs back yet a fraction of a year farther. The onslaught of Jason was probably in May, 169 B.C. The period named in our passage (six years, three months, and twenty days) should begin about September 5, 170 B.C. The author of the second book of Maccabees, in his fourth chapter, immediately preceding that quoted above, records the murder of the good Onias, long time a high priest, a "star" of the first magnitude, whose influence had long withstood the wickedness of the times; and the murder of the three Jewish deputies who went to meet the king at Tyre, and obtain his interposition against Menelaus. This Menelaus was a vile apostate; a minion of Antiochus, subserving his interests by drawing the people into Grecian customs and idolatry. Indirectly what he did in the way of persecuting the Jews was done by Antiochus himself. Hence this murder of four distinguished Jewish leaders should be set to the account of this "little horn." They all seem to have occurred in the year 170 B.C. Moreover it was in the year B.C. 170 that Antiochus made his first expedition into Egypt, in which he naturally passed through Judea. It is not strange that a period intended to cover the whole time of casting down "some of the hosts of the stars" unto the "cleansing of the sanctuary" should embrace the murder of Onias, and of the three deputies to Tyre, and also the period of his first military expedition through the country. "This is the amount of historical verification which I am able to obtain from any authentic source at my command. . . . This paucity of historic material is an ample apology for any apparent deficiency in making out the precise historic verification of this time period which refers to events so remote, and which gives us periods so minute as the number of days. And even this number (2,300) may be round and general, and not precise and particular. Yet the approximation which is obtained, despite such difficulties, will satisfy fair-minded readers."

"And it came to pass, when I, even I Daniel, had seen the vision, and sought for the meaning, then, behold, there stood before me as the appearance of a man. And I heard a man's voice between the banks of Ulai, which called, and said, Gabriel, make this man to understand the vision. So he came near where I stood: and when he came, I was afraid, and fell upon my face: but he said unto me, Understand, O son of man: for at the time of the end shall be the vision. Now as he was speaking with me, I was in a deep sleep on my face toward the ground: but he touched me, and set me upright. And he said, Behold, I will make thee know what shall be in the last end of the indignation: for at the time appointed the end shall be."

These verses describe the way in which Daniel obtained from the angel Gabriel an explanation of the vision. God was angry with his people for their sins. Never was there a time in the history of this people when there seemed to be more probability of their being carried away by the customs and false religion of the heathen. The Greeks, with all their refinement of manners and the attractiveness of their religious rites, their customs and their games, seemed likely to bear the whole nation away from the God and worship of their fathers. "Nor was their social position less perilous. The influence of Greek literature, of foreign travel, of extended commerce had made itself felt in daily life. At Jerusalem the mass of the inhabitants seemed to have desired to imitate the exercises of the Greeks, and a Jewish embassy attended the games of Hercules at Tyre." For these things God's indignation was kindled. And now, as Daniel desired to know of the final issue, Gabriel is sent to make him "know what should be in the last end of the indignation," assuring him that " at the time appointed the end shall be." He therefore begins to unfold the entire vision.

"The ram which thou sawest having two horns are the kings of Media and Persia. And the rough goat is the king of Grecia: and the great horn that is between his eyes is the first king. Now that being broken, whereas four stood up for it, four kingdoms shall stand up out of the nation, but not in his power."

This is so plain, especially in view of what has already been said, that it needs no further explanation.

"And in the latter time of their kingdom, when the transgressors are come to the full, a king of fierce countenance, and understanding dark sentences, shall stand up. And his power shall be mighty, but not by his own power: and he shall destroy wonderfully, and shall prosper, and practice, and shall destroy the mighty and the holy people. And through his policy also he shall cause craft to prosper in his hand; and he shall magnify himself in his heart, and by peace shall destroy many: he shall also stand up against the Prince of princes; but he shall be broken without hand."

When Daniel was describing what he saw, he says (verse 9): "Out of one of them [kingdoms] came forth a little horn." Gabriel says: "In the latter time of their kingdom a king shall stand up." Thus it is assumed that this king is a king of one of these four kingdoms, and the angel locates him in point of time. " In the latter time of their kingdom, when the transgressors [of the Jews] are come to the full." This king can be none other than Antiochus Epiphanes. The portrait of him is true to the life. He and he alone sat for the picture. No other can claim it. Two of the four kingdoms built out of the wreck of Alexander's empire had already run their course and become extinct when Antiochus ascended the throne. As a whole, these kingdoms were in "their latter time." His "fierce countenance" indicates the cruelty of his character. His command to put all the Jews to the sword, and his last threat to make Jerusalem a grave-yard, are a full answer to this feature of his character as pointed out by the angel. He was a most ferocious, passionate, cruel man. Moses describes the Romans, who were to effect the final overthrow of the Jews (Deut. xxviii. 50), as "a nation of *fierce countenance*, which shall not regard the person of the old, nor show favor to the young." That he should " understand dark sentences" refers to his resources of cunning, craft, and policy, as is more fully indicated in verse 25: "Through his policy also he shall cause craft to prosper in his hand." "His power shall be mighty, but not by his own power"—that is, he was not the rightful heir to the throne. He, by his unscrupulous craft, rooted up three other kings, thus taking their power. It was not his own. "And he shall destroy wonderfully." This he did wherever he went, but especially in Judea, and the wars and troubles he originated among them continued for nearly a quarter of a century after his death. "Craft prospered in his hand." He was ever planning and scheming, and was usually successful, not only in times of war, but "by peace [in time of peace] he destroyed many." "He shall also stand up against the Prince of princes." It was in his plan to overthrow the religion of the Jews, and not only did he issue his command to this end, but enforced it at the point of the sword. His last impulse was to return to Jerusalem and overthrow their religion, or annihilate them as a people. Thus he stood " up against the Prince of princes; but he shall be broken without hand." The author of Second Maccabees, chapter ix., when Antiochus was stricken with his last sickness and knew he must die, says: "Here therefore being plagued, he began to leave off his great pride, and to come to the knowledge of himself, by the scourge of God, his pain increasing every moment. And when he himself could not abide his own smell, he said these words, It is meet to be subject unto

God, and that a man that is mortal should not proudly think of himself, as if he were God." Also in his distress and remorse he vowed that if God would spare him, he would become a Jew himself, and go through all the world declaring the power of God. "This shows that he had arrayed himself against God with his eyes open, standing up intelligently against the Prince of princes. No wonder, therefore, that he was suddenly 'broken without hand.'"

"And the vision of the evening and the morning which was told is true: wherefore shut thou up the vision; for it shall be for many days. And I Daniel fainted, and was sick certain days; afterward I rose up, and did the king's business; and I was astonished at the vision, but none understood it."

" This vision is spoken of as 'the vision of the evening and the morning,' with reference to this phrase in the Hebrew of verse 14: 'Twenty-three hundred evening morning.' There can be no doubt that 'the vision of the evening and the morning,' mentioned in verse 26, is the vision of this eighth chapter, especially that part of it in which this phrase occurs, and which shows how long the little horn shall tread down 'the sanctuary' and the sacramental 'host.'"

In the 14th verse, where the two thousand three hundred *days* are given, the word translated days is "evening morning;" and the meaning is no doubt merely *day* in the sense of twenty-four hours, the time of one revolution of the earth upon its axis. This expression means a full day, made up of night and day, as if the inspiring Spirit intended that men should never fall into the error of claiming that a day here meant a year, or three hundred and sixty days.

Daniel is commanded to "shut up the vision; for it shall be for many days." Men of his day were not specially interested in these persecutions because they were so far off. As the time drew near then men would read them to profit. "Daniel fainted, and was sick certain days." The strain upon his nervous system was so great, the revelations so startling and important to him as a lover of God and his people, that he was completely overcome, was incapacitated for business for "certain days;" then he "rose up, and did the king's business." Doubtless he was, as he had been for many years, the Prime Minister at the court. He "was astonished at the vision, but none understood it." The things revealed in it were so strange, so wonderful, so unlike any thing ever revealed before, that it was not fully understood. And, as we shall find, it requires other visions and other explanations to enable him to understand it. One more vision, parallel to the three he had already had, with the plain and explicit explanation of the revealing angel, who dropped all figure and symbol, and gave the grand play of events, and then he could and would understand it.

So many have fallen into the error of applying

the little horn of this chapter to papal Rome that I cannot withhold some judicious remarks on this subject by Rev. Henry Cowles. He says: "A few words are due here respecting the theory of interpreting this chapter, which makes the little horn papal Rome. This little horn of chapter viii. cannot be papal Rome: 1. Because he is Antiochus Epiphanes, as has been shown. 2. Because this horn is a king; and therefore *is not a Church*, is not a great religious organization, is not even a kingdom. Let it be remembered that this is put especially on the ground of God's own interpretation. The current strain of the vision proper (verses 9-14) most fully implies that this horn is a king; but the interpretation (verses 20-25) affirms it, and so describes him throughout. This authority ought to be respected. Of course it will be by those who admit that he who presents thoughts to others, whether by symbols or in ordinary speech, is the best interpreter of his own thought; and that this universal law is *pre-eminently applicable to the omniscient God*. He surely ought to know what he himself means, and ought to be trusted to give his own meaning fairly. Consequently this argument settles the question. More is really gratuitous, useful mainly to show how many things seem to have been overlooked, or at least unaccountably disposed of, that should have compelled every student of these prophecies to reject the theory that makes the little horn papal Rome. 3. This king rises in one of the four kingdoms into which Alexander's empire was cleft. Papal Rome did not; in fact papal Rome could not, for the reason that every one of these four kingdoms had ceased some time before the Christian era—*i. e.*, some seven hundred years before any historian dates the rise of papal Rome. 4. He pushes his conquests 'toward the south [Egypt], toward the east [Persia], and toward the pleasant land [Palestine].' But papal Rome had on the south the Mediterranean Sea; made no footing in Egypt or Africa; had to give up the East to the Greek Church; never made any show in the 'pleasant land'—all her crusades through two fearful centuries of blood and toil becoming a magnificent failure. Yet she did push her conquests in precisely every other direction, thus reversing this description of the little horn. 5. This horn persecuted the Jews while yet Judaism was in force, and the Jews were the only known people of God. This papal Rome did not do, and *could* not, for the reason that they had ceased to be the recognized 'saints' of God, and Judaism 'had waxed old and vanished away' long before papal Rome was born. 6. This horn takes away 'the daily sacrifice,' which papal Rome never did, for God had taken it away forever at least six hundred years before papal Rome came into being. After a definite period of these persecutions and desecrations by the little horn, his power is broken and 'the sanctuary is cleansed'—in all which papal Rome was not, for the same very sufficient reason as above:

she was not yet in existence. 7. Finally, there is not one solitary point in this description which applies to papal Rome so specifically as to define her and distinguish her from any other persecuting power. Nothing in this chapter applies to papal Rome except those very general features which must pertain to any persecutor of the Church. The papal Rome theory, therefore, violates all just principles of interpreting prophecy. Especially it goes in the very face of God's own interpretation of this little horn as a king; hence *it cannot possibly be true*. It has absolutely nothing in its support, and every thing against it. From this position I infer that the little horn of chapter vii. cannot be papal Rome, for that horn and this are identical. As this cannot be papal Rome, neither can that. This entire course of reasoning applies in every particular with equal force against the theory that this little horn of chapter viii. is the Mohammedan power. There is not the first shade of an argument in its support."

CHAPTER IV.

Daniel's Confession and Prayer—Gabriel Comes to Explain—When Christ Is to Suffer and Die—His Kingdom Established.

CHAPTER IX. is an important one, and closely connected with the vision contained in the eighth. At the close of the vision there recorded there were important matters not yet understood. He says: "I was astonished at the vision, but none understood it." He saw the sore and dreadful punishment to which his people were doomed on account of transgressions. He saw that the king symbolized by the little horn, after stamping the saints of God under his feet, and standing up against the Prince of princes, should be broken without hand; and now he desired to know the full meaning of the matter. He first began by searching the writings of the prophets; and when he had read all that they contained on the subject, he set himself to find out the rest from God himself.

"In the first year of Darius the son of Ahasuerus, of the seed of the Medes, which was made king over the realm of the Chaldeans; in the first year of his reign, I Daniel understood by books the number of the years, whereof the word of the Lord came to Jeremiah the prophet, that he would accomplish seventy years in the desolations of Jerusalem. And I set my face unto the Lord God, to seek by prayer and supplications, with fasting, and sackcloth, and ashes: and I prayed unto the Lord my God, and made my confession, and said, O Lord, the great and dreadful God, keeping the covenant and mercy to them that love him, and to them that keep his commandments; we have sinned, and have committed iniquity, and have done wickedly, and have rebelled, even by departing from thy precepts and from thy judgments: neither have we hearkened unto thy servants the prophets, which spake in thy name to our kings, our princes, and our fathers, and to all the people of the land."

In Jeremiah xxv. 11, 12 he found this prophecy: "And the whole land shall be a desolation, and an astonishment; and these nations shall serve the king of Babylon seventy years. And it shall come to pass, when seventy years are accomplished, that I will punish the king of Babylon," etc. And in verse 14: "For many nations and great kings shall serve themselves of them also: and I will recompense them according to their deeds, and according to the works of their own hands."

This whole chapter of Jeremiah's prophecy is full of what God will do to those nations that "shall serve themselves" of the Jews. In reading this the whole soul of Daniel was stirred, and he set himself to find out all about it. The visions he had seen indicated that at the coming of the Messiah these things should be fulfilled.

The first thing he did was to lay the sins of the people, by confession, before God. This he does in the most thorough and humble manner, keeping nothing back, exonerating neither himself, the people, or their rulers. And while he confesses he draws the contrast between their unfaithfulness and the faithfulness of God " keeping the covenant and mercy to them that love him, and to them that keep his commandments.

"O Lord, righteousness belongeth unto thee, but unto us confusion of faces, as at this day; to the men of Judah, and to the inhabitants of Jerusalem, and unto all Israel, that are near, and that are far off, through all the countries whither thou hast driven them, because of their trespass that they have trespassed against thee. O Lord, to us belongeth confusion of face, to our kings, to our princes, and to our fathers, because we have sinned against thee. To the Lord our God belong mercies and forgivenesses, though we have rebelled against him; neither have we obeyed the voice of the Lord our God, to walk in his laws, which he set before us by his servants the prophets. Yea, all Israel have transgressed thy law, even by departing, that they might not obey thy voice; therefore the curse is poured upon us, and the oath that is written in the law of Moses the servant of God, because we have sinned against him. And he hath confirmed his words, which he spake against us, and against our judges that judged us, by bringing upon us a great evil: for under the whole

The Kingdom and Comings of Christ. 65

heaven hath not been done as hath been done upon Jerusalem. And it is written in the law of Moses, all this evil is come upon us: yet made we not our prayer before the Lord our God, that we might turn from our iniquities, and understand thy truth. Therefore hath the Lord watched upon the evil, and brought it upon us: for the Lord our God is righteous in all his works which he doeth: for we obeyed not his voice."

In this whole prayer Daniel keeps prominent the sins they had committed against light and knowledge, and God's righteousness in sending upon them the calamities against which he had so faithfully forewarned them by Moses and the prophets. (See this warning in Lev. xxvi. 14-46, and Deut. xxviii.-xxx.) And yet, in view of all these aggravating sins, he stands up to plead for forgiveness.

"And now, O Lord our God, that hast brought thy people forth out of the land of Egypt with a mighty hand, and hast gotten thee renown, as at this day; we have sinned, we have done wickedly. O Lord, according to all thy righteousness, I beseech thee, let thine anger and thy fury be turned away from thy city Jerusalem, thy holy mountain: because for our sins, and for the iniquities of our fathers, Jerusalem and thy people are become a reproach to all that are about us. Now therefore, O our God, hear the prayer of thy servant, and his supplications, and cause thy face to shine upon thy sanctuary that is desolate, for the Lord's sake. O my God, incline thine ear, and hear; open thine eyes, and behold our desolations, and the city which is called by thy name: for we do not present our supplications before thee for our righteousnesses, but for thy great mercies. O Lord, hear; O Lord, forgive; O Lord, hearken and do; defer not, for thine own sake, O my God: for thy city and thy people are called by thy name."

No more earnest prayer was, perhaps, ever offered by man. The whole soul of the prophet seems as if it would break away from the body in its ardent longings and absorbing supplications. He pleads in view of God's mercies, in view of his love to his people, in view of the fact that his own honor is involved, Jerusalem and the people are called by his name, in view of the desolations of the one and the distresses of the other, and then he pleads "for the Lord's sake," the Lord who had redeemed Israel, their Messiah, his Son. And then with a triple supplication he pleads with the Lord to defer not, for his own sake, and for the sake of the city and people called by his name. Such a prayer touched the heart of God, and a heavenly messenger was sent to reveal to him the hope of Israel and the world, the coming of Christ and the redemption he should accomplish through his death and sufferings. He says:

"And while I was speaking, and praying, and confessing my sin and the sin of my people Israel, and presenting my supplication before the Lord my God for the holy mountain of my God; yea, while I was speaking in prayer, even the man Gabriel, whom I had seen in the vision at the beginning, being caused to fly swiftly, touched me about the time of the evening oblation. And he informed me, and talked with me, and said, O Daniel, I am now come forth to give thee skill and understanding. At the beginning of thy supplications the commandment came forth, and I am come to shew thee; for thou art greatly beloved: therefore understand the matter, and consider the vision."

Every indication of Gabriel here shows that he had come to finish the explanation of the vision seen by Ulai, where he had appeared to Daniel, and given him some light. Daniel recognizes him as the same whom he "had seen in the vision at the beginning." And the angel announces to him that he had "come forth to give him skill and understanding." He tells Daniel that he is "greatly beloved: therefore understand the matter, and consider the vision." This puts it beyond a doubt that he had come to explain the vision, at the close of which Daniel had "fainted, and was sick certain days." He was physically too weak to bear more at the time, and he says: "I was astonished at the vision, but none understood it." It had lain heavy on his heart ever since, and now he set himself to find it out. God was to break the power of all the enemies of his people, and to set up a kingdom that never should be destroyed. His dominion was to be an everlasting dominion, and Daniel wanted to know just how it was to be accomplished. He had seen the little stone cut out of the mountain without hands break down and grind to dust the kingdoms of earth. He had heard that the last great foe to God and his people was to be broken without hand. But when? how? were the great questions that troubled him; and as he stood panting with the fervor of his petitions, Gabriel stood by him with full authority to give him all the information he asked for. It comes in the following language:

"Seventy weeks are determined upon thy people and upon thy holy city, to finish the transgression, and to make an end of sins, and to make reconciliation for iniquity, and to bring in everlasting righteousness, and to seal up the vision and prophecy, and to anoint the Most Holy. Know therefore and understand, that from the going forth of the commandment to restore and to build Jerusalem, unto the Messiah the Prince, shall be seven weeks, and threescore and two weeks: the street shall be built again, and the wall, even in troublous times. And after threescore and two weeks shall Messiah be cut off, but not for himself: and the people of the prince that shall come shall destroy the city and the sanctuary; and the end thereof shall be with a flood, and unto the end of the war desolations are determined. And he shall confirm the covenant with many for one week: and in the midst of the week he shall cause the sacrifice and the oblation to cease, and for the overspreading of abominations he shall make it desolate, even until

The Kingdom and Comings of Christ. 69

the consummation, and that determined shall be poured upon the desolate."

Before entering upon a full explanation of this wonderful passage we desire to give you what Rev. Henry Cowles says of the "seventy weeks," and in fact all the "weeks" contained in it:

" This English phrase suggests only the ordinary week of seven days, making the whole duration four hundred and ninety days. Inasmuch as the fulfillment seems to require instead four hundred and ninety *years*, it has been often assumed that this passage at least must be admitted to be a case of a prophetic day used for a year. A closer examination removes this case from the list of those proofs, explaining the phrase in another and much more reliable way. A Hebrew reader coming to this phrase would say at once: ' This first word is not the usual form for weeks of days.' The word means a seven, a heptad, and is formed from the numeral seven. The feminine plural is the form which is constantly used to denote weeks of days. This is the masculine plural, indicating at least something different from a mere week of seven days. There is no instance in the Hebrew Bible where this masculine plural form is used alone for *weeks* of days. In a few cases, where it means sevens of days, the word for days follows it to make the sense clear, showing that of itself it would not be taken in this sense of seven days. (See these cases, Dan. x. 2, 3.) In Ezekiel xlv. 21 the feminine plural has the word *days* after it, meaning the feast of sevens of days—*i. e.*, the Passover, which was held seven days—a case which shows that the primary sense of even the feminine plural is a *heptad*, and not properly a *week*. The use of the feminine plural in the sense of our common week may be seen in Exodus xxxiv. 22; Numbers xxviii. 26; Deuteronomy xvi. 9, 10, 16; 2 Chronicles viii. 13; Jeremiah v. 24. Further, when any thoughtful reader should meet the word *sevens* he would naturally ask: 'Sevens of what? Is this sevens of *days*, or sevens of *years*, or sevens of *centuries?*' He would expect to find the clew to his answer in the context. 'What has the writer been saying? There must be something in what he has said to give a definite clew to his meaning, for to say only "sevens" is to leave his meaning entirely indefinite.' Pursuing this train of inquiry, he would see in the present case a manifest allusion to the seventy years of captivity which is so vividly before Daniel's mind. It cannot be overlooked that Daniel is praying with the great thought of the seventy years' captivity before his mind. When the Lord sends his answer by Gabriel, he too understands that the seventy years of captivity are present to Daniel's thought, and therefore he only needs to say: 'Not that seventy *years* are assigned before the next great event, but seventy sevens.' On the strength, then, of these two considerations, either of them sufficient alone, and both entirely decisive, I account this period precisely seventy sevens *of years*, or four hundred and ninety years. The same usage prevails throughout this passage in the 'seven weeks,' the 'sixty-two weeks,' and the 'one week.' The word 'heptad,' transferred from the Greek language, precisely translates the original Hebrew. Or we might say *a seven*, meaning a period of seven units, leaving the particular sense of the unit to be learned from the contexts. Hence this is not by any means a case of a day for a year. It is only a case of using a Hebrew word meaning a seven, a heptad, a period of seven units, selecting a form that does not suggest a unit of days, but a unit of years."

Here then is the meaning of this passage as we understand it. The thought centers upon the setting up of the kingdom of Jesus Christ, the means by which it is accomplished, and the results to the Jewish people that will follow.

Daniel's thoughts in his scriptural research is upon the seventy years of the captivity and its termination. Gabriel tells him *seven seventies* or four hundred and ninety years are determined upon his people, and the holy city for the sacrifice of Jesus Christ for the sins of the world. By the death of Jesus he will finish the transgression, make an end of sins, and make reconciliation for iniquity. In other words, he will atone for sins. The word atonement means to cover. He will, with his blood, cover sins and bring in everlasting righteousness. The Mosaic economy was to pass away, but the purely spiritual worship to be brought in by Christ was never to be changed: it was "everlasting." When he should come, the great prophet like unto Moses, they should hearken unto him: no more should visions be needed, no more should prophets be required. He "was the true light, which lighteth every man that cometh into the world." Men were now to go into all the world and preach his gospel, tell what he said, call men to him as the only Saviour; hence he would seal up the vision and prophecy. But he would pour out his spirit upon the Church, thus anointing the Most Holy, enduing it with his power. All nations should come unto him, and righteousness should cover the earth as the waters cover the sea. His kingdom not being of this world, any man could hold allegiance to his earthly government and yet belong to his kingdom.

Now Gabriel begins to fix certain points in history from which to count. "From the going forth of the commandment to restore and to build Jerusalem, unto the Messiah the Prince, shall be seven weeks, and threescore and two weeks." Let us remember that this is not the decree issued by Cyrus (B.C. 536) to rebuild the temple, or, as he expresses it, to "build a house for God in Jerusalem;" but the one by Artaxerxes (B.C. 454), when he gave commandment to Nehemiah to go and rebuild, not the temple (for that had been built already), but Jerusalem. (See the first and second chapters of Nehemiah.) From this commandment (454 B.C.) "unto the Messiah the Prince, shall be seven weeks, and threescore and two weeks," making sixty-nine weeks of years, or four hundred and eighty-three years. Then it shall be four hundred and eighty-three years from that commandment to the commencement of the ministry of Jesus. Jesus began his ministry in A.D. 29. 454+29=483. Again Luke iii. 1 tells us that John commenced his ministry in the fifteenth year of Tiberius Cæsar—*i. e.*, in the year of Rome 782. The birth of Jesus Christ is usually put in the year of Rome 753. Now if we add twenty-nine to that, we have 782.

There is a division of the first number "seven weeks [49], and threescore and two [62] weeks." It is thought the forty-nine weeks of years indicate the time in which the city of Jerusalem was building. "The street [houses along the street] shall be built again, and the wall, even in troublous times." We have but to refer to the book of Nehemiah to see the truth of this when "half of the men wrought in the work, and the other half of them held both the spears, the shields, and the bows, and the habergeons;" and where all that wrought "worked with one hand and with the other hand held a weapon." "And after threescore and two weeks shall Messiah be cut off, but not for himself." Christ was crucified just at this time, "but not for himself." We find the New Version to read "and shall have nothing." His people rejected him. "He came unto his own, and his own received him not." They cried: "Crucify him!" "We have no king but Cæsar." So he rejects them, and gives them up to their doom. Hear what that is: "And the people of the prince that shall come shall destroy the city and the sanctuary; and the end thereof shall be with a flood, and unto the end of the war desolations are determined." The prince here is Titus, and the people of the prince the Roman army. They did come, and destroyed the city and the sanctuary, rolling over their ruined homes like a "flood." Their whole land was made desolate. Greater distresses no people ever endured.

"And he shall confirm the covenant with many for one week: and in the midst of the week he shall cause the sacrifice and the oblation to cease." The Jews were in the habit of dividing their time into "sevens," and the ministry of Christ is reckoned to take place in a week of years. But in the midst of it he, the great sacrifice for sin, was offered, and this ended forever the virtue of Jewish sacrifices and oblations. He caused them to cease, not as under Antiochus—for "time and times and the dividing of time"—but forever. "And for the overspreading of abominations he shall make it desolate, even until the consummation, and that determined shall be poured upon the desolate." This indicates that God had given up the city to the desolator because of the abominations there were in the midst of it. Corruption was in all her borders, and now the Roman eagle would swoop down upon it until its full desolation was consummated. Three times now had God, in visions, revealed the same things to Daniel, and through him to his people. Each vision brings him more and more into the light of his purposed dealing with his people, and yet the soul of this great man was not satisfied. He would know it all; and having succeeded by prayer and supplication before, he tries it again. He says: "I Daniel was mourning three full weeks. I ate no pleasant bread, neither came flesh nor wine in my mouth, neither did I anoint myself at all, till three whole weeks were fulfilled." Such earnestness as that must bring the desire of his heart. He is now an old man. He had been in the East now about seventy-four years; had been the prime minister under the several kings of Chaldea and Medo-Persia from Nebuchadnezzar to Cyrus. Many of his brethren had, under the decree of Cyrus, gone back to Jerusalem, and were busy building the temple; but he was still retained in the service of the king, whom, doubtless, he had influenced to liberate his brethren. Perhaps he felt that he could serve his people to better advantage in the court of their king than in Jerusalem, especially at his advanced age. That he still loved his country and his people is evidenced by this all-prevailing prayer, with which he obtained information for them more valuable than gold.

CHAPTER V.

The Fourth Parallel Vision—The Angel Comes to Explain What Should Befall the Jews—Michael the Archangel.

"IN the third year of Cyrus king of Persia a thing was revealed unto Daniel, whose name was called Belteshazzar; and the thing was true, but the time appointed was long: and he understood the thing, and had understanding of the vision." A thing was revealed. Not only were the symbols given, but the revealing angel at last dropped all figure of speech, and talked to him as a man talks to his fellow-man. "The time appointed was long" does not give the idea. The New Version has it more correctly: "And the thing was true, even a great warfare." As we shall find, the subject-matter of this vision pertains to great wars. It was so plain as revealed to him that he understood it. This vision is the fourth and last of the great parallel visions of Daniel. We will find it going over the same ground and revealing the same facts, with some additions, with less of symbols, and more of plain revelations.

"In those days I Daniel was mourning three full weeks. I ate no pleasant bread, neither came flesh nor wine in my mouth, neither did I anoint myself at all, till three whole weeks were fulfilled."

"The 'three full weeks' and the 'three whole

weeks' here are the same, and literally mean ' three sevens' (or heptads) as to days, the word 'days' being added to exclude what otherwise a Hebrew reader would think of: a week of years. The word for ' seven ' is precisely the same in form that occurred repeatedly in the passage of chapter ix. 24-27."

"And in the four and twentieth day of the first month, as I was by the side of the great river, which is Hiddekel; then I lifted up mine eyes, and looked, and behold a certain man clothed in linen, whose loins were girded with fine gold of Uphaz: his body also was like the beryl, and his face as the appearance of lightning, and his eyes as lamps of fire, and his arms and his feet like in color to polished brass, and the voice of his words like the voice of a multitude."

Hiddekel is another name for the Tigris River. This was a heavenly visitant revealing himself to Daniel for the purpose of communicating certain facts to him with reference to his people.

"And I Daniel alone saw the vision: for the men that were with me saw not the vision; but a great quaking fell upon them, so that they fled to hide themselves."

His companions, terrified at the sight that was presented to them, left him alone.

" Therefore I was left alone, and saw this great vision, and there remained no strength in me: for my comeliness was turned in me into corruption, and I retained no strength."

He stood his ground, although overcome by the sight, and hence he alone saw it all.

"Yet I heard the voice of his words: and when I heard the voice of his words, then was I in a deep sleep on my face, and my face toward the ground. And, behold, a hand touched me, which set me upon my knees and upon the palms of my hands. And he said unto me, O Daniel, a man greatly beloved, understand the words that I speak unto thee, and stand upright: for unto thee am I now sent. And when he had spoken this word unto me, I stood trembling. Then said he unto me, Fear not, Daniel: for from the first day that thou didst set thine heart to understand, and to chasten thyself before thy God, thy words were heard, and I am come for thy words. But the prince of the kingdom of Persia withstood me one and twenty days: but, lo, Michael, one of the chief princes, came to help me; and I remained there with the kings of Persia."

For three weeks Daniel had been mourning and desiring a full revelation of certain events concerning his people, much of which had already been revealed unto him. He was now nearing the end of life. God had blessed him with three visions or revelations, each one giving more of light and knowledge than the former, and now he set his heart to find out all that God was willing to reveal to him. The scene manifested as the heavenly instructor approaches is grand in the extreme, and the effect upon the old prophet is overpowering. He explains to him the cause of his delay in coming to his call. The prince of the kingdom of Persia withstood him one and twenty days. It does not lie within our province now to inquire into the nature and meaning of this invisible contest. It is sufficient for our purpose to know that the contest did take place, and that this was the cause of the delay. But the difficulty had been cleared away, and he says:

"Now I am come to make thee understand what shall befall thy people in the latter days: for yet the vision is for many days."

This is the key to the entire vision. It was to reveal to Daniel what should befall his people, the Jews, not some other remote nation. If we will bear this in mind, it will help us much in arriving at the truth of the vision. Then it was what was to befall his people in the latter days. This term has various meanings, or refers to various times. Jacob, when he had called his sons about him just before dying, said: "Gather yourselves together, that I may tell you that which shall befall you in the last days." The great body of the facts in this prophecy refers to events long prior to the coming of Christ. Baalam advertises Balak what Israel shall do to his people in the latter days. These events transpired in the days of David. (Num. xxiv. 14.) Isaiah (ii. 2), when prophesying of the days of Christ, calls the time "the last days." Micah (iv. 1) uses the same term with reference to the same time and event. But these are sufficient to justify us in placing the events of this prophecy, especially as the facts demand it, at a time prior to the coming of Jesus Christ in the flesh. In fact, the events prophesied transpired about three hundred and sixty years after the revelation made to Daniel. The last clause does not change this construction, for the word " many " is not in the original; it is " for yet the vision is for days," meaning that it was not to transpire immediately, but some time in the future. Some years must elapse before the main events should transpire.

"And when he had spoken such words unto me, I set my face toward the ground, and I became dumb. And, behold, one like the similitude of the sons of men touched my lips: then I opened my mouth, and spake, and said unto him that stood before me, O my lord, by the vision my sorrows are turned upon me, and I have retained no strength. For how can the servant of this my lord talk with this my lord? for as for me, straightway there remained no strength in me, neither is there breath left in me."

Daniel had thought and prayed so much and so earnestly for his people, and he had already had revealed to him so much of their coming sorrows, that now as another heavenly messenger stood before him with fresh revelations, in his age and the excitement of the hour, he was utterly prostrate: no strength, and hardly breath, was left in him. He was overcome at the prospect of receiving an answer to his prayer of three weeks' duration. But as he lay breathless upon the ground he says:

"Then there came again and touched me one like the appearance of a man, and he strengthened me, and said, O man greatly beloved, fear not: peace be unto thee; be strong, yea, be strong. And when he had spoken unto me, I was strengthened, and said, Let my lord speak; for thou hast strengthened me."

He was thus prepared and strengthened to receive the vision.

"Then said he, Knowest thou wherefore I come unto thee? and now will I return to fight with the prince of Persia: and when I am gone forth, lo, the prince of Grecia shall come. But I will show thee that which is noted in the Scripture of truth: and there is none that holdeth with me in these things, but Michael your prince."

The angel interpreter had not come without opposition, nor did this opposition cease with his coming. The prince of the kingdom of Persia, as we learn from verse 13, had hindered his coming for three weeks, and now while engaged in fighting with the prince of Persia, lo! the prince of Greece came upon the scene. But this valiant angel gives Daniel to understand that, notwithstanding this opposition, he would show him what was noted in the scripture of truth—not the Bible as we possess it, but what God had written with reference to his people. He also informed Daniel that he had a strong ally in the person of Michael, his prince. There have been various opinions with reference to Michael. Without reference to these opinions, we believe Michael to be none other than the Lord Jesus Christ. Twice only is the term "archangel" used in the Scripture, and each time preceded by the definite article, thus showing that there is but one archangel, and that this archangel is Michael. Jude says: "Michael the archangel, when contending with the devil," etc. Paul says (1 Thess. iv. 16): "For the Lord himself shall descend from heaven with a shout, with the voice of the archangel, and with the trump of God." Jesus says (John v. 28, 29): "All that are in the graves shall hear his voice, and shall come forth." Then the voice of the archangel and the voice of Jesus must be the same.

Here the revealing angel calls Michael Daniel's prince, and in chapter xii. he says of him: "Michael shall stand up, the great prince which standeth for the children of thy people." Taking all these things together, we are assured that this great prince, this archangel whose voice is to wake the dead at the last day, is Jesus Christ. He then stands with this revealing angel, and the assurance is enough to comfort Daniel in his ardent desire to know what shall befall his people.

CHAPTER VI.

The Kings of Persia—Xerxes—Alexander—Egypt and Syria, Their Wars and Intrigues—Antiochus Epiphanes; His Vileness; His Punishment of the Jews; He Profanes the Temple—The Daily Sacrifice Taken Away—Persecutions of the Jews—Judas Maccabeus—Death of Antiochus Epiphanes.

WE come now in this eleventh chapter to the explanation of the fourth and last parallel vision made to Daniel.

It does not begin with Nebuchadnezzer. He and his kingdom had passed away. The vision reaches back but a few years, only for the purpose of forming the connecting link. After the introductory remarks of the angel, "Also I in the first year of Darius the Mede, even I, stood to confirm and strengthen him," as Darius was carrying out the purpose of God as developed in his history, this good angel stood to confirm and strengthen him. In the second verse the revelation properly begins.

"And now will I show thee the truth. Behold, there shall stand up yet three kings in Persia; and the fourth shall be far richer than they all; and by his strength through his riches he shall stir up all against the realm of Grecia." This vision is not like the former, given in symbols, but in plain language, narrating briefly the great events that are to take place. Three kings after Cyrus, from whose reign the prophecy begins, were to sit on the throne before Xerxes—viz., Cambyses, Simerdis, and Darius Hystaspis. They are only mentioned to give the proper place to the fourth, who by his strength and riches stirred up all against the realm of Grecia. No fact in history is better attested than this; that Xerxes gathered to his standard nearly all of Asia for the purpose of invading the little kingdom of Greece. Various estimates have been made of the wealth of his armament and the number of his soldiers. The lowest estimate gives the number at five millions of men, while untold wealth was lavished upon the outfit. History gives account of no such display as this. There was nothing in the shape of soldiers or money that this monarch did not command. All Asia gathered to his standard as they never did to any other man's. So he actually "*stirred up all* against the realm of Grecia," but this is all that is said about it. Never was there a more signal failure. Hence the revealing angel passes on.

"And a mighty king shall stand up, that shall rule with great dominion, and do according to his will. And when he shall stand up, his kingdom shall be broken, and shall be divided toward the four winds of heaven; and not to his posterity, nor according to his dominion which he ruled: for his kingdom shall be plucked up, even for others besides those."

With rapid touches the angel brings the conqueror of the Persians to view, Alexander the

The Kingdom and Comings of Christ. 85

Great, and in few but forcible words tells that he shall stand up, rule with great dominion, and do according to his will, and then while in the midst of his power and dominion his kingdom shall be broken and divided to the four winds of heaven, and not to his posterity, etc. The Greeks never could forgive the wrong done them by Xerxes, and when Alexander proposed to invade Persia thousands of eager, willing soldiers flocked to his standard, and with one fell blow he broke the power of Persia, and during his life did according to his will. But just as he had made selection of Babylon as his capital and was planning for extensive commerce he died, and at once his kingdom was broken and divided among his four generals, not a son of his ever coming to the throne or holding sway over any part of his vast dominions.

"And the king of the south shall be strong, and one of his princes; and he shall be strong above him, and have dominion; his dominion shalt be a great dominion."

The angel interpreter only deals with those nations that were to come in contact with Daniel's people, or whose movements were to affect them; so he begins a rapid sketch of the two kingdoms, Egypt and Syria, filling the interval between their rise and the reign of Antiochus Epiphanes with their wars, intrigues, treaties, and perfidies.

The king of the south is Ptolemy Lagus, a man of great wisdom and power. He was one of Alexander's chief generals. He founded his kingdom of Egypt B.C. 323. But there was another stronger than he. This is Seleucus Nicator, another one of Alexander's generals, who founded the Syrian kingdom B.C. 312. His kingdom was indeed very powerful, embracing almost all that Alexander ever held in Asia. The angel mentions these two particularly, because in their movements they affected more or less the Jewish nation, Daniel's people.

"And in the end of years they shall join themselves together; for the king's daughter of the south shall come to the king of the north to make an agreement: but she shall not retain the power of the arm; neither shall he stand, nor his arm: but she shall be given up, and they that brought her, and he that begat her, and he that strengthened her in these times."

Here we find the angel interpreter passing over a considerable period of time, as nothing particularly affecting the Jews occurred in this time. He brings the narrative down to the time of Antiochus Theos, King of Syria. "This Theos, after long and fruitless wars with his Egyptian rival, Ptolemy Philadelphus, at last patched up a compromise ('they joined themselves together'), which, being utterly iniquitous, could not stand. The historical facts are these: He divorced his wife, Laodice, and married Berenice, daughter of Philadelphus. Two years after, Philadelphus, now aged, died. Theos soon divorced his Egyptian wife and restored his Syrian. But the latter had lost confidence in her husband, and, stung by his abuse, took him off by poison. She then secured the kingdom for her own son, Seleucus Callinicus, who managed to murder his mother's rival, Berenice, with her son and servants. Thus the compromise availed only to the ruin of both the guilty parties to this infamous marriage. Neither of them 'retained the power of the arm,' the military power, not even to the extent of self-protection."

"But out of a branch of her roots shall one stand up in his estate, which shall come with an army, and shall enter into the fortress of the king of the north, and shall deal against them, and shall prevail: and shall also carry captives into Egypt their gods, with their princes, and with their precious vessels of silver and of gold; and he shall continue more years than the king of the north. So the king of the south shall come into his kingdom, and shall return into his own land."

The third Ptolemy, brother of Berenice, is here spoken of as one "out of a branch of her roots." They came from the same parentage. His wars with the King of Syria were very successful. He defeated him in every engagement, and ravaged the greater portion of his kingdom, taking great spoils. He also removed and took back into Egypt twenty-five hundred idols (see verse 8), most of which Cambyses had carried from Egypt into Persia nearly three hundred years before. This fixes with unerring certainty these facts of history upon this time and upon this man. It is one of the threads that guides us unerringly through the mazes of this prophecy. Ptolemy reigned twenty-five years; his rival, Seleucus Callinicus, but twenty, thus he "continued more years than the king of the north."

"But his sons shall be stirred up, and shall assemble a multitude of great forces: and one shall certainly come, and overflow, and pass through: then shall he return, and be stirred up, even to his fortress."

The two sons of this king, Seleucus Ceraunus and Antiochus the Great, made great efforts and raised large armies, and pursued their conquests even to the fortresses of Egypt.

"And the king of the south shall be moved with choler, and shall come forth and fight with him, even with the king of the north: and he shall set forth a great multitude; but the multitude shall be given into his hand. And when he hath taken away the multitude, his heart shall be lifted up; and he shall cast down many ten thousands: but he shall not be strengthened by it."

Ptolemy Philopater, the King of Egypt, exasperated by the near approach of this vast army that stood at his very doors and threatened this key to his kingdom, went forth to fight with the king of the north; and at the battle of Raphia, near Gaza (B.C. 217), he overcame the army of Antiochus the Great, and the power passed into his hands; but he was not permanently strengthened by it, though he "cast down many ten thousands."

"For the king of the north shall return, and shall set forth a multitude greater than the former, and shall certainly come after certain years with a great army and with much riches. And in those times there shall many stand up against the king of the south: also the robbers of thy people shall exalt themselves to establish the vision; but they shall fall."

Antiochus the Great raises another army and comes again against the Egyptians. The King of Egypt, at this time a mere child, was assailed by many enemies. Philip of Macedon formed an alliance with Antiochus, while some of the violent men among the Jews threw off their allegiance to Egypt. But they failed, and only established the vision, while they themselves were overwhelmed with disaster.

"So the king of the north shall come, and cast up a mount, and take the most fenced cities: and the arms of the south shall not withstand, neither his chosen people, neither shall there be any strength to withstand. But he that cometh against him shall do according to his own will, and none shall stand before him: and he shall stand in the glorious land, which by his hand shall be consumed."

Antiochus besieged and took Zidon, Gaza, and other strong cities. He, overcoming all opposition, pressed his way even into Palestine, "the glorious land," and laid waste a great portion of it. He besieged Jerusalem, subsisting his army in the meantime in the land of Palestine, thus "consuming" it.

"He shall also set his face to enter with the strength of his whole kingdom, and upright ones with him; thus shall he do: and he shall give him the daughter of women, corrupting her: but she shall not stand on his side, neither be for him."

Antiochus sets his heart on invading Egypt, many of the better class of the Jews joining his standard. But the Romans' interfered and frustrated his plans. He then made a treaty with Ptolemy, giving him his own daughter Cleopatra in marriage, with the provinces of Phœnicia as her dower. He hoped that she would be true to him, her father, and play into his hands; but in this he was mistaken, for she was true to her husband, and thus did not stand on his (her father's) side, nor be for him.

"After this shall he turn his face unto the isles, and shall take many: but a prince for his own behalf shall cause the reproach offered by him to cease; without his own reproach he shall cause it to turn upon him. Then shall he turn his face toward the fort of his own land: but he shall stumble and fall, and not be found."

Antiochus made war against Greece and took many of the isles of that kingdom, but the Roman prince came to the rescue and gained a signal victory over him at Thermopylæ (B.C. 191), and still another at Magensia the following year. This completely broke the power of Antiochus the Great. Compelled to relinquish all his possessions west of Mount Taurus, a heavy tribute was laid upon him, exhausting all of his wealth and resources. To raise money to meet his pressing wants he made a raid into Elymais, which cost him his life.

"Then shall stand up in his estate a raiser of taxes in the glory of the kingdom: but within few days he shall be destroyed, neither in anger, nor in battle."

This was Seleucus Philopater, the son of Antiochus the Great. The great burden of paying the tribute of a thousand talents per year to the Romans left him nothing else to do but "raise taxes in the glory of his kingdom." After a brief reign of eleven years he was poisoned, thus dying "neither in anger, nor in battle."

"And in his estate shall stand up a vile person, to whom they shall not give the honor of the kingdom: but he shall come in peaceably, and obtain the kingdoms by flatteries."

This rapid sketch of the revealing angel brings us to the main figure of this prophecy, Antiochus Epiphanes. He came in the "estate" of his brother. He is a "vile person to whom they shall not give the honor of the kingdom." The kingdom was not his of right, but belonged legitimately to the son of Seleucus Philopater. Antiochus had been a hostage at Rome for thirteen years, and was now at Athens on his way home when he heard of the death of his brother. He at once laid his plans to secure the crown. Heliodorus, who had poisoned his master and usurped the throne, was at once expelled by the aid of Eumenes, King of Pergamos. Elsewhere we have spoken of the three horns plucked up by him in his ascent to the throne.

That he was a " vile person " we have only to look at the pages of history that record his deeds. " His delight was to play the buffoon, in getting half drunk, and then putting himself below the common level of even tipsy, silly drunkards. It is hard to believe that a king would rise from his dinner table heated with wine, strip himself stark naked, and dance round the hall as one frantic, with the lowest comedians. History can scarcely produce another like case of a man wearing a crown who debased himself so low, and made himself so vile as this same Antiochus Epiphanes."

"And with the arms of a flood shall they be overflown from before him, and shall be broken; yea, also the prince of the covenant."

Though he came in by flatteries, yet he was not long in raising an army and asserting his authority at the point of the sword.

" The prince of the covenant " was the high priest of the Jews, one of the most excellent and venerable of men. He soon fell before this vile king through the machinations of his apostate countrymen.

And after the league made with him he shall

work deceitfully: for he shall come up, and shall become strong with a small people. He shall enter peaceably even upon the fattest places of the province; and he shall do that which his fathers have not done, nor his fathers' fathers; he shall scatter among them the prey, and spoil, and riches: yea, and he shall forecast his devices against the strongholds, even for a time.

The revealing angel here shows that Antiochus made a league with that apostate Jew, Jason, whom he made high priest instead of the good Onias. He was to pay him a large sum for this office. When he sent his younger brother, Menelaus, to carry to Antiochus the money he had promised for the high priesthood, these two "worked deceitfully," for Menelaus bidding higher than his brother for the priesthood, Antiochus repudiated the league he had made with Jason, and gave the priesthood to him. Thus with "a small people" he gained a foothold in Judea and became strong.

He entered upon the "fattest places of the province," Arminia, where he found rich booty, and he scattered it with a recklessness and prodigality that excelled any thing of the kind ever done by his ancestors. This waste of treasure seemed merely to gratify a silly ambition to be thought more liberal than any one before him.

"And he shall stir up his power and his courage against the king of the south with a great army; and the king of the south shall be stirred up to battle with a very great and mighty army; but he shall not stand: for they shall forecast devices against him. Yea, they that feed of the portion of his meat shall destroy him, and his army shall overflow: and many shall fall down slain. And both these kings' hearts shall be to do mischief, and they shall speak lies at one table; but it shall not prosper: for yet the end shall be at the time appointed."

In the year B.C. 170 Antiochus raised a great army with which to invade Egypt. For four successive years he carried on this war of invasion, at last subjugating the whole country. He became the nominal protector of the young king, Ptolemy Philometor, and had precisely the intrigues spoken of in verse 27: "Both these kings' hearts shall be to do mischief, and they shall speak lies at one table"—yet in neither case availing to frustrate the great results which God in his providence had in view, "for yet the end would surely be at the time appointed." The Egyptian king was young, and imbecile even for his youth. He was formally inaugurated at the age of fourteen; had been kept in ignorance and inefficiency by the artful management of his tutors, who loved and sought to retain the regal power which his minority and incompetence gave them. 'They that feed of the portion of his meat shall destroy him.'"

"Then shall he return unto his land with great riches; and his heart shall be against the holy covenant; and he shall do exploits, and return to his own land."

While Antiochus Epiphanes was in Egypt, a rumor was circulated in Judea that he was dead, at which the Jews made every demonstration of joy. This being reported to Antiochus, with many exaggerations, he returned in a furious state of mind, fully bent on taking vengeance of the Jews. With the spoils of Egypt, with which he had been enriched, he hastened to Judea, and at once assailed Jerusalem. Of this terrific onslaught the author of 2 Maccabees (v. 11-16) says: "Removing out of Egypt in a furious mind, he took the city by force of arms, and commanded his men of war not to spare such as they met, and to slay such as went up upon the houses. Thus there was killing of young and old, making away of men, women, and children, slaying of virgins and infants. And there were destroyed within three whole days four score thousand, whereof forty thousand were slain in the conflict; and no fewer sold than slain. Yet was he not content with this, but presumed to go into the most holy temple of all the world; Menelaus, that traitor to the laws, and to his own country, being his guide: and taking the holy vessels with polluted hands, and with profane hands pulling down the things that were dedicated by other kings to the augmentation and glory and honor of the place, he gave them away." "In this scene of pillage and sacrilege, Antiochus found and took away from the temple eighteen hundred talents of gold [$41,304,000], and then offered swine's flesh on the altar, and sprinkled the whole temple with the broth of this flesh. After these exploits he returned to his own land."

"At the time appointed he shall return, and come toward the south; but it shall not be as the former, or as the latter. For the ships of Chittim shall come against him: therefore he shall be grieved, and return, and have indignation against the holy covenant: so shall he do; he shall even return, and have intelligence with them that forsake the holy covenant."

Philometor, who was the son of Cleopatra, and therefore the nephew of Antiochus Epiphanes, was so completely under the control of Antiochus that the Egyptians placed his brother, Physcon, on the throne. Antiochus therefore undertook another expedition to Egypt to subdue this prince. In his first battle with Physcon he was successful. Physcon then sought the help and intervention of the Romans. By Chittim, as Josephus affirms, we are to understand the Romans. "An embassy of three men from the Roman Senate met him just as he was about to lay siege to Alexandria; told him they had taken young Physcon under their protection, and that he must desist, or have war with Rome. Antiochus indicating a wish to procrastinate, Tophilius drew a circle in the sand about his feet, and said: 'Give me an answer before you cross that circle.' He yielded, and pledged himself to do all the Senate should require. He dared not offend the Roman power. But he chafed like a tiger under his chain, and came back to vent his rage on a fallen people, the Jews. He was '*grieved*,' in this very selfish sense, and let loose his indignation against the holy covenant and its people. At this time, and for several years previous, he had intelligence with Jewish apostates, kept up a mutual understanding and co-operation with them, and made great use of their aid to further his designs."

"And arms shall stand on his part, and they shall pollute the sanctuary of strength, and shall take away the daily sacrifice, and they shall place the abomination that maketh desolate. And such as do wickedly against the covenant shall he corrupt by flatteries: but the people that do know their God shall be strong, and do exploits."

In the year B.C. 167 Antiochus sent an army of twenty-two thousand, under Apollonius, against Jerusalem. He took it and kept it as his stronghold. The command to Apollonius was to kill all the Jews who were of full age, and to sell the women and young men. These orders were pnnctually executed. The author of the Maccabees says: "Who [Appolonius] coming to Jerusalem, and pretending peace, did forbear till the holy-day of the Sabbath, when taking the Jews keeping holy-day, he commanded his men to arm themselves. And so he slew all them that were gone to the celebrating of the Sabbath, and running through the city with weapons slew great multitudes. But Judas Maccabeus with nine others, or thereabout, withdrew himself into the wilderness, and lived in the mountains after the manner of beasts, with his company, who fed on herbs continually, lest they should be partakers of the pollution." (2 Mac. v. 25–27.)

These misfortunes were only the preludes of what they were to suffer, for Antiochus, apprehending that the Jews would never be constant in their obedience to him unless he obliged them to change their religion and to embrace that of the Greeks, issued an edict, enjoining them to conform to the laws of other nations, and forbidding their usual sacrifices in the temple, their festivals, and their Sabbaths. The statue of Jupiter Olympus was placed upon the altar of the temple, and thus the abomination of desolation was seen in the temple of God.

Again the author of the Maccabees says: "Not long after this the king sent an old man of Athens to compel the Jews to depart from the laws of their fathers, and not to live after the laws of God: and to pollute also the temple in Jerusalem, and to call it the temple of Jupiter Olympius; and that in Garizim, of Jupiter the Defender of Strangers, as they did desire that dwelt in the place. The coming in of this mischief was sore and grievous to the people. . . . The altar also was filled with profane things, which the law forbiddeth. Neither was it lawful for a man to keep Sabbath-days or ancient feasts, or to profess himself at all to be a Jew. And in the day of the king's birth, every month they were brought by bitter constraint to eat of the sacrifices; and when the feast of Bacchus was kept, the Jews were compelled to go in procession to Bacchus, carrying ivy." (2 Mac. vi. 1-7.)

And again, in the 11th verse of the same chapter: "And others, that had run together into caves near by, to keep the Sabbath-day secretly, being discovered to Philip, were all burnt together, because they made a conscience to help themselves for the honor of the most sacred day." And that you may see what these men had to endure during this period, see verses 18-31 of the same chapter: "Eleazer, one of the principal scribes, an aged man, and of a well-favored countenance, was constrained to open his mouth, and to eat swine's flesh. But he, choosing rather to die gloriously, than to live stained with such an abomination, spit it forth, and came of his own accord to the torment, as it behooved them to come, that are resolute to stand out against such things, as are not lawful for love of life to be tasted. But they that had the charge of that wicked feast, for the old acquaintance they had with the man, taking him aside, besought him to bring flesh of his own provision, such as was lawful for him to use, and make as if he did eat of the flesh taken from the sacrifice commanded by the king; that in so doing he might be delivered from death, and for the old friendship with them find favor. But he began to consider discreetly, as became his age, and the excellency of his ancient years, and the honor of his gray head, whereunto he was come, and his most honest education from a child, or rather the holy law made and given by God: therefore he answered accordingly, and willed them straightways to send him to the grave. For it becometh not our age, said he, in anywise to dissemble, whereby many young persons might think that Eleazar, being fourscore years old and ten, were now gone to a strange religion: and so they through mine hypocrisy, and desire to live a little time and a moment longer, should be deceived by me, and I get a stain to mine old age, and make it abominable. For though for the present time I should be delivered from the punishment of men: yet should I not escape the hand of the Almighty, neither alive nor dead. Wherefore now, manfully changing this life, I will show myself such a one as mine age requireth, and leave a notable example to such as be young, to die willingly and courageously for the honorable and holy laws. And when he had said these words, immediately he went to the torment: they that led him changing the good-will they bare him a little before into hatred, because the aforesaid speeches proceeded, as they thought, from a desperate mind. But when he was ready to die with stripes, he groaned, and said, It is manifest unto the Lord, that hath the holy knowledge, that whereas I might have been delivered from death, I now endure sore pains in body by being beaten: but in soul am well content to suffer these things, because I fear him. And thus this man died, leaving his death for an example of a noble courage, and a memorial of virtue, not only unto young men, but unto all his nation."

In the next chapter is found an account of the constancy and cruel death of seven brothers and their mother, one of the most remarkable and memorable in the annals of martyrs. It is doubtless those of these times of whom the author of the Hebrews speaks when he says: "They were stoned, they were sawn asunder, were tempted, were slain with the sword: they wandered about in sheep-skins and in goat-skins; being destitute, afflicted, tormented; of whom the world was not worthy: they wandered in deserts, and in mountains, and in dens and caves of the earth."

By the decree of Antiochus the temple was not only profaned, but the "daily sacrifice was taken away." The book of Maccabees makes it very plain that many of the Jews were utterly apostate from the service and worship of God. They were bribed by the flatteries of this vile king. While those people who do know their God stood firm, and did "exploits," Mattathias of Modin, and Judas Maccabeus, and others, are noble examples of courage, strength, and constancy. Hear what the aged Mattathias said: "Woe is me! wherefore was I born to see this misery of my people, and of the holy city, and to dwell there, when it was delivered into the hand of the enemy, and the sanctuary into the hand of strangers? Her temple is become as a man without glory. Her glorious vessels are carried away into captivity, her infants are slain in the streets, her young men with the sword of the enemy. . . . Behold, our sanctuary, even our beauty and our glory, is laid waste, and the Gentiles have profaned it. To what end therefore shall we live any longer?"

When the king's officers came to Modin and plied Mattathias with flatteries and with bribes, pressing him to be the first to fulfill the king's command as all the heathen had done, he cried with a loud voice: " Though all the nations that are under the king's dominion obey him, and fall away every one from the religion of their fathers, and give consent to his commandments: yet will I and my sons and my brethren walk in the covenant of our fathers. God forbid that we should forsake the law and the ordinances. We will not hearken to the king's words, to go from our religion, either on the right hand, or the left. Now when he had left speaking these words, there came one of the Jews in the sight of all to sacrifice on the altar which was at Modin, according to the king's commandment, which thing when Mattathias saw, he was inflamed with zeal, and his reins trembled, neither could he forbear to show his anger according to judgment: wherefore he ran, and slew him upon the altar. Also the king's commissioner, who compelled men to sacrifice, he killed at that time, and the altar he pulled down." Then he cried throughout the city, "Whoever is zealous of the law, and maintaineth the covenant, let him follow me." He and his followers retired to the mountain fastnesses of southern Palestine, where they struck many valiant blows for their country and their religion. With such evidence as this who could ever think of applying this prophecy to any other than to Antiochus Epiphanes and the men and events of his times?

"And they that understand among the people shall instruct many: yet they shall fall by the sword, and by flame, by captivity, and by spoil, many days. Now when they shall fall, they shall be holpen with a little help; but many shall cleave to them with flatteries. And some of them of understanding shall fall, to try them, and to purge, and to make them white, even to the time of the end: because it is yet for a time appointed."

How true this was of these times! The leaders who instructed many fell one after another: the venerable Mattathias first, then Jonathan, Eleazar, Judas, and Simon; a noble band. Occasionally they were victorious, and were thus "holpen with a little help." But time and again their cause suffered from the treachery of false friends who were won over to their enemies by flatteries. By the fall of their leaders and bravest men God seemed "to purge and make them white even to the time of the end"—the time when he would deliver his people entirely from their foes. Why should men conversant with the history of these times ever look anywhere else for the fulfillment of this prophecy?

Here, and here only, do we find every feature of the prophecy fulfilled.

"And the king shall do according to his will; and he shall exalt himself, and magnify himself above every god, and shall speak marvelous things against the God of gods, and shall prosper until the indignation be accomplished: for that that is determined shall be done. Neither shall he regard the God of his fathers, nor the desire of women, nor regard any god: for he shall magnify himself above all. But in his estate shall he honor the God of forces: and a god whom his fathers knew not shall he honor with gold, and silver, and with precious stones, and pleasant things. Thus shall he do in the most strong holds with a strange god, whom he shall acknowledge and increase with glory: and he shall cause them to rule over many, and shall divide the land for gain."

This can be no other than the king spoken of before—Antiochus Epiphanes. God had his purpose in chastising his people, and delivered them up to the will of this king. We are told in the seventeenth Psalm, verse 13, that "the wicked is God's sword." So this vile king is used as God's sword to afflict and punish his unfaithful people. Hence he shall prosper until the "indignation be accomplished." The king is proud and self-conceited; thinks himself above every god, speaks marvelous things against the God of gods—things that for their horrid blasphemy excite the wonder of mankind. Hear what the author of the Maccabees says on this point: "Having spoken very proudly." And again, commenting on his fall from his chariot, he says: "Thus he who a little afore thought he might command the waves of the sea [so proud was he above the condition of man] and weigh the high mountains in a balance, was now cast on the ground, and carried in a horse-litter, showing unto all the manifest power of God." And again; "The man who thought a little afore that he could reach to the stars of heaven," etc. He had no reverence for any God, not even the god of his fathers, but made the effort to introduce the religion of the Greeks in all his dominions. No pleadings of men or women could turn him from his purpose of overthrowing the religion of the countries conquered by him. Every feature of this man as portrayed by the angel to Daniel is fully pointed out by the historian as he writes of Antiochus. He, and he only, is revealed to us here.

"And at the time of the end shall the king of the south push at him: and the king of the north shall come against him like a whirlwind, with chariots, and with horsemen, and with many ships; and he shall enter into the countries, and shall overthrow and pass over. He shall enter also into the glorious land, and many countries shall be overthrown: but these shall escape out of his hand, even Edom, and Moab, and the chief of the children of Ammon. He shall stretch forth his hand also upon the countries: and the land of Egypt shall not escape. But he shall have power over the treasures of gold and of silver, and over all the precious things of Egypt: and the Libyans and the Ethiopians shall be at his steps. But tidings out of the east and out of the north shall trouble him: therefore he shall go forth with great fury to destroy, and utterly to make away many. And he shall plant the tabernacles of his palace between the seas in the glorious holy mountain; yet he shall come to his end, and none shall help him."

"At the time of the end" is the period at which this scourge of God's people shall be destroyed, and that people be relieved from their terrible punishment. Now the curtain lifts from the last act in the grand drama of his life. Antiochus is provoked to war by Ptolemy Philometor, the "king of the south pushing at him." The fighting of the king of the north is compared to a storm—a whirlwind coming down in its fury, sweeping all before it. He was successful in this war, only a few named escaping his hand. The Libyans and Ethiopians ally their armies with his, and help him in the war. But while prosecuting it successfully, tidings from Persia, Armenia, and Palestine—the east and the north—reach and trouble him. Judas Maccabeus was constantly growing stronger, and while he was trying to crush his heroic band he heard of the rebellion of Persia and Armenia, and he at once divided his forces, leaving part under the leadership of Lysias to prosecute the war against the Jews, he took the rest and pushed toward the east. The rebellion there was caused by his effort to supplant the ancient religion of the Magians with Greek idolatry. He had planted the "tabernacle of his palace" in Palestine between the seas of the glorious mountain; but now he goes east. While there he meets his death.

Knowing that very great riches were lodged in the temple of Elymais, he determined to carry it off. But the inhabitants of the country made so vigorous a resistance that he was forced to retreat toward Babylonia. When he was come to Ecbatana, he was informed of the defeat of Nicanor and Timotheus, and that Judas Maccabeus had retaken the temple of Jerusalem and restored the worship of the Lord and the usual sacrifices. On receiving this intelligence the king was transported with indignation, and threatened to make Jerusalem a grave for the Jews, commanded the driver of his chariot to urge the horses forward and to hasten his journey. He fell from his chariot, receiving such injuries that he died a short time after in the most excrutiating pain, acknowledging in his last moments that his death was from God. So he died not in battle, but came to his end with none to "help him."

CHAPTER VII.

Trials and Persecutions of the Jews—The Seven Brethren and Their Mother Martyred—The Resurrection to Joy and Shame—The Thousand Two Hundred and Ninety Days—The Sanctuary Cleansed—The Kingdom of Christ.

WE come now to the closing chapter of this wonderful prophecy. At the death of this vile king, Antiochus Epiphanes, it is said:

"And at that time shall Michael stand up, the great prince which standeth for the children of thy people: and there shall be a time of trouble, such as never was since there was a nation even to that same time: and at that time thy people shall be delivered, every one that shall be found written in the book. And many of them that sleep in the dust of the earth shall awake, some to everlasting life, and some to shame and everlasting contempt. And they that be wise shall shine as the brightness of the firmament; and they that turn many to righteousness, as the stars forever and ever."

The Jews had never passed through such persecutions before. They had been slain by tens of thousands. Their sacred temple had been invaded, the daily sacrifice taken away. Swines' flesh had been offered in the house of God, and the abominable broth poured over every sacred spot and vessel in the blessed sanctuary. Men and women, irrespective of age or station, had been

The Kingdom and Comings of Christ. 109

submitted to rack, fire, and sword in the most inhuman manner.

The author of the Maccabees says: "It came to pass also, that seven brethren with their mother were taken, and compelled by the king against the law to taste swine's flesh, and were tormented with scourges and whips. But one of them that spake first said thus, What wouldst thou ask or learn of us? we are ready to die rather than to transgress the laws of our fathers. Then the king, being in a rage, commanded pans and caldrons to be made hot: which forthwith being heated, he commanded to cut out the tongue of him that spake first, and to cut off the utmost parts of his body, the rest of his brethren and his mother looking on. Now when he was thus maimed in all his members, he commanded him, being yet alive, to be brought to the fire, and to be fried in the pan: and as the vapor of the pan was for a good space dispersed, they exhorted one another with the mother to die manfully, saying thus, The Lord looketh upon us, and in truth hath comfort in us, as Moses in his song, which witnessed to their faces, declared, saying, And he shall be comforted in his servants. So when the first was dead after this manner, they brought the second to make him a mocking-stock: and when they had pulled off the skin of his head with the hair, they asked him, Wilt thou eat, before thou be punished throughout every member of thy body? But he answered in his own language, and said, No. Wherefore he also received the next torment in order, as the former did. And when he was at the last gasp, he said, Thou like a fury takest us out of this present life, but the King of the world shall raise us up, who have died for his laws, unto everlasting life. After him was the third made a mocking-stock: and when he was required, he put out his tongue, and that right soon, holding forth his hands manfully, and said courageously, These I had from heaven; and for his laws I despise them; and from him I hope to receive them again. . Insomuch that the king, and they that were with him, marveled at the young man's courage, for that he nothing regarded the pains. Now when this man was dead also, they tormented and mangled the fourth in like manner. So when he was ready to die, he said thus, It is good, being put to death by men, to look for hope from God to be raised up again by him: as for thee, thou shalt have no resurrection to life. Afterward they brought the fifth also, and mangled him. Then looked he unto the king, and said, Thou hast power over men, thou art corruptible, thou doest what thou wilt; yet think not that our nation is forsaken of God; but abide awhile, and behold his great power, how he will torment thee and thy seed. After him also they brought the sixth, who, being ready to die, said, Be not deceived without cause: for we suffer these things for ourselves, having sinned against our God: therefore marvelous things are done unto us. But think not thou, that takest in hand to strive against

God, that thou shalt escape unpunished. But the mother was marvelous above all, and worthy of honorable memory: for when she saw her seven sons slain within the space of one day, she bare it with a good courage, because of the hope she had in the Lord. Yea, she exhorted every one of them in her own language, filled with courageous spirits; and stirring up her womanish thoughts with a manly stomach, she said unto them, I cannot tell how ye came into my womb; for I neither gave you breath nor life, neither was it I that formed the members of every one of you; but doubtless the Creator of the world, who formed the generation of man, and found out the beginning of all things, will also of his own mercy give you breath and life again, as ye now regard not your own selves for his laws' sake. Now Antiochus, thinking himself despised, and suspecting it to be a reproachful speech, whilst the youngest was yet alive, did not only exhort him by words, but also assured him with oaths, that he would make him both a rich and happy man, if he would turn from the laws of his fathers; and that also he would take him for his friend, and trust him with affairs. But when the young man would in no case hearken unto him, the king called his mother, and exhorted her that she would counsel the young man to save his life. And when he had exhorted her with many words, she promised him that she would counsel her son. But she bowing herself to him, laughing the cruel tyrant to scorn, spake in her country language on this manner; O my son, have pity upon me that bare thee nine months in my womb, and gave thee suck three years, and nourished thee, and brought thee up unto this age, and endured the troubles of education. I beseech thee, my son, look upon the heaven and the earth, and all that is therein, and consider that God made them of things that were not; and so was mankind made likewise. Fear not this tormentor, but, being worthy of thy brethren, take thy death, that I may receive thee again in mercy with thy brethren. While she was yet speaking these words, the young man said, Whom wait ye for? I will not obey the king's commandment: but I will obey the commandment of the law that was given unto our fathers by Moses. And thou that hast been the author of all mischief against the Hebrews, shalt not escape the hands of God. For we suffer because of our sins. And though the living God be angry with us a little while for our chastening and correction, yet shall he be at one again with his servants. But thou, O godless man, and of all other most wicked, be not lifted up without a cause, nor puffed up with uncertain hopes, lifting up thy hand against the servants of God; for thou hast not yet escaped the judgment of Almighty God, who seeth all things. For our brethren who have now suffered a short pain, are dead under God's covenant of everlasting life: but thou through the judgment of God, shalt receive just punishment for thy pride. But I, as my brethren, offer up my body and life for the laws of our fathers, beseeching God that he would speedily be merciful to our nation; and that thou by torments and plagues mayest confess, that he alone is God and that in me and my brethren the wrath of the Almighty, which is justly brought upon all our nation, may cease. Then the king, being in a rage, handled him worse than all the rest, and took it grievously that he was mocked. So this man died undefiled, and put his whole trust in the Lord. Last of all, after the sons, the mother died."

We have given this long and interesting quotation to show that this was the "time of trouble, such as never was since there was a nation even to that same time: and at that time thy people shall be delivered, every one that shall be found written in the book."

Verse 2 is highly symbolic. It means that when Michael shall stand up for his people there shall be a mighty change. Those that were as in the dust of death on account of the dreadful persecutions shall be delivered, and it will be, as Paul expresses it when speaking of the conversion of the Jews, "What shall the receiving of them be, but life from the dead?" The figure of the resurrection is often used to express joy after sorrow. While the faithful saints shall wake to joy, their persecutors and the apostate Jews who, to save their life, gave up their faith, will now "awake to shame and everlasting contempt." Such men as Mattathias, Judas, Eleazar, Simon, the seven brothers and their faithful mother, "shall shine as the brightness of the firmament; and they that turn many to righteousness, as the stars forever and ever."

As we conceive, this has no reference whatever to a literal resurrection, but it is wholly figurative, and it comes in just at the point where such joy on the one hand and such confusion and contempt would be found on the other.

Those "found written in the book" was a familiar expression to the Jews. When God counted one worthy of eternal life, it was as if he wrote the name of such a one in the Book of Life. Moses felt that his name was written there, for while praying for his people he uses this language: "Yet now, if thou wilt, forgive their sin; and if not, blot me, I pray thee, out of thy book which thou hast written." David, in the 69th Psalm, when speaking of certain wicked ones, says: "Let them be blotted out of the book of the living, and not be written with the righteous." The time of deliverance was coming, and all who were worthy, all whose names should be found written in this book, should meet with signal deliverance. A mighty change was to take place. The wicked who had terrorized the good for so long were themselves to be in terror. The slayer should be slain, while the good, that had been hunted down as they hid in dens and caves of the earth, were now to be exalted; and so signal was to be the manifestation of God's favor that all the world should see it. They should "shine as the brightness of the firmament; and they that turn many to righteousness, as the stars forever and ever."

Daniel is commanded to "shut up the words, and seal the book, even to the time of the end." This prophecy would not be understood until the power of the wicked under Antiochus should be broken and the mighty deliverance wrought, so the words should be shut and the book sealed till the time of the end, then should it all appear to them. The joyous news of their deliverance should fly from place to place: "Many shall run to and fro, and knowledge shall be increased." As the knowledge of this deliverance should spread and increase, joy should abound, and men would run everywhere with the good news. This was literally the case at the death of Antiochus.

But God intends to give yet more information to his beloved servant. Hence he sees two other angels standing, "the one on this side of the bank of the river, and the other on that side of the bank of the river. And one said to the man clothed in linen, which was upon the waters of the river. How long shall it be to the end of these wonders?" The man clothed in linen, lifting his hand, swears "by him that liveth forever, that it shall be for a time, times, and a half"—that is, as we have seen elsewhere, three years and a half. Daniel did not fully comprehend it, and he asks: "What shall be the end of these things? And he said, Go thy way, Daniel: for the words are closed up and sealed till the time of the end." Between the time of this vision and the end, especially during the fierce persecutions under Antiochus, "many shall be purified, and made white, and tried." This was literally the case. Persecutions, such as this people endured, if properly received, purify those who endure them, and at the same time "the wicked shall do wickedly." Those engaged in the persecutions would increase in wickedness as a natural result.

Now the angel becomes more specific as to time. In round numbers, all along through these parallel prophecies, three years and a half has been given; now the very number of the days is announced, and the point from which to calculate them: "And from the time that the daily sacrifice shall be taken away, and the abomination that maketh desolate set up, there shall be a thousand two hundred and ninety days." This time, when "the daily sacrifice was taken away," is not accurately recorded in history; but the time when the abomination was set up is December 10, 167 B.C., and the time when the sanctuary was cleansed and the sacrifice restored is also recorded. It was December 25, 164 B.C. But the time when the sacrifice was taken away is not so clearly recorded. No doubt this was done some time before the abomination of desolation was set up—that is, when an idol altar was erected on the altar of sacrifice in the temple. If we could get this date, no doubt from it to the cleansing of the sanctuary

The Kingdom and Comings of Christ. 117

would be twelve hundred and ninety days. We know that it was early in June of the year B.C. 167 that Antiochus returned from Egypt and sent Apollonius with an army into Judea. He seized Jerusalem, and put a stop to the temple worship. This much we do know: that Josephus distinctly states in two passages that the daily sacrifices were suspended three and a half years; and this, accurately calculated, would make twelve hundred and seventy-nine days, lacking just eleven of the number given by the revealing angel. Josephus may have put it in round numbers three and a half years, while it was eleven days longer than this.

The death of Antiochus was an event that sent a thrill of joy through all the land of Judea. It virtually ended the persecutions of this people. When the Jews cleansed their sanctuary and restored the daily sacrifice, Antiochus was far away in Persia. When these tidings reached him, he was greatly affected by them, and set off at once for home, and brought on the fall from his chariot, and the violent sickness of which he died. "Now if we allow a reasonable time for this news to reach him, and for the journey, the fall, and the sickness which preceded his death, we shall find that forty-five days is a fair estimate. The testimony of the second book of Maccabees (chapter ix.) corresponds with that of the first book in these particulars, as far as it goes. Well might the revealing angel say, 'Blessed is he that waiteth' in patient hope so long, for there would be great joy over the death of that arch-enemy of the people of God." The angel adds these forty-five days, saying: "Blessed is he that waiteth, and cometh to the thousand three hundred and five and thirty days." Then they should know certainly that their enemy was dead, and their long night of sorrow was over.

The last verse of the chapter, and of the prophecy of Daniel, was addressed to him. "But go thou thy way till the end be: for thou shalt rest, and stand in thy lot at the end of the days." For seventy years he had been from time to time receiving these wonderful visions, and now he is gently dismissed. His work was done, he must now rest, and stand in his lot.

The four great parallel visions of this book, as we have seen, commencing with Nebuchadnezzar and ending with Antiochus Epiphanes, deal only with the features of the Jewish nation to within a few years of the coming of Christ in the flesh. We have found nothing beyond this, and we feel assured that we are right. Our purpose has not been to speculate, but to give a plain, simple interpretation of the visions of this great prophet. We have not found any great antichrist of the present age. Neither the pope nor the Roman Catholic Church has appeared to our mind. The times spoken of in the prophecy have not been stretched to our age and time, but have been interpreted in their natural and legitimate periods. This prophecy furnishes the New Testament idea and expressions of the "kingdom of God" and the "kingdom of heaven." It points men to the time " when the God of heaven shall set up a kingdom." It prepared men for the *first coming of Christ*. Other prophets had written of this same coming. Some more, and some less clearly.

The long night was passing, and the last prophet of the Jewish Church had announced that "the Sun of righteousness shall arise with healing in his wings," and all the world was looking for the promised Messiah. When at last the birth of Christ was announced, angels proclaimed it to the shepherds. Wise men came from the East inquiring for him born "King of the Jews." And soon he began "preaching the gospel of the kingdom of God, and saying, "The time is fulfilled, and the kingdom of God is at hand." He gathered his disciples on the mount, and delivered to them a sermon, in which he laid down the great principles of the kingdom of heaven, of which he was the head and ruler. He took the reins of government in his own hands, and with an authority that astonished the people he announced in the conclusion of his sermon: "Therefore whosoever heareth these sayings of mine, and doeth them," etc. He entered the temple, claiming it as his father's house, and drove out the buyers and sellers, announcing the fact that it was to be regarded of all nations as the house of prayer. By the wonderful miracles he wrought he gave the most indubitable proof of his claim to the Messiahship, and by numerous parables revealed the true nature of his kingdom. By some of these parables he showed that the Gentiles were to be admitted into his kingdom upon the same terms as the Jews, and that he wronged no man by admitting them. See the parable of the laborers, as found in Matthew xx. 1-16. Those hired at the eleventh hour represented the Gentiles, while those who murmured were the Jews. Jesus claims that it "is lawful for me to do what I will with mine own," and announces the fact that "the last shall be first, and the first last." The Gentiles who had been last called were to come to the front rank and take possession of his kingdom and be first in all respects, while the Jews, his first people, were to drop behind in all things and be last.

CHAPTER VIII.

The Prophecies of the Old Testament Center in Israel—False Interpretations—The Triumphal Entry of Jesus into Jerusalem—Its Object—The Fig-tree Cursed—The Two Sons—Parable of the Vineyard—Marriage of the King's Son—Scribes, Pharisees, and Herodians Assail Jesus—Their Hypocrisy Unveiled—Prophecy Concerning the Destruction of Jerusalem.

PERHAPS no single prophecy of scripture has called forth more wild and visionary interpretations than the predictions of Jesus as contained in Matthew xxiv., Mark xiii., and Luke xxi. The signs pointed out by the Saviour as contained in these chapters have been seen in all ages of the world, and men are still straining their vision to catch sight of others of them yet unfulfilled.

We do not claim to be wiser than others who have written, and to be able to sift out all error and to give the true interpretation, but having carefully studied the subject for years, and read expounders of almost every class—read them with a special eye to seeing what was true—we think that we are at least entitled to a hearing. It shall be our constant aim to let scripture interpret scripture wherever this can be done. And in all cases to give a common-sense view of whatever prophecies we may attempt to explain.

No prophecy was ever written merely to satisfy the curiosity of men, or to tell the fate of nations or individuals. But in every instance the benevolent designs of the Father of us all are manifest. His unbounded love to us moved him to do all in his power consistent with our free moral agency to save us from the snares of the devil and bring us back to himself. Hence we find every single prophecy of the Scripture centering in his people. Is the doom of Babylon, Egypt, Tyre, or any other nation revealed? It is only as these nations are connected with his people. Some thread of their history binds them vitally to this wonderful family of nations, to whom were committed the oracles of God that were to lighten and enlighten all the people of earth down to the end of time. The word of God must be established as such, beyond the shadow of a question.

Selecting the family of Abraham from among the tribes of the earth, he makes them the burning focus to which he bends every single ray of prophecy, whether it pass through nations or individuals. If we will hold this in mind, we will be enabled to follow each individual prediction with perfect assurance. And difficulties that have hung like a cloud over many portions of God's word will vanish as mists of the morning before the rising sun.

Christ is the soul and center of all spiritual light. He, the son of David, the glory of the house of Israel, is also the desire of all nations. He it is whose voice comes ringing through the ages: "I am the Lord, and there is none else, there is no

God beside me. . . . I am the Lord, and there is none else. . . . Ask me of things concerning my sons, and concerning the work of my hands command ye me. . . . Who hath declared this from ancient time? who hath told it from that time? have not I the Lord? and there is no God else beside me; a just God and a Saviour; there is none beside me. Look unto me, and be ye saved, all the ends of the earth: for I am God, and there is none else."

As Christ is the soul and center of all spiritual light, so the period of his manifestation on earth, the time of the offering of his soul for sin, was the center of time. And about this period we see the completion of the written word, the closing up of all the predictions that were uttered for its full and complete establishment. When the last book of the sacred volume was written, then God sealed up the vision and the prophecy. There was then no longer any need of them. Holding to this as our central orb, we will find but little difficulty in unraveling the mysteries of interpretation. When men have broken away from this and wandered off into other fields they have filled their writings with the wildest and most contradictory theories. Every crime, every war, every earthquake, every plague is to them a fulfillment of prophecy. With them the folds of Revelation and Daniel are wide enough to wrap about all the nations of the earth, and far-reaching enough to cover all time.

The prophecy of Jesus with reference to his

second coming has had innumerable interpreters, many of them losing sight of the fact we have already presented, that all the prophecies of scripture centered in God's chosen people, or those connected immediately with them, or were intended to forever fix the claims of Jesus to the Messiahship and establish the truth of the Bible, and that none were needed to reach beyond the full and satisfactory establishment of these two great facts. As the Bible is to be for all time and for all people, and as Jesus Christ is the Saviour of all men, especially of them that believe, all predictions and prophecies, whether uttered before or after the incarnation of Jesus, were designed to establish these facts. We will never find any single prophecy bearing on any other point. Nor will we find them reaching to a period not necessary to the fulfillment of this design.

The very first ray of prophecy that ever shot athwart the gloom of our lost estate can be traced unerringly to the Sun of righteousness as he comes with healing in his wings, and each subsequent ray only added to the splendors of his shining.

Men have set out with preconceived notions with reference to certain prophecies, and they have drawn from Old and New Testament predictions and with them have constructed a mosaic that has the appearance of unity and solidity; but somewhere there is a loose stone that no amount of adjustment can make fit, and on this account the whole fails of its design and becomes worthless.

Beforehand they have concluded that Christ is coming once more in the flesh to set up a kingdom on earth, and that here among his saints in visible person he is to reign a thousand years, having his throne somewhere—most of them say at Jerusalem. Upon this idea they have built up a separate sect, and have set to work to calculate the time of his coming, notwithstanding the declaration of Jesus: "But of that day and hour knoweth no man, no, not the angels of heaven, but my Father only." Yet these prophecy-mongers have time and again set the day. Nearly every year in the last half century has been fixed upon by some one or another of them as the time of his coming. Nor do mistakes and disappointments discourage them. When time has demonstrated the error of their calculations, immediately they begin again from some other stand-point, and with unshaken confidence figure out another time.

In examining the prophecy of Jesus it will aid us somewhat to go back to what is known as his triumphal entry into Jerusalem, for it was during the week that followed this entry that he delivered this wonderful prophecy. The disciples having seated him upon the ass secured by his direction, they gathered about him, "and a very great multitude spread their garments in the way; others cut down branches from the trees, and strewed them in the way." And when he was come nigh, even now at the descent of the Mount of Olives, the whole multitude of the disciples, and the multitudes that went before, and that followed, began to rejoice and praise God with a loud voice, for all the mighty works that they had seen, and cried, saying: "Hosanna to the Son of David! Hosanna in the highest! Blessed be the king that cometh in the name of the Lord! peace in heaven, and glory in the highest! Blessed be the kingdom of our father David, that cometh in the name of the Lord! Hosanna in the highest!"

This scene is unlike any other in the history of our Lord. Once or twice the multitude had become excited and were ready to lift him to the throne of his father David; but this excitement had been suppressed, and the multitude sent away. Now he submits to all they do. While in the midst of this triumph the Pharisees asked him to "rebuke his disciples," but he said: "I tell you that, if these should hold their peace, the stones would immediately cry out."

The question arises, What was the object of this movement? why did Jesus now submit to this display? why did he give loose rein to the multitude to shout him king? It was the last grand effort that he was making to reach the heart of his people and bring them back to God. He had gone among them in humility, not suffering "his voice to be heard in the streets," yet working the most stupendous miracles among them; spreading out his hand of compassion over them, he had "borne their sorrows and carried their griefs;" and yet he had failed to reach them. Now for one brief hour, in the fulfillment of a well-known and signal prophecy recorded in Zachariah ix. 9, 10, he gives his disciples and the multitude full rein to send their echoing shouts over the wall into the city that lay at his feet. Methinks I see, for one brief moment, an expectant flush upon his cheek as he waits the effect of this movement, but ere the hosannas have ceased to reverberate among the hills a change sweeps over him. Let us draw near and look upon this king—this triumphal one—as the people shout him welcome to the throne of his father David. Wonder of wonders! *he is in tears!* Lost to all his surroundings, heeding not the glad hosannas that fall upon his ears, he gazes down upon the city that lay like a jewel upon the brow of Moriah. He had come unto his own, and his own received him not. While some were ready to acknowledge him as their Saviour and king, the great heart of the people was not his, and he knew it. All, all is in vain! They understood not the rustle of his wings, they felt not the yearning of his heart. They knew not the things which belonged unto their peace. And through these blinding tears he caught sight of their desolation. He saw the horizon flecked with the eagles which with beak and talons would tear their quivering flesh with relentless cruelty. He heard the thundering shock of Roman battering-rams breaking down their walls to let in the relentless soldiery who should roll like a resistless tidal wave of woe over the shattered stones to the slaughter through every street and alley of the doomed city. Through the intervening years he heard the dying groans of the million one hundred thousand helpless, hapless ones that should perish in the siege. Upon his eyes flashed the fires that should wrap like a shroud all the magnificence and splendor of her temple and palaces, sending down into the grave all the accumulated wealth, pride, glory, and hope of centuries, covering up in blood and ashes the form that once leaned upon the bosom of Jehovah as his peculiar treasure. No wonder this mighty king wept and wailed out the anguish of his loving heart. "If thou hadst known, even thou, at least in this thy day, the things which belong unto thy peace! but now they are hid from thine eyes. For the days shall come upon thee, that thine enemies shall cast a trench about thee, and compass thee round, and keep thee in on every side, and shall lay thee even with the ground, and thy children within thee; and they shall not leave in thee one stone upon another; *because thou knewest not the time of thy visitation.*"

When the echo of his voice that now sounded in mercy should die away, there would be nothing more for him to do than to pronounce their doom and die.

Again the procession moved. Think you their shouts were as joyous now as before that sad wail and that bitter weeping? Surely some of his spirit must have been communicated to those about him! They enter the city, press on to the temple, and go in. Here the scene was indescribable. "All the city was moved." A throb pulsed along her thronged thoroughfares such as had never been felt before. Many felt that "the desire of all nations" was the central figure of that procession. The Prince of Peace was in their midst and about to be acknowledged. He himself was about to uncover his glory and let the multitude adore him. From mouth to mouth the question flew: " Who is this?"

With a majestic wave of his hand he casts out all that bought and sold in the temple. He overthrew the table of the money-changers and the seats of them that sold doves and said: "It is written, My house shall be called the house of prayer; but ye have made it a den of thieves." The blind and lame came to him in the temple, and he healed them. The very children caught the spirit of the occasion and shouted: " Hosanna to the Son of David." And when the chief priests and scribes, with deep displeasure, said to him, " Hearest thou what these say?" he replied: " Yea; have ye never read, Out of the mouth of babes and sucklings thou hast perfected praise?"

As he taught in the temple from day to day during this eventful week it is said: " The chief priests and the scribes and the chief of the people sought to destroy him, and could not find what they might do: for all the people were very attentive to hear him." He was asked by those rulers: " By what authority doest thou these things? and who gave thee this authority?" thus utterly rejecting him. Moreover, they made special attacks on him. First, the Pharisees banded with the Herodians; then the Sadducees; then again the Pharisees alone. After all these were met and put to silence he began to show them where they stood and to read to them their doom. But first he reveals it to his disciples. And he does it on this wise. On their way to Bethany he seeks fruit on a certain fig-tree, and finds nothing but leaves. He pronounces the fatal words: "Let no fruit grow on thee henceforward forever." This fig-tree represented the barren Church. He had come seeking fruit, and while they had all the outward show of piety—the altars smoking with sacrifices, the temple ringing with song, scribes and priests all in their places—yet it was but "leaves:" no fruit appeared. And now the curse of the Master falls: "Let no fruit grow on thee henceforward forever," and it "withers." From that day to this this tree stands not only fruitless, but "dried up from the roots."

The next day in the temple, when they press upon him, he asks: "But what think ye? A certain man had two sons; and he came to the first, and said, Son, go work to-day in my vineyard. He answered and said, I will not; but afterward he repented, and went. And he came to the second, and said likewise. And he answered and said, I go, sir; and went not. Whether of them twain did the will of his father? They say unto him, The first. Jesus saith unto them, Verily I say unto you, That the publicans and the harlots go into the kingdom of God before you. For John came unto you in the way of righteousness, and ye believed him not; but the publicans and the harlots believed him: and ye, when ye had seen it, repented not afterward, that ye might believe him."

Now this first son was the Gentiles who first refused to do God's will, but now repented and were ready to accept salvation through him; while the second son represented the Jews, who said, "I go, sir," and went not. Still further he presses the matter with the parable of the vineyard contained in Matthew xxi., Luke xx., and Mark xii. This parable represents the Lord as planting a vineyard, setting a hedge about it, digging a wine-press, building a tower, and letting it out to husbandmen. At the time of fruit he sent his servants, and they were shamefully handled: some beaten, some stoned, and some killed. Last of all he sends his son, "saying, They will reverence my son. But when the husbandmen saw the son, they said among themselves, This is the heir; come, let us kill him, and let us seize on his inheritance. And they caught him, and cast him out of the vineyard, and slew him." Jesus then asked them the direct question: "When the lord therefore of the vineyard cometh, what will he do unto those husbandmen?" They answered: "He will miserably destroy those wicked men, and will let out his vineyard unto other husbandmen, which shall render him the fruits in their seasons." It would seem that they had not discovered the nature and bearing of the parable. The vineyard was the Church or kingdom of God, which had been committed to their hands. They had played the part of these husbandmen, and now he (the Son and Heir) was among them; and they were plotting his death, and would accomplish their purpose before the next Sabbath should dawn. And the judgment they had pronounced against themselves should be literally carried out, for Jesus said unto them: "Therefore say I unto you, The kingdom of God shall be taken from you, and given to a nation bringing forth the fruits thereof." Jesus said: "What is this then that is written, The stone which the builders rejected, the same is become the head of the corner?" "This is the Lord's doing, and it is marvelous in our eyes."

"And whosoever shall fall on this stone shall be broken: but on whomsoever it shall fall, it will grind him to powder. And when the chief priests and Pharisees had heard his parables, they perceived that he spake of them."

But they were not convinced. Will nothing open their eyes and melt their hearts? Now he begins to uncover the armory of his wrath, and lets them look upon what awaits them. Here is retribution for rejecting him. "The falling upon this stone" suggest great injury from falling over something in the way, bruising the flesh and breaking the bones. They rush upon him to destroy him. They had been plotting all the week to take him, but "feared the multitude." In this they should be broken, forever broken. But when this stone should fall upon them, in the awful judgments that were soon to come, it would "grind them to powder." No pen can ever portray the horrors of the siege of Jerusalem, when Christ, this rejected stone, was falling upon them in wrath; when he came "with his armies to miserably destroy" this nation of murderers, and to "burn up their city."

"To measure the awful meaning of 'grind him to powder,' one must know all the horrors, the frenzies, unutterable degradations, and overwhelming miseries that were felt in that prolonged siege. He must be in full sympathy with the intestine strifes, the rapine, the bloodshed, and cannibalism to which they were driven in 'the sraightness of the siege, wherewith their enemies besieged them.' Horrors, driven by the breath of God, clouding the day, and hanging like a pall over the night, until they would say at night, 'Would God it were day!' and in the day, as if they could not bear the sight, they would cry, 'Would God it were night!' You must feel their helplessness as the awful calamity came upon them. Sun, moon, and stars sympathized with them in their crushing, grinding calamity."

That there might be no mistaking his meaning, he spake another parable unto them: that of the marriage of the king's son. This parable forcibly represents the position of these rejecters of Jesus.

With a long-standing invitation, when all is ready and they are told to come, they made light of the invitation and the opportunity, and even insulted and slew the innocent servants. Now the wrath of the king is revealed, and he sends forth his armies (the Romans) and destroys these murderers and burns up their city. The munificent provision for the royal feast must not be wasted. He has other subjects, and these at the last moment must be bidden, and messengers are sent into the "highways" for guests. Thus Jesus shows these scribes and Pharisees how certainly and how justly their treatment of the gospel invitation must seal their doom hopelessly and forever, and how that which was provided for them shall be given to others.

After this the Pharisees and Herodians, acting as "spies," "feigning to be just men," came to entrap him. They adroitly, as they thought, placed him between two fires in the question they asked. See their hypocrisy in the manner of address: "Master, we know that thou art true, and teachest the way of God in truth, neither carest thou for any man: for thou regardest not the person of men. Tell us, therefore, What thinkest thou? Is it lawful to give tribute unto Cæsar or not?" They thought whatever his answer might be he would involve himself. If he said it was right, the Jews, who were chaffing under this tribute, would be offended at him; and the multitude, whom they feared, would at once

The Kingdom and Comings of Christ. 135

array themselves on their side, and they could take him without trouble. If he should say it was not right, this would put him squarely against the Roman power, and they would arrest him for treason.

"But Jesus perceived their wickedness, and said, Why tempt ye me, ye hypocrites? Show me the tribute money. And they brought unto him a penny. And he saith unto them, Whose is this image and superscription? They say unto him, Cæsar's. Then saith he unto them, Render therefore unto Cæsar the things which are Cæsar's; and unto God the things that are God's." Thus they were foiled, "and left him, and went their way."

When these had departed "then came to him [the same day] certain of the Sadducees, which deny that there is any resurrection." They propounded to him a question involving, as they thought, unanswerable difficulties with reference to the resurrection. But he is as ready for them as for the Pharisees, and in answering them gives some overwhelming evidence from their own scripture concerning this doctrine.

When the Pharisees heard that he had put the Sadducees to silence, they again rallied their forces, and "one of them, which was a lawyer, asked him a question, tempting him, and saying, Master, which is the great commandment in the law?" Jesus answered and said: "The first of all the commandments is, Hear, O Israel! The Lord our God is one Lord: and thou shalt love the Lord thy God with all thy heart, and with all thy soul, and with all thy mind, and with all thy strength: this is the first commandment. And the second is like unto it, Thou shalt love thy neighbor as thyself. On these two commandments hang all the law and the prophets." By this answer he lifted himself above their reach, and it is said "no man after that durst ask him any question."

Having silenced them effectually, he then takes the offensive and overwhelms them with facts concerning their own Messiah as revealed in the one hundred and tenth Psalm. And now he proceeds to unveil their hypocrisy, and to roll away the stone from the sepulcher of their moral corruption and rottenness. Such words never before fell from the lips of Jesus. They burn like the fires of doom. Like hot thunder-bolts of wrath from an overcharged tempest they strike, and wither, and blast irresistibly. Like the awful judge that he is, he commands these criminals whom he is about to sentence to a most terrible death to stand up while he recounts their crimes and tells them for what they are doomed. Never in the history of the world was there such an arraignment. As a preliminary he calls upon his disciples in the "audience of all the people." "The scribes and Pharisees sit in Moses' seat: all therefore whatsoever they bid you observe, that observe and do; but do not ye after their works: for they say, and do not." "Beware of the scribes," "for they bind heavy burdens and grievous to be borne, and lay them on men's shoulders; but they themselves will not move them with one of their fingers. But all their works they do for to be seen of men:" "they love to go in long clothing," and "make broad their phylacteries, and enlarge the borders of their garments, and love the uppermost rooms at feasts, and the chief seats in the synagogues, and greetings in the markets, and to be called of men, Rabbi, Rabbi!" which "devour widow's houses, and for a pretense make long prayer;" the same "shall receive greater damnation." "But be not ye called Rabbi: for one is your master, even Christ; and all ye are brethren."

Then, turning to the culprits whose sentence he was about to pronounce, he addresses them thus: "But woe unto you, scribes and Pharisees, hypocrites! for ye shut up the kingdom of heaven against men: for ye neither go in yourselves, neither suffer ye them that are entering to go in. Woe unto you, scribes and Pharisees, hypocrites! for ye devour widow's houses, and for a pretense make long prayer: therefore ye shall receive the greater damnation. Woe unto you, scribes and Pharisees, hypocrites! for ye compass sea and land to make one proselyte, and when he is made, ye make him twofold more the child of hell than yourselves. Woe unto you, ye blind guides, which say, Whosoever shall swear by the temple, it is nothing; but whosoever shall swear by the gold of the temple, he is a debtor! Ye fools and blind: for whether is greater, the gold, or the temple that sanctifieth the gold? And, Whosoever shall swear by the altar, it is nothing; but whosoever sweareth by the gift that is upon it, he is guilty. Ye fools and blind: for whether is greater, the gift, or the altar that sanctifieth the gift? Whoso therefore shall swear by the altar, sweareth by it, and by all things thereon. And whoso shall swear by the temple, sweareth by it, and by him that dwelleth therein. And he that shall swear by heaven, sweareth by the throne of God, and by him that sitteth thereon. Woe unto you, scribes and Pharisees, hypocrites! for ye pay tithe of mint and anise and cummin, and have omitted the weightier matters of the law, judgment, mercy, and faith: these ought ye to have done, and not to leave the other undone. Ye blind guides, which strain at [out] a gnat, and swallow a camel. Woe unto you, scribes and Pharisees, hypocrites! for ye make clean the outside of the cup and of the platter, but within they are full of extortion and excess. Thou blind Pharisee, cleanse first that which is within the cup and platter, that the outside of them may be clean also. Woe unto you, scribes and Pharisees, hypocrites! for ye are like unto whited sepulchers, which indeed appear beautiful outward, but are within full of dead men's bones, and of all uncleanness. Even so ye also outwardly appear righteous unto men, but within ye are full of hypocrisy and iniquity. Woe unto you, scribes and Pharisees, hypocrites! because ye build the tombs of the prophets, and garnish the sepulchers of the righteous, and say, If we had been in the days of our fathers, we would not have been partakers with them in the blood of the prophets. Wherefore ye be witnesses unto yourselves, that ye are the children of them which killed the prophets. Fill ye up then the measure of your fathers. Ye serpents, ye generation of vipers, how can ye escape the damnation of hell? Wherefore, behold, I send unto you prophets, and wise men, and scribes: and some of them ye shall kill and crucify; and some of them shall ye scourge in your synagogues, and persecute them from city to city: that upon you may come all the righteous blood shed upon the earth, from the blood of righteous Abel unto the blood of Zacharias son of Barachias, whom ye slew between the temple and the altar. Verily I say unto you, All these things shall come upon this generation. O Jerusalem, Jerusalem, thou that killest the prophets, and stonest them which are sent unto thee, how often would I have gathered thy children together, even as a hen gathereth her chickens under her wings, and ye would not! Behold, your house is left unto you desolate. For I say unto you, Ye shall not see me henceforth, till ye shall say, Blessed is he that cometh in the name of the Lord."

Thus he arrayed their crimes before their faces and in the eyes of the world, that all might see the justness of their punishment. The cup of their iniquity was nearly full, and they were rapidly filling the measure of their corruption, until some forty years from the delivery of this sentence the cloud of vengeance broke over the guilty city; and as peal after peal echoed through the land, and the smoke of their torment ascended in the sight of the nations, they stood aghast before the awful terror of exterminating desolations.

"Not in wrath, but in grief; not in malice, but in sorrow, born of real love, came forth these exposures of Pharisaic hypocrisy and vileness." He who three days before, in the midst of exultant shouts, wept over them and grieved at their persistent refusal to take shelter under his wings, could not now in wrath and malice hurl his denunciations on them. Retribution for their wickedness was mustering its forces for the final blow, and between them and the destroyer he stood, and told them of their sins, if mayhap he might lead them to repentance and to safety. *But they would not!*

Shelterless he was about to leave them. Said he, "I go my way, ye shall die in your sins;" and it was only when the storm should be at its worst that they would gladly welcome any one "in the name of the Lord." But there was no protection in the wings of those who claimed to be the Messiah, as they found to their sorrow, as we shall see when we come to notice more fully the prophecies of Jesus on this point. We consider this the sentence of Jesus, as pronounced against these criminals. It is the most remarkable of all his predictions. As he turned and went out and

The Kingdom and Comings of Christ. 141

departed from the temple, his disciples called his attention to the grandeur and beauty of the buildings on Mount Moriah, saying: "See what manner of stones, and what buildings are here." They seem to understand that the temple and city were to be destroyed, and they call the attention of Jesus to the extent and apparent durability of the buildings. Everything about them denoted permanence. The stones were of the most durable and massive character. Josephus tells us of the stupendous size of some of them—sixty-seven feet long, seven feet high, and nine broad, and of the whitest marble. Herod had rebuilt the temple, and of it as rebuilt by him Josephus says: "The temple was built of stones that were white and strong, and their length was twenty-five cubits, height eight, and breadth about twelve; and the whole structure, as also the structure of the royal cloister, was on each side much lower; but the middle was much higher, till they were visible to those that dwelt in the country for a great many furlongs, but chiefly to such as lived over against them, and those that approached to them. He also encompassed the entire temple with very large cloisters, contriving them to be in a due proportion thereto; and he laid out larger sums of money upon them than had been done before him, till it seemed that no one else had so greatly adorned the temple as he had done. There was a large wall to both the cloisters, which wall was itself the most prodigous work that was ever heard of by man. It was covered all over with plates of gold of great weight, and at the first rising of the sun reflected back a very fiery splendor, and made those who forced themselves to look upon it to turn their eyes away, just as they would have done at the sun's own rays. But this temple appeared to strangers, when they were at a distance, like a mountain covered with snow; for as to those parts of it that were not gilt, they were exceedingly white. Of its stones, some of them were forty-five cubits in length, five in height, and six in breadth."

It was to these massive and magnificent buildings that the disciples called the attention of our Lord, when he said: "See ye not all these things? verily I say unto you, There shall not be left here one stone upon another, that shall not be thrown down." These words of Jesus were fulfilled to the letter. Titus ordered his soldiers to demolish the temple utterly, and the very site was plowed over.

The disciples asked him: "When shall these things be? and what shall be the sign of thy coming, and of the end of the world?" They had seen and heard enough to be convinced that what he said was true; that he himself would come to accomplish this awful destruction; that when he did come it would be to put an end to the Jewish nation as such, and they are solicitous to know when *this second coming* should be. They also wanted to know what signs should presage this coming. He first puts them on their guard against false Christs. When troubles should begin to thicken about the land, there would arise many in his name, saying, "I am Christ," and should deceive many.

He then tells them: "Ye shall hear of wars and rumors of wars; see that ye be not troubled: for all these things must come to pass, but the end is not yet. For nation shall rise against nation, and kingdom against kingdom: and there shall be famines, and pestilences, and earthquakes, in divers places. All these are the beginning of sorrows." As to the false Christs, there were many. Josephus says: "While Fadus was procurator (A.D. 45 or 46) a certain magician whose name was Theudas persuaded many to follow him to the river Jordan; for he told them that he was a prophet, and that he would by his own command divide the river, and afford them an easy passage; and many were deluded by his words." "The country was again filled with robbers and impostors, who deluded the multitude; yet did Felix catch and put to death many of these impostors every day." "These impostors and deceivers persuaded the multitude to follow them into the wilderness, and pretended that they would exhibit manifest wonders and signs, that should be performed by the providence of God. There came out of Egypt about this time one who said he was a prophet, and advised the multitude to go along with him to Mount Olivet, which lay over against the city at the distance of five furlongs. He said he would show them from thence how at his command the walls of Jerusalem would fall down. Felix slew four hundred of them, and took two hundred alive; but the Egyptian escaped." We could mention many others from the history of these times, but these are sufficient for our purpose.

The "wars and rumors of wars" were not wars in different parts of the world, but there right in their midst or very near them—wars that would affect them. The whole East was in a ferment, and Judea in open insurrection; while the armies of Spain and Gaul and Germany, Illyricum, and Syria converged upon Italy, to decide who should succeed to Nero's purple. The throes of inanimate nature seemed to sympathize with the travail of the world. The histories of the age are full of "famines, pestilences, and earthquakes in divers places." "Fearful sights and great signs from heaven appeared to mark the very spot at which the great judgment was to descend. A comet shaped like a scimitar hung over the devoted city during the whole year before the war. Other portents are recorded, in the very exaggeration of which we trace how 'men's hearts failed them for fear, and for looking after those things which were to come on the earth.'"

Josephus tells us of "a light at the ninth hour of the night, that shone round the altar and the holy house, so that it appeared to be bright daytime;" that the "eastern gate of the inner court of the temple, which was of brass and vastly heavy, and had been with difficulty shut by twenty men, and rested upon a basis armed with iron, and had bolts fastened very deep into the firm floor which was there made of one entire stone, was seen to be opened of its own accord about the sixth hour of the night."

"Moreover at that feast which we call Pentecost, as the priests were going by night into the inner court of the temple, as their custom was, to perform their sacred ministrations, they said that in the first place they felt a quaking and heard a great noise, and after that they heard a sound as of a great multitude saying, ' Let us remove hence.' "

Then he tells us of one Jesus, the son of Ananus, who four years before the war "began of a sudden to cry aloud, 'A voice from the east, a voice from the west, a voice from the four winds, a voice against Jerusalem and the holy house, a voice against the bridegrooms and the brides, and a voice against the whole people.' He was whipped until his bones were laid bare, yet did he not make any supplication for himself nor shed any tears, but, turning his voice to the most lamentable tones possible, at every stroke of the whip his answer was, 'Woe, woe to Jerusalem!' He continued this cry for seven years and five months, without growing hoarse. He was at last slain by a stone from one of the engines, just as he uttered 'Woe, woe to the city again, and to the people, and to the holy house; woe, woe to myself also!'" These are enough to fix this prophecy of Jesus on this time.

"Then shall they deliver you up to be afflicted, and shall kill you: and ye shall be hated of all nations for my name's sake. And then shall many be offended, and shall betray one another, and shall hate one another. And many false prophets shall rise, and shall deceive many. And because iniquity shall abound, the love of many shall wax cold. But he that shall endure unto the end, the same shall be saved."

It will not be necessary to go beyond the record found in the New Testament to find these persecutions. But as the day for the destruction of Jerusalem approached these persecutions became more severe, and many suffered their love to grow cold on their account. We have already seen that very many false prophets arose and deceived many.

"And this gospel of the kingdom shall be preached in all the world for a witness unto all nations; and then shall the end come."

This verse has been looked upon by some as an insurmountable difficulty in the way of applying this prophecy of Jesus to the destruction of Jerusalem and the Jewish nation. It was not that the gospel was to be embraced by all nations, but it was to be preached "in all the world for a witness unto all nations," and this was literally fulfilled. "Doddridge is authority for the statement that ' It appears from credible records that the gospel was

The Kingdom and Comings of Christ. 147

preached in Idumea, Syria, and Mesopotamia by Jude; in Egypt, Marmorica, Mauritania, and other parts of Africa by Mark, Simon, and Jude; in Ethiopia by Candice's eunuch and Matthias; in Partus, Galatia, and the neighboring parts of Asia by Peter; in the territories of the seven Asiatic Churches by John; in Parthia by Matthew; in Scythia by Philip and Andrew; in the northern and western part of Asia by Bartholomew; in Persia by Simon and Jude; in Media, Carmania, and several eastern parts by Thomas; through the vast tract from Jerusalem round about unto Illyricum by Paul; as also in Italy, and probably in Spain and Gaul — in most of which places Christian Churches were planted in less than thirty years after the death of Christ—*i. e.*, before the destruction of Jerusalem.'"

We have proof from the Acts of the Apostles of the wide extent of territory visited and preached in by one man—Paul—and we cannot think the twelve were less active. There is no inspired record of their deeds and preaching, but doubtless they were preaching the conquests of the cross to the ends of the earth. Enough had been done during the lifetime of the apostles to stand as a witness to all nations that the long-promised Messiah had appeared in the person of Jesus Christ. Paul wrote to the Romans (x. 18) that "their sound went into *all the earth*, and their words unto the ends of the world;" and to the Colossians (i. 6, 23) that the truths of the gospel had come not to them only, but to "*all the world,*" being "*preached to every creature which is under heaven.*"

Thus we have the evidence from inspired writers, as well as from Church history, that these words of Jesus were literally fulfilled, that "this gospel of the kingdom had been preached in all the world for a witness unto all nations;" and thus is this passage cleared of all difficulty.

"When ye therefore shall see the abomination of desolation, spoken of by Daniel the prophet, stand in the holy place, (whoso readeth, let him understand,) then let them which be in Judea flee unto the mountains: let him which is on the housetop not come down to take any thing out of his house: neither let him which is in the field return back to take his clothes. And woe unto them that are with child, and to those that give suck in these days! But pray ye that your flight be not in the winter, neither on the Sabbath-day."

Luke throws light on this passage by giving a sentence in this prophecy of Jesus omitted by Matthew and Mark. It is: "When ye shall see Jerusalem compassed with armies, then know that the desolation thereof is nigh." The Roman armies spoken of here that were to encompass Jerusalem and destroy it bore upon their standards their idols, which was specially abominable to the Jews, and as these standards were borne at the head of these destroying armies they are called "the abomination of desolation." And as this was to be one of the signs by which the disciples of Jesus were to know when to fly from the doomed city, Jesus adds for their admonition: "Whosoever readeth, let him understand." This was to be their signal for immediate and hasty flight. Now as to the history of this flight we are told that "full two years before the final investment of the city, Cestius Gallus marched a Roman army upon the city, and commenced its siege. Why he did not push the siege is historically unaccountable. Josephus says: 'If he had continued the siege but a little longer, he would have taken the city. But Cestius removed his army, and having received no loss, departed from the city.' This warning had been given; the opportunity for flight came. The Christians, remembering these words, fled to the mountains of Pella, east of the Jordan."

See how distinctly Jesus puts his finger on the place where this is to occur. "Let them which be in Judea." The prophecy was local, and referred to Judea and Jerusalem, and to no other place. No doubt the disciples obeyed the suggestion of Jesus to " pray that their flight be not in the winter, neither on the Sabbath-day," and received an answer; for this flight took place in October, and the day after Cestius raised the siege on Tuesday, giving the disciples time to escape before the Sabbath.

"For then shall be great tribulation, such as was not since the beginning of the world to this time, no, nor ever shall be. And except those days should be shortened, there should no flesh be saved: but for the elect's sake those days shall be shortened."

It would seem that all the facts in the case not only fix this on Jerusalem and its fall under Titus, but exclude all others. No one can read the history of this event written by Josephus without being impressed that the Saviour's prediction had a literal fulfillment in this siege. Strange to say, Josephus, in trying to describe the horrors of this siege, uses the identical idea, and much of the language of Jesus. He says: "Of all the cities which were subjected to the Romans, ours was advanced to the highest felicity, and was thrust down again to the extremest misery; for if the misfortunes of all from the beginning of the world were compared with those of the Jews, they would appear much inferior. No other city ever suffered such things, as no other generation from the beginning of the world was ever more fruitful of wickedness."

Here is but a passage or two to give some idea of these times as seen by the same author. Speaking of the seditious, he says: "They agreed in nothing but this, to kill those that were innocent. The voice also of those that were fighting [this was the Jews among themselves] was incessant, both by day and by night; but the lamentation of those that mourned exceeded the other. Nor was there ever any occasion for them to leave off their lamentations: because their calamities came perpetually one upon another; although the deep consternation they were in prevented their outward wailing. But being constrained by their fear to conceal their inward passions, they were inwardly tormented: without daring to open their lips in groans. Nor was any regard paid to those that were still alive by their relations: nor was there any care taken of burial for those that were dead. The occasion of both which was, that every one despaired of himself. For those that were not among the seditious had no great desires of any thing; as expecting for certain, that they should very soon be destroyed. But for the seditious themselves, they fought against each other while they trod upon the dead bodies, as they lay heaped one upon another; and taking up a mad rage from these dead bodies that were under their feet, became the fiercer thereupon."

Again, when the Romans broke into the city, he says of them: "And when they were come into the houses to plunder them, they found in them entire families of dead men; and the upper rooms full of corpses of such as died by the famine. They then stood in horror at the sight; and went out without touching any thing. But although they had this commiseration for such as were destroyed in that manner, yet had they not the same for those that were still alive: but they ran every one through whom they met with; and obstructed the very lanes with their dead bodies: and made the whole city run down with blood, to such a degree, indeed, that the fire of many of the houses was quenched with these men's blood."

We might greatly multiply the evidence from this author to prove just what Jesus said: that there "shall be tribulation, such as was not since the beginning of the world to this time." And we feel satisfied that nothing has equaled it since. As these tribulations extended to all parts of the Jewish nation, it was well for "the elect" (Christian Jews) to pray for the shortening of these days, and God heard and answered their prayers, or the whole nation would have perished. Titus himself felt and acknowledged that God had helped them, or they never could have taken Jerusalem. When he examined the strong towers, constructed of such immense stones, so well put together, he said: "We have certainly had God for our assistant in this war; and it was no other than God who ejected the Jews out of these fortifications. For what could the hands of men, or any machines, do toward overthrowing these towers." And again: "We have fought with God on our side; and it is God who hath pulled the Jews out of these strongholds; for what could the hands of men or machines do against these towers." Thus we see "God shortened the days by helping the Romans."

Christ also said, " There shall arise false Christs, and false phrophets," etc. There is abundant proof that there arose at this time men who claimed to be Christ, and did deceive many.

Josephus says, in describing the final struggle: "A false prophet was the occasion of these peo-

The Kingdom and Comings of Christ. 153

ple's destruction: who had made a public proclamation in the city, that very day, that 'God commanded to get up upon the temple; and that there they should receive miraculous signs of their deliverance.' Now there was then a great number of false prophets suborned by the tyrants to impose on the people, who told them that they should wait for deliverance from God." Thus does this historian confirm the words of Jesus, and fix the fulfillment of this prediction on the destruction of Jerusalem under Titus.

"For as the lightning cometh out of the east, and shineth even unto the west; so shall also the coming of the Son of man be."

This coming of Christ was to be in judgment, with the Romans as his sword. Moses had predicted this very thing, even describing the nation with which God was to punish them before that nation had an existence. "The Lord shall bring a nation against thee from far, from the end of the earth, as swift as the eagle flieth," etc. (Deut. xxviii. 49-52.) He tells them that this enemy shall besiege them in all their gates. Again, in the second Psalm, we are told that Christ should break them with a rod of iron; that he should dash them in pieces as a potter's vessel. When Christ should come to judgment, they would have no need to ask where is he. He would be in all parts of their land, dealing blows on every place. Like a bright flash of lightning, illuminating the heavens and the earth from horizon to horizon, so would he be. The

Roman army did follow the very course marked out by this prophecy of Jesus. Instead of coming from the west, they came from the east, and swept over to the west, laying waste the land everywhere.

"For wheresoever the carcass is, there will the eagles be gathered together." The whole body of the Jewish nation was despoiled by the Roman eagles. So completely was their whole country laid waste, that when the citizens of Antioch met Titus and besought him to expel them from their city, his notable answer was: "How can this be done, since that country of theirs, whither the Jews must then be obliged to retire, is destroyed, and no place will receive them besides?" The Jewish nation was morally and judicially dead, and God sent these eagles to prey upon them. Josephus says there was no part of Judea which did not partake of the calamities of the capital.

"Immediately after the tribulation of those days shall the sun be darkened, and the moon shall not give her light, and the stars shall fall from heaven, and the powers of the heavens shall be shaken: and then shall appear the sign of the Son of man in heaven: and then shall all the tribes of the earth mourn, and they shall see the Son of man coming in the clouds of heaven with power and great glory."

This is strong symbolic language, intended to show that the whole Jewish polity, civil and ecclesiastical, shall be whelmed in ruin, and that it shall be the work of Christ. This was to follow "immediately after the tribulation of those days." The language of the Saviour forces us to look for this fulfillment immediately upon the destruction of Jerusalem. Christ was not to be seen with the natural eye; but the work of the utter overthrow of the Jewish nation and Church, according to his prediction, was to be so plainly his that all should see it and know it. It is no uncommon thing for the prophets to use just such expressions as these with reference to the sun, moon, and stars, when speaking of great calamities. Christ in the heavens above, as upon the clouds, should direct the storm that should work this dreadful overthrow of his people.

"And he shall send his angels with a great sound of a trumpet, and they shall gather together his elect from the four winds, from one end of heaven to the other."

Immediately upon sweeping the Jewish nation out of the way, Christ's ministers (often called angels) went out into all the world to call the Gentiles—now the elect—to come together unto him. To show that the calamities spoken of by Christ in this wonderful prophecy would soon come, Jesus uses the parable of the budding fig-tree as the harbinger of summer. So the portents spoken of should be evidence to them that the day of destruction was near at hand; and as if to fix it beyond all danger of misapprehension, he says:

"Verily I say unto you, This generation shall not pass, till all these things be fulfilled."

Christ meant just what he said. There were men then living who should see the calamities spoken of by him come to pass—yea, should see their entire fulfillment. His councils were fixed, and heaven and earth would sooner pass away than his words should fail. And yet, near at hand as the time was, no man knew it; nor did the angels: only the Father.

He then compares the suddenness of his coming to the coming of the flood in the days of Noah, and uses an expression that exactly describes the events of that time:

"Then shall two be in the field; the one shall be taken, and the other left. Two women shall be grinding at the mill; the one shall be taken, and the other left."

At the given signal, "the abomination of desolation standing in the holy place," they were to flee to the mountains, not taking time for any thing. If two men were at work side by side in the field, one a Christian and the other not, and the Christian saw the signal of flight, he was to leave his companion and fly. So of the women—one should "be taken, and the other left;" just as Noah and his family were taken into the ark, and the rest left to their destruction. How natural, then, the exhortation to *watch* for the signal.

Jesus then uses the parable of the ten virgins to illustrate this fact. The wise virgins represented the Christians who watched for the sign of the Son of man, and were safely housed from destruction

The Kingdom and Comings of Christ. 157

in the mountains of Pella; while the foolish virgins represented those who were left in the city, encompassed by the Roman armies. Again he repeats the command: "*Watch!*"

This parable is intimately connected with the following one of the talents, which is to show that the Jewish nation had hid their talent in the earth, and thus proved themselves utterly unworthy to take care of the Church of Jesus Christ. It should therefore be taken from them, and given to the Gentiles. Not only so, but the unprofitable servant should be cast into outer darkness. Then it was easy and natural to speak of the final coming of the Son of man to judge all men at the last day. This he does in Matthew xxv. 31-46.

But we have to deal especially with the wonderful predictions found in the previous chapter. The very things spoken of by Jesus in this prophecy were foretold by Isaiah. No doubt in the remarkable sermon delivered in Nazareth, that first enchanted and then angered his hearers to such an extent as to incite them to try and take his life, Jesus referred to this prophecy. Luke only gives us a few of the verses of this prophecy, all of which we believe was read and commented on by the Saviour. We can account for the sudden change of demeanor of the people in no other way. The prophet first speaks of the blessing of Christ's coming; tells us plainly that "the Gentiles shall see thy righteousness, and all kings thy glory: and thou shalt be called by a new name, which the mouth of the Lord shall name." Then, referring to the Christian age, he says: "I have set watchmen upon thy walls, O Jerusalem, which shall never hold their peace day nor night." Jerusalem in this place does not mean the city in Palestine, but it is the New Jerusalem, the Church of Jesus Christ. After speaking of the establishment of this Church, he then refers to the judgments that he will bring upon Jerusalem proper and the Jewish people. The prophet sees him coming with "dyed garments," and he asks the question: "Wherefore art thou red in thine apparel, and thy garments like him that treadeth in the winefat?" And the answer comes as from Jesus himself: "I have trodden the wine-press alone; and of the people there was none with me: for I will tread them in mine anger, and trample them in my fury; and their blood shall be sprinkled upon my garments, and I will stain all my raiment. For the day of vengeance is in mine heart, and the year of my redeemed is come. . . . They rebelled, and vexed his Holy Spirit: therefore he was turned to be their enemy, and he fought against them." Then, after referring to the fact that they had been his people, and offering one of the most touching prayers, concluding with the declaration: "Our holy and our beautiful house, where our fathers praised thee, is burned up with fire: and all our pleasant things are laid waste. Wilt thou refrain thyself for these things, O Lord? wilt thou hold thy peace, and afflict us very sore?" Jesus an-

The Kingdom and Comings of Christ. 159

swers: "I am sought of them that asked not for me; I am found of them that sought me not: I said, Behold me, behold me, unto a nation that was not called by my name. I have spread out my hands all the day unto a rebellious people, which walketh in a way that was not good, after their own thoughts; a people that provoketh me to anger continually to my face."

When Jesus, in his sermon at Nazareth, came to this prophecy, and they felt its application to them, "they were filled with wrath, and rose up, and thrust him out of the city, and led him unto the brow of the hill whereon their city was built, that they might cast him down headlong." But we shall see this thing more clearly revealed in Revelation, when we come to examine that book.

We can see nothing in this whole prophecy of Jesus that cannot be applied to the coming of Christ for the destruction of Jerusalem. Any other interpretation is far-fetched and unnatural. Once break away from this application, and we open the flood-gates of wild speculation to pour out an endless stream of conflicting views and interpretations that will even whelm faith in the Book of of God itself.

CHAPTER IX.

The Book of Revelation—Letters to the Seven Churches—The Book Sealed with Seven Seals—Sealing of the Saints—The Seven Trumpets.

LET us come to the examination of the closing book of Revelation, the book that has been the innocent cause of more wild speculations than perhaps all the rest of the Bible combined; and yet when held in the proper light is as easy of explanation as almost any other part of God's word.

And let me say in the beginning that we shall be disappointed if we expect to find the Roman Catholic Church in this book. The main prophecies of the book had their immediate fulfillment. It is a scenic representation of the overthrow of the first two great persecuting powers of Christianity—namely, the Jews, with their center of power at Jerusalem; and the Romans, with theirs at Rome—the whole closing with a grand representation of the Church of Jesus Christ, as it shall go forth in its prosperity after these two great persecuting powers are broken and destroyed.

John strikes the prelude to this grand drama when he says: "Behold, he cometh with clouds; and every eye shall see him, and they also which pierced him: and all kindreds of the earth shall wail because of him. Even so, Amen."

Jesus had told Caiaphas: "Hereafter shall ye see

the Son of man sitting on the right hand of power, and coming in the clouds of heaven." It was to this coming of Jesus to judge Jerusalem that he refers. All should see and know that these judgments were from him—not of men—as he sits at the right hand of power in the heavens. Every eye should see him, both friend and foe, and they also which pierced him. It was only forty years after the crucifixion that Jerusalem was destroyed, and no doubt there were many of those who took part in the condemnation and crucifixion of Jesus still alive. They had pierced him, had heard his dying groans, and saw his head fall upon his lifeless bosom; saw him wrapped in the cerements of the grave and laid away in the chambers of the dead. But for years they had heard his followers declaring that he had risen from the dead and gone up on high, where he sitteth at the right hand of God, expecting till his enemies be made his footstool. Now they were to see him, see him "coming in the clouds of heaven" with power and great glory. And when the blow should fall upon the second great persecuting power—pagan Rome—all nations should feel the effect, "and all kindreds of the earth shall wail because of him." How graphic is the description of the fulfillment of this prediction, as found in the eighteenth chapter: "And the kings of the earth, who have committed fornication and lived deliciously with her, shall bewail her, and lament for her, when they shall see the smoke of her burning, standing afar off for the fear of her torment, saying, Alas, alas, that great city Babylon, that mighty city! for in one hour is thy judgment come. . . . And the merchants of these things, which were made rich by her, shall stand afar off for the fear of her torment, weeping and wailing, and saying, Alas, alas, that great city, that was clothed in fine linen, and purple, and scarlet, and decked with gold, and precious stones, and pearls! For in one hour so great riches is come to nought. And every ship-master, and all the company in ships, and sailors, and as many as trade by sea, stood afar off, and cried when they saw the smoke of her burning, saying, What city is like unto this great city! And they cast dust on their heads, and cried, weeping and wailing, saying, Alas, alas, that great city, wherein were made rich all that had ships in the sea by reason of her costliness! for in one hour is she made desolate." And we must not forget the expression of satisfaction, "Even so, Amen," as uttered by God's people; for it is said in immediate connection with this wailing of the kings and merchants. "Rejoice over her, thou heaven, and ye holy apostles and prophets; for God hath avenged you on her." Let us not anticipate, but come to a careful examination of this book.

John, as if to put us on our guard against referring the revelations of this book to future ages, tells us that this is a revelation of "things which must shortly come to pass." They are not of things that lie thousands of years remote, but he repeats the

The Kingdom and Comings of Christ. 163

idea, "for the time is at hand." He tells us that he is in the isle called Patmos, for the word of God and for the testimony of Jesus Christ. Jesus appears to him, commanding him to write what he should see "in a book, and send it to the seven Churches which are in Asia." It is evident that he is to send all that is written unto these Churches, and not just the several special messages addressed to each by name, as found in the second and third chapters. These Churches lay just where they would be subject to the greatest trials; and as there were certain facts connected with each of them that required a separate message, John was directed to write to them, and stir them up to preparation for the coming calamities and trials. Their faults and weaknesses are faithfully pointed out, and a special promise made to those of them who should overcome:

"To him that overcometh," in Ephesus, Jesus says, "will I give to eat of the tree of life, which is in the midst of the paradise of God." This tree is specially described in the closing scenes of the book.

To him that overcometh, in Smyrna, he promises that "he shall not be hurt of the second death." This second death we also find amid the closing scenes.

To him that overcometh, in Pergamos, he promises to give "to eat of the hidden manna, and will give him a white stone, and in the stone a new name written, which no man knoweth saving he that receiveth it." We also find the promise: "For the Lamb which is in the midst of the throne shall feed them.". As to the new name, we naturally turn our thought to the great Conqueror, of whom it is said: "He had a name written that no man knew but he himself."

To him that overcometh, in Thyatira, the promise is to "give power over the nations." This was a glorious promise. The nations of earth were persecuting the followers of Jesus, and often destroying them. The promise, then, that he should have power over these nations was very full of comfort.

To him of Sardis who should overcome, the promise was that "the same shall be clothed in white raiment; and I will not blot out his name out of the book of life, but I will confess his name before my Father, and before his angels." In the body of the book we see the great multitude which no man can number, "clothed with white robes, and palms in their hands."

To him of Philadelphia that overcometh is the promise: "I will make a pillar in the temple of my God, and he shall go no more out: and I will write upon him the name of my God, and the name of the city of my God, which is New Jerusalem, which cometh down out of heaven from my God: and I will write upon him my new name."

We find the description of this New Jerusalem in the last chapters of the book, as well as the company that stood with the Lamb upon Mount Zion, "having his Father's name written in their foreheads."

To him of Laodicea who should overcome, the promise is: "I will grant to sit with me in my throne, even as I also overcame, and am set down with my Father in his throne."

In the last chapter of this Revelation we have the blessed declaration: "And there shall be no more curse: but the throne of God and of the Lamb shall be in it; and his servants shall serve him: and they shall see his face; and his name shall be in their foreheads."

From these promises, all of which are to be found in the latter part of the book, we are fully satisfied that the whole of Revelation was intended for and addressed to the Seven Churches.

In the opening vision the great Alpha and Omega, their glorified Lord and Saviour, appears in surpassing majesty—a majesty that he is to sustain throughout the grand panorama that passes in review from this opening manifestation to the closing scene. To each of the Churches he holds up some special feature of this manifestation; but to all of them he is the Almighty, walking among the golden candlesticks (the Churches), holding in his right hand the stars (ministers) of these Churches. What we find in this opening chapter, and in the letters to the Churches, we find in the body of the work. In a word, the whole thing is so connected that one must do violence to all laws of unity to separate it. Every word written must be read by all. The mighty Conqueror, and the avenger of the blood of his saints, had risen and girded his sword upon his thigh; had mounted his white steed, and the shout of battle was soon to be on his lips The season of tribulation, such as the world had never seen, was just at hand; and ere the bugle blast that should sound to the charge should fall upon the ears of the startled world the faithful, loving Jesus would warn his followers and house them from the slaughter. The last earnest warning he gave them while in the flesh—to "watch therefore; for ye know neither the day nor the hour wherein the Son of man cometh"—he would now repeat, that they might not be involved in the great calamity. Grand and glorious as he appeared, yet they were to know that he was none other than their crucified, risen Lord, he that was dead but now alive for evermore, holding in his right hand the "keys of hell and of death." Though long sealed, and only in the knowledge of the Father, the hour was at hand when that Father would deliver the sealed book into the hand of his Son, who should break one seal after another, and unroll the awful secret in time for the safety of his beloved.

Most writers on this book have referred the prophecies to times long after the writing of them, bringing many of them down to our times; and others leave some of them to be fulfilled near the end of time. But should we not listen to the frequent declarations of the book itself. The opening sentence is, "The Revelation of Jesus Christ, which God gave unto him, to show unto his servants *things which must shortly come to pass.*" "Blessed is he that readeth, and they that hear the words of this prophecy, . . . *for the time is at hand.*" Books were only written in those days, and hence there were but few copies; and people had to depend upon readers, and the inditing Spirit, knowing that the time was short, pronounces a special blessing upon the *reader*, and also upon the *hearer*. If its contents be not soon known, it will be too late.

Mr. Henry Cowles says: "'Write the things which thou hast seen, and the things which are, and the things which shall be hereafter' (i. 19); but this 'hereafter' is not the remote, indefinite future, but, according to the original (*meta tauta*), the things which follow *closely after*, in the closest connection with present events. The same language and in the same sense appears (iv. 1): 'Come up hither [into this open heaven], and I will show thee things which must be hereafter'— *i. e.*, in close connection with the present, things which must be *very soon.*"

Near the close of the book we have similar declarations showing that these are times that apply to all the book. In the last chapter John is commanded to "Seal not the sayings of the prophecy of this book: *for the time is at hand.*" We cannot close our eyes to such plain declarations as these.

After the letters to the seven Churches, Jesus

stands ready to reveal the things that must shortly come to pass. He begins with the revelations concerning the first great persecuting power, the Jewish nation.

John sees an open door in heaven, and hears the first voice calling him to "Come up hither, and I will show thee things which must be hereafter," or soon, as it is in the original. In the former vision he sees the Son of man walking amid the candlesticks as if for the assurance and protection of the Churches. Now he sees things in heaven; one upon a throne. He attempts no description of this being. It is evidently God the Father. Round about this throne he sees four and twenty elders sitting, clothed in white raiment, with crowns of gold upon their heads, and out of the throne proceeded lightnings, and thunderings, and voices. Before the throne the seven Spirits of God. Round about the throne, four living creatures (unfortunately called beasts in the Authorized Version). They each had four faces, and six wings, " and they rest not day and night, saying, Holy, holy, holy, Lord God Almighty, which was, and is, and is to come. And when these living creatures give glory and honor and thanks to him that sat on the throne, who liveth forever and ever, the four and twenty elders fall down before him " also.

These twenty-four elders perhaps represent the patriarchs and apostles, or the heads of the two dispensations, while the four living creatures are no doubt the seraphim seen in the vision of Isaiah;

for the descriptions are almost identical. At any rate, they are intelligent creatures that minister before the throne.

This chapter only prepares us for the revelations to be made. John says: "I saw in the right hand of him that sat on the throne a book written within and on the back side, sealed with seven seals." This was a parchment roll that was written on both sides, "within and on the back side," and it was sealed in seven sections or parts.

The prophet now advances a step farther. A strong angel makes a proclamation with a loud voice: "Who is worthy to open the book and to loose the seals thereof?" This book is evidently the book containing the things that must shortly come to pass. No man, either in heaven or earth, neither under the earth, is able to open the book, neither to look thereon. John is overcome with grief at this fact, when one of the elders assures him that "the Lion of the tribe of Juda, the Root of David, hath prevailed to open the book, and to loose the seven seals thereof.'" Just then he makes a discovery: "In the midst of the throne and of the four living creatures, and in the midst of the elders, stood a Lamb as it had been slain, having seven horns and seven eyes, which are the seven Spirits of God sent forth into all the earth. And he came and took the book out of the right hand of him that sat upon the throne." Then the four living creatures and the twenty-four elders fall before the Lamb, and sing a new song, saying: "Thou art worthy to take the book, and to open the seals thereof." Then an almost countless number of angels join in the song, and to this is added the song of every creature in heaven and earth and under the earth and in the sea. And as their song concludes, the four living creatures say, "Amen," showing that all the intelligent creatures of God are deeply interested in the revelations to be made when the seals of this wonderful book shall be loosed.

When the Lamb opened one of the seals, one of the living creatures, with a voice of thunder, said: "Come." It is not "Come and see," as is found in the Authorized Version as addressed to John, but it is a command to the rider on the white horse. At the thundering voice, "Come," there leaped forth "a white horse: and he that sat on him had a bow; and a crown was given unto him: and he went forth conquering, and to conquer." This is a symbol of *the Messiah* riding forth to victory. He had been at the right hand of God the Father waiting the time when he should "make his enemies his footstool." This time had now come, and he, as a conqueror, should "strike through kings in the day of his wrath." He was armed with a bow: he was ready for battle; "and a crown was given unto him," showing that he had full authority as a king to execute judgment, as he says in his parable: "He sent forth his armies, and destroyed those murderers, and burned up their city." He had now mounted for the destruction of Jerusalem and its inhabitants.

The Kingdom and Comings of Christ. 171

"And when he had opened the second seal, I heard the second living creature saying, Come. And there went out another horse that was red; and power was given to him that sat thereon to take peace from the earth, and that they should kill one another: and there was given unto him a great sword."

This is a symbol of war. We are now at a period immediately preceding the destruction of Jerusalem. It did seem just at this time that peace had fled the earth. "Nero had perished; and first Otho, then Vitellus, and then Vespatian—each with his influence setting the whole Roman empire into conflicts. Army against army! These armies, sometimes going forth in the interest of one claimant to the imperial purple, would espouse the cause of another on the eve of battle; and thus like contending winds on a stormy sea they tore the empire into factions and deluged the land with blood. Then there was war between Jews and Romans, between John of Giscala and Simon; men should slay one another in internecine and civil discord. It was an epoch of massacres. There had been massacres at Alexandria, massacres at Seleucia, massacres at Jamnia, massacres at Damascus, massacres at Cæsarea, massacres at Bedriacum. There had been wars in Britain, wars in Armenia, wars in Gaul, wars in Italy, wars in Arabia, wars in Parthia, wars in Judea. Disbanded soldiers and marauding troops filled the world with rapine, terror, and massacre. The world was like an aceldama, or field of blood. The red horse and its rider are but a visible image of the words of our Lord: 'For nation shall rise against nation, and kingdom against kingdom;' and 'ye shall hear of wars and rumors of wars,' which things 'are the beginnings of sorrows.'" This rider upon the red horse, as well as all the others, is under the command of the Messiah, who heads the list on his white horse. In a word, it is Jesus now gone forth with all his instruments to judge and punish his people for their rejection of him and all their added crimes. The time had come for him to " break them with a rod of iron," to "dash them in pieces as a potter's vessel."

At the opening of the third seal the third living creature shouted, " Come;" and there leaped forth " a black horse; and he that sat on him had a pair of balances in his hand. And I heard a voice in the midst of the four living creatures say, A measure of wheat for a penny, and three measures of barley for a penny; and see thou hurt not the oil and the wine."

This is a symbol of famine. When Jerusalem was besieged, there was an abundant supply of corn; but the several parties in the city burned these stores of corn and other provisions, thus, as Josephus expresses it, "cutting off the nerves of their own power." He also says: "Almost all the corn was burned, which would have been sufficient for a siege of many years. So they were taken by the famine, which it was impossible they should have been unless they had thus prepared the way for it by this procedure."

Speaking of this famine, he says: "Many there were, indeed, who sold what they had for one measure. It was of wheat, if they were of the richer sort; but of barley, if they were poorer. . . . A table was nowhere laid for a distinct meal, but they snatched the bread out of the fire, half-baked, and devoured it very hastily. It was now a miserable case, and a sight that would justly bring tears into your eyes, how men stood as to their food. . . . Children pulled the very morsels that their fathers were eating out of their mouths; and, what was still more to be pitied, so did the mothers do to their infants. And when those that were most dear were perishing under their hands, they were not ashamed to take from them the very last drops that might preserve their lives. . . . The old men who held their food fast were beaten: and if the women hid what they had within their hands, their hair was torn for so doing. Nor was there any commiseration shown either to the aged or to the infants; but they lifted up children from the ground as they hung upon the morsels they had gotten, and shook them down upon the floor. Moreover, their hunger was so intolerable that it obliged them to chew every thing, while they gathered and ate such things as the most sordid animals would not touch; nor did they at length abstain from girdles and shoes; and the very leather which belonged to their shields they pulled off and gnawed. Even whisps of old hay became food to some, and some gathered up fibers and sold a very small weight of them for four Attic drachmas [one shekel]." And yet, strange to say, in Jerusalem, where such a famine at this time prevailed, "John of Giscala and his zealots had access to the sacred stores of *wine and oil* in the temple, and wasted it with reckless extravagance; and Simon's followers were even hindered from fighting by their perpetual drunkenness."

We are bold to say that this symbol can be applied to no other time or place than this memorable siege of Jerusalem. As the coin to the die every feature of it applies, and any attempt to apply this seal to any other time or place can but be vain. Let us in this, as in other things, apply the rules of common sense and just interpretation, and be done with the wild vagaries that have filled the world with false doctrines.

"And when he had opened the fourth seal, I heard the voice of the fourth living creature say, Come. And I looked, and behold a pale horse: and his name that sat on him was Death, and Hell followed with him. And power was given unto them over the fourth part of the earth, to kill with sword, and with hunger, and with death, and with the beasts of the earth."

Here is a symbol with its very name announced. The rider is Death, going forth with his four faithful allies—sword, famine, pestilence, and wild beasts—while Hell followed to garner the harvest as it fell before these mighty reapers. Of course the term "earth," as used here, as is often the case in the Scriptures, refers to Palestine, that portion of the earth being dealt with in the symbol. We have no means of determining accurately as to the fourth part, but from the massacres all over the land we are fully persuaded that a full fourth of the Jews perished. Josephus estimates the loss of life in Jerusalem alone at 1,100,000, while multitudes perished in other cities also: "At Alexandria, 50,000; at Cæsarea, 10,000; at Scythopolis, 13,000; at Damascus, 10,000; at Jotapata, 30,000." This list might be multiplied almost indefinitely. "In every city there were hostile armies, and there was no safety for any one but in the strength of the party to which he belonged. At Askelon, Ptolemais, Tyre, Hippo, and Gadara the Jews were involved in one general massacre," etc. (Jahn.) "And when in A.D. 67 Vespasian swept through Galilee and Samaria, and city after city fell before him, the scenes of horror and carnage were fearful; the merciless sword spared neither age nor sex; cities were left without inhabitants."

The opening of the fifth seal is a very important one, as it shows what has moved this conqueror to "send forth his armies" for this work of death and destruction. No lesson is more plainly taught in the Scriptures than that God is moved by the prayers of his people. Bearing on this very point our Saviour spoke a parable to this end, that men ought always to pray, and not to faint; and in the application of the parable he says: "And shall not God avenge his own elect, which cry day and night unto him, though he bear long with them? I tell you that he will avenge them speedily."

Let us listen to the teaching of the fifth seal: "And when he had opened the fifth seal, I saw under the altar the souls of them that were slain for the word of God, and for the testimony which they held: and they cried with a loud voice, saying, How long, O Lord, holy and true, dost thou not judge and avenge our blood on them that dwell on the earth? And white robes were given unto every one of them; and it was said unto them, that they should rest yet for a little season, until their fellow-servants also and their brethren, that should be killed as they were, should be fulfilled."

These souls of the martyrs were under or at the foot of the altar praying to be avenged. They had been slain for the word of God and for the testimony which they held, slain for their very righteousness. And their foes, encouraged by their success in putting out of the way these good men, were still at their bloody work. And these martyrs, who knew that the promise had been given that "He would avenge them speedily," were lifting their cry, "How long, O Lord, holy and true, dost thou not judge and avenge our blood on them that dwell on the earth?" White robes of victory, as petitioners, were given unto every one of them, and they were assured that as soon as a few more of their fellow-servants should be killed, then he would rise in vengeance against their enemies.

The Kingdom and Comings of Christ. 177

There were martyrs of that period. Jesus, in encouraging the Church at Pergamos, calls one of these (Antipas) by name as a faithful martyr. And it is folly to be looking along down the ages for seasons of persecution to find the souls of those under the altar. When the seal is opened, they are seen. Having been slain before it, therefore it cannot apply to those slain centuries afterward. To suppose that they are souls to be slain centuries afterward, "in the days of the Waldenses and Albigenses, is simply to wrest the words from their obvious sense and application, and force upon them a meaning which could not have entered the mind of John or of those whom he addressed. Such methods of interpretation cannot be too severely censured. They practically destroy all confidence in prophecy by ignoring the legitimate principles and laws of prophetic interpretation."

Giving John time to record the scenes revealed under this seal, the Lamb proceeds to break another.

"And I beheld when he had opened the sixth seal, and, lo, there was a great earthquake; and the sun became black as sackcloth of hair, and the moon became as blood; and the stars of heaven fell unto the earth, even as a fig-tree casteth her untimely figs, when she is shaken of a mighty wind. And the heaven departed as a scroll when it is rolled together; and every mountain and island were moved out of their places. And the kings of the earth, and the great men, and the rich men, and the chief captains, and the mighty men, and every bond man, and every free man, hid themselves in the dens and in the rocks of the mountains; and said to the mountains and rocks, Fall on us, and hide us from the face of him that sitteth on the throne, and from the wrath of the Lamb: for the great day of his wrath is come; and who shall be able to stand?"

The Lamb, at the foot of whose altar the souls of the martyrs kneeled and prayed, now moves heaven and earth with mighty convulsions as assurances that he has heard their prayers and "will avenge them speedily." This is all symbolic language, and we need not look for any facts or phenomena in nature analogous to it. We need not look for any special earthquake, no "dark day" in the history of the ages, no showers of meteors, or any thing of the kind. The time had come when altar and temple should be thrown down; and not only the Jewish Church, but the nation itself was to fall under the shivering stroke of the "rod of iron" in the hands of the angry Lamb, whose precious blood had been trampled upon by their unhallowed feet. The old city of Jerusalem, that had become a Sodom, was to be removed to give place to the new Jerusalem that should come down from God out of heaven.

Paul refers to this in Hebrews xii. 22–29: " But ye are come unto mount Sion, and unto the city of the living God, the heavenly Jerusalem, and to an innumerable company of angels, to the general assembly and Church of the First-born, which are written in heaven, and to God the Judge of all, and to the spirits of just men made perfect, and to Jesus the Mediator of the new covenant, and to the blood of sprinkling, that speaketh better things than that of Abel. See that ye refuse not him that speaketh: for if they escaped not who refused him that spake on earth, much more shall not we escape, if we turn away from him that speaketh from heaven: whose voice then shook the earth: but now he hath promised, saying, Yet once more I shake not the earth only, but also heaven. And this word, Yet once more, signifieth the removing of those things that are shaken, as of things that are made, that those things which cannot be shaken may remain. Wherefore we receiving a kingdom which cannot be moved, let us have grace, whereby we may serve God acceptably with reverence and godly fear: for our God is a consuming fire." Here the apostle shows that Christ will remove the tottering Jewish Church and forever establish the Christian Church. The civil and ecclesiastical rulers, with all their officers and priests, shall be swept away like the darkening of the sun, turning the moon to blood, and the hurling down of the stars.

"And the heavens departed like a scroll when it is rolled together." Every vestige of the ceremonial worship was to be rolled away. Isaiah, in prophesying of this, says: " Thus saith the Lord, The heaven is my throne, and the earth is my footstool: where is the house that ye build unto me? and where is the place of my rest? For all those things hath mine hand made, and all those things have been, saith the Lord: but to this man will I look, even to him that is poor and of a contrite spirit, and trembleth at my word. He that killeth an ox is as if he slew a man; he that sacrificeth a lamb, as if he cut off a dog's neck; he that offereth an oblation, as if he offered swines' blood; he that burneth incense, as if he blessed an idol. Yea, they have chosen their own ways, and their soul delighteth in their abominations." This shows the utter abhorrence with which God will regard the sacrifices that these Jews shall offer. The great antitype had come; and now he that should still cling to these types and sacrifices, though once acceptable to God, would by them manifest his unbelief in Christ the Lamb of God that had been crucified among them, and hence God would despise them. And as they persisted in offering them, and in persecuting and murdering those who did believe in Jesus, they were to be destroyed, and with them every form of their religion.

Farther on in this same chapter he says, after saying some comforting things concerning those that "trembleth at his word:" "The hand of the Lord shall be known toward his servants, and his indignation toward his enemies. For, behold, the Lord will come with fire, and with his chariots like a whirlwind, to render his anger with fury, and his rebuke with flames of fire. For by fire and by his

The Kingdom and Comings of Christ. 181

sword will the Lord plead with all flesh: *and the slain of the Lord shall be many."* The history of this period shows that this was literally fulfilled when all the land was filled with their dead bodies, and the stench of their unburied carcasses bred pestilence and plague that added to the awful list.

"And every mountain and island were moved out of their places." So thorough should be the work of the Lamb that Jewish ceremonies should never be restored. Since that awful period, when city and temple went down under the power of the Lamb, no altar has ever been erected, and no sacrifice has ever been offered. The only notes heard from Jewish lips in Jerusalem are the sad wailings outside the walls.

The last words of the prophecy of Isaiah, in the chapter from which we have quoted, are: "And it shall come to pass, that from one new moon to another, and from one Sabbath to another, shall all flesh come to worship before me, saith the Lord. And they shall go forth, and look upon the carcasses of the men that have transgressed against me: for their worm shall not die, neither shall their fire be quenched; and they shall be an abhorring unto all flesh." The awful judgments that befell this people are known by all flesh, and the just retribution heaped upon them in their utter overthrow is looked upon by all. There is no mitigation of their woes, but they are scattered and torn and peeled. They have been driven to the ends of the earth; fragments of them are found among all nations, and wherever they have gone they are looked upon as a people cursed of God. "Their worm dieth not, and their fire is not quenched." No wonder that "the kings of the earth, and the great men, and the rich men, and the chief captains, and the mighty men, and every bond man, and every free man, hid themselves in the dens and in the rocks of the mountains; and said to the mountains and rocks, Fall on us, and hide us from the face of him that sitteth on the throne, and from the wrath of the Lamb: for the great day of his wrath is come; and who shall be able to stand?"

Kings, mighty men, captains, rich and poor, bond and free, went down alike under the glittering sword of this Lamb of God, when he arose to judgment; when Roman legions encompassed them without, and internal discords, famine, and pestilence rent and tore and withered them within. When they despaired of life within the city, and went to the Romans, they were crucified until, as Josephus tells us, "So the soldiers, out of the wrath and hatred they bore to the Jews, nailed those they caught—one after one way, and another after another—to the crosses, by way of jest, when their multitude was so great that room was wanting for the crosses, and crosses wanting for bodies." What were the horrors within that could induce people to go out among such merciless fiends in human shape? Let us see. Josephus says: "The citizens themselves were under terrible consternation. The zealots agreed in nothing but this: to kill those that were innocent. The noise, also, of those that were fighting was incessant, both by day and by night; but the lamentation of those that mourned exceeded the other. Nor was there any occasion to leave off their lamentation, because their calamities came perpetually one upon another." And again: "The upper rooms were full of women and children that were dying of famine, and the lanes of the city were full of the dead bodies of the aged. The children, also, and the young men wandered about the market-places like shadows, all swelled with the famine, and fell down dead wheresoever their misery seized them. As for burying them, those that were sick were not able, and those that were well were deterred from doing it by the great multitude of these dead bodies, and by the uncertainty as to how soon they should die themselves; for many died as they were burying others, and many went to their coffins before that fatal hour was come." No wonder they called to the mountains and rocks to fall upon them, and hide them from the wrath of the Lamb.

The next scene is one of deep interest. The wrath of the Lamb is just ready to break upon the guilty; but all over the land there are the righteous. They are found even in the city of Jerusalem, that second Sodom, upon which he is just ready to pour his vengeful fires. Will the righteous perish with the wicked? If not, how are they to be delivered? John tells us: "And after these things I saw four angels standing in the four corners of the earth, holding the four winds of the earth, that the wind should not blow on the earth, nor on the sea, nor on any tree. And I saw another angel ascending from the east, having the seal of the living God: and he cried with a loud voice to the four angels, to whom it was given to hurt the earth and the sea, saying, Hurt not the earth, neither the sea, nor the trees, till we have sealed the servants of our God in their foreheads. And I heard the number of them which were sealed: and there were sealed a hundred and forty and four thousand of all the tribes of the children of Israel. Of the tribe of Juda were sealed twelve thousand. Of the tribe of Reuben were sealed twelve thousand. Of the tribe of Gad were sealed twelve thousand. Of the tribe of Aser were sealed twelve thousand. Of the tribe of Nephthalim were sealed twelve thousand. Of the tribe of Manassas were sealed twelve thousand. Of the tribe of Simeon were sealed twelve thousand. Of the tribe of Levi were sealed twelve thousand. Of the tribe of Issachar were sealed twelve thousand. Of the tribe of Zabulon were sealed twelve thousand. Of the tribe of Joseph were sealed twelve thousand. Of the tribe of Benjamin were sealed twelve thousand. After this I beheld, and, lo, a great multitude, which no man could number, of all nations, and kindreds, and people, and tongues, stood before the throne, and before the Lamb, clothed with white robes, and palms in their hands; and cried with a loud voice, saying, Salvation to our God which sitteth upon the throne, and unto the Lamb. And all the angels stood round about the throne, and about the elders, and thé four beasts, and fell before the throne on their faces, and worshiped God, saying, Amen: Blessing, and glory, and wisdom, and thanksgiving, and honor, and power, and might, be unto our God forever and ever. Amen. And one of the elders answered, saying unto me, What are these which are arrayed in white robes? and whence came they? And I said unto him, Sir, thou knowest. And he said to me, These are they which came out of great tribulation, and have washed their robes, and made them white in the blood of the Lamb. Therefore are they before the throne of God, and serve him day and night in his temple: and he that sitteth on the throne shall dwell among them. They shall hunger no more, neither thirst any more; neither shall the sun light on them, nor any heat. For the Lamb which is in the midst of the throne shall feed them, and shall lead them unto living fountains of water: and God shall wipe away all tears from their eyes."

This scene follows immediately *(meta tauta)*. God intends to protect his people. Hence the four angels, standing on the four corners of the earth, hold back the winds until this protection is secured. It is a remarkable fact that winds have more to do with the destructive elements than anything else. It is the winds that form the tempests in all their varied manifestations. They sweep the earth in their destructive force; they lash the waves of the sea into billows of power, and hurl them along with irresistible force. It is the winds that bear the clouds along as war chariots of the King of heaven. Their friction generates the lightning's bolt, that leaps with the thunder's voice on its mission of death. It is the winds that as a mighty catapult hurl death-dealing hail-stones to the earth; hence they are symbolic of the mighty agencies that the Lamb shall employ in displaying his wrath on the guilty.

A distinguishing mark must be set upon God's servants. An angel is seen ascending from the east, having the seal of the living God. Jesus, when he sent his disciples into all the world to preach his gospel to every creature, said, "Whosoever believeth and is baptized shall be saved." This seal, then, is baptism, wherewith is written the name of the "Father, and of the Son, and of the Holy Ghost" on the forehead of him that believeth. This, then, is to be the sign to the destroying angel to spare, just as the blood of the paschal lamb, sprinkled on the door-posts and on the lintels, was to be a sign to the destroying angel in Egypt to pass over that house. Men might not be able to read this wonderful name on the forehead of his servants, but those who were commissioned to destroy could. Jesus refers to this same scene in that wonderful prophecy that foretold the destruction of Jerusalem. He said: "And he shall send his angels with a great sound of a trumpet, and they shall gather together his *elect from the four winds*, from one end of heaven to the other."

As the disciples who were to go into all the world to preach were to begin at Jerusalem, so this angel begins his sealing among the Israelites. Round numbers only are given, and for some reason twelve is the number. There were twelve tribes, as there were twelve apostles, and there were twice twelve elders prominent in all these symbols. So twelve thousand are announced for each of the twelve tribes. Dan is omitted on account of his idolatry. His tribe went almost wholly away from God. Joseph has two, one in his own name and one in Manassas's name. The patriarch, Jacob, said to Joseph on his death-bed: "Moreover I have given to thee one portion above thy brethren, which I took out of the hand of the Amorite with my sword and with my bow."

There were very many of the Jews that were obedient to the faith. James said to Paul when he went up to Jerusalem, "Thou seest, brother, how many thousands [myriads, 10,000, as in the margin] of Jews there are which believe;" and there were converts among this people in all parts of the land. Here a hundred and forty and four thousand are mentioned as sealed, no doubt a definite for an indefinite number, as is frequently the case in Scripture. In addition to these there were a great multitude, which no man could number, of Gentile converts. These were shouting: "Salvation to our God which sitteth upon the throne, and unto the Lamb." When all the angels that stood round about the throne, and the elders, and the four living creatures heard it, they fell before the throne in their joy, and worshiped, and said: "Blessing, and glory, and wisdom, and thanksgiving, and honor, and power, and might, be unto our God forever and ever. Amen." There was general joy in earth and heaven.

One of the elders calls John's attention to this countless multitude, and asks him who they are and whence they came. John said: "Sir, thou knowest." Then the elder told him they were those that had stood the fires of persecution, and had been washed in the blood of the Lamb, and this entitled them to the special care and protection of God. This, too, is symbolic language. These men were not in heaven; they were still alive on earth, but under the special protection of God and the Lamb. These, both Jews and Gentiles, who had the seal of God in their foreheads were to be as much protected on earth as if they were in heaven. Jesus said: "But there shall not a hair of your head perish." He gave his disciples the sign by which they should know of the destruction and make their escape; and it is a noted fact that all the Christians of Jerusalem did escape to Pella, and not a single Christian perished in that dreadful siege. And we have no reason to think that he would be less careful of those in other parts of the land, or those of other nations who were recognized as his servants

With reference to the salvation of the Christians at the siege of Jerusalem let us see the warning and the escape. Jesus said: "When ye therefore shall see the abomination of desolation, spoken of by Daniel the prophet, stand in the holy place, (whoso readeth, let him understand,) then let them which be in Judea flee into the mountains." Josephus tells us: "When Cestius Gallus came with his army against Jerusalem, many fled from the city as if it would be taken presently, and after his retreat many of the noble Jews departed out of the city, as out of a sinking ship: and a few years afterward, when Vespasian was drawing his forces toward Jerusalem, a great multitude fled from Jericho into the mountainous country for their security." That some of these were Christians appears from Eusebius, who says: "The whole body of the Church at Jerusalem, having been commanded by a divine revelation, removed from the city, and dwelt at a certain town beyond the Jordan called Pella. Here those who believed in Christ, having removed from Jerusalem, as if holy men had entirely abandoned the royal city itself, and the whole land of Judea, the divine justice, for their crimes against Christ and his apostles, finally overtook the Jews," etc. Thus those of Israel that were sealed escaped.

The Gentiles were equally protected. Wherever they were, God was among them. The Lamb which is in the midst of the throne (the good Shepherd) fed and watered them; and God wiped away all tears from their eyes—that is, the religion of Jesus gave them comfort in all the afflictions of life. "Earth had no sorrow that God could not heal."

We must ever remember that symbolic language can never be interpreted literally. The prophets of the Old Testament used just this class of symbols in their writings. Isaiah, in prophesying against Babylon, uses this language: "Behold, the day of the Lord cometh, cruel both with wrath and fierce anger, to lay the land desolate: and he shall destroy the sinners thereof out of it. For the stars of heaven and the constellations thereof shall not give their light: the sun shall be darkened in his going forth, and the moon shall not cause her light to shine." And again: "Their slain also shall be cast out, and their stink shall come up out of their carcasses, and the mountains shall be melted with their blood. And all the hosts of heaven shall be dissolved, and the heavens shall be rolled together as a scroll: and all their host shall fall down, as the leaf falleth off from the vine, and as a falling fig from the fig-tree."

No one thinks of making this literal in its signification. We might multiply these passages almost indefinitely. We will take but one more, and take that because of its known use. It is found in Joel, and is quoted by Peter on the day of Pentecost: "And on my servants and on my handmaidens I will pour out in those days of my Spirit; and they shall prophesy: And I will show wonders in the heaven above, and signs in the earth beneath; blood, and fire, and vapor of smoke: the sun shall be turned into darkness, and the moon into blood, before that great and notable day of the Lord come."

Every one knows that this was not literally fulfilled. The sun was not really darkened, nor did the moon turn to blood before the day of Pentecost. But a great change was to be made in the Church of God and in its operations. Jewish sacrifices were to cease to be offered, and the temple services to close. Christ, the great High Priest, was to enter into heaven, the true tabernacle, and there, in the presence of God, to offer the blood that he, as the Lamb of God, had shed on the altar of the cross; and fresh heralds were to be sent out into all the world to preach the gospel to every creature, and it must be made manifest that this change was wrought of God. The first, or Mosaic, dispensation, was established amid the blackness and darkness and tempest that rested upon Mount Sinai. Every supernatural evidence that was necessary was given, that men might know that God did it. Now when a radical change is to take place, there are signs not only on earth, but in heaven. All understood the figurative nature of this language, and the pouring out of God's Spirit and the gift of tongues that was bestowed satisfied all who believed in Jesus that the prophecy was fulfilled. Peter did not go into any elaborate explanation of the symbol, for he knew that his hearers were familiar with just such expressions in their prophets; in fact, that their writings abounded in them.

It was the constant custom of Jesus to use symbolic language. Who would take as literal such an expression as this: "Except ye eat my flesh and drink my blood, ye have no life in you?" and again, "Destroy this temple, and in three days I will raise it up?" One great error in many expounders of these prophecies is that they are hunting for a literal fulfillment of things that are only symbolical.

"And when he had opened the seventh seal, there was silence in heaven about the space of half an hour. And I saw the seven angels which stood before God; and to them were given seven trumpets. And another angel came and stood at the altar, having a golden censer; and there was given unto him much incense, that he should offer it with the prayers of all saints upon the golden altar which was before the throne. And the smoke of the incense, which came with the prayers of the saints, ascended up before God out of the angel's hand."

Upon the opening of this seal, which was to reveal so many and such awful woes, there was silence in heaven about the space of half an hour. This betokens the reluctance of God in letting fall the long-suspended blow. God has sworn, "As I live, I have no pleasure in the death of the wicked;" and while it was but just that this blow should fall, and God avenge his people, yet God had no pleasure in it. The calamities revealed under this seal are presented more in detail and are more elaborate than any of the preceding. The seven angels which stand before God are given each a trumpet, symbols of war. The Jews were familiar with this: "If ye go to war in your land against the enemy that oppresseth you, then ye shall blow an alarm with the trumpets." These trumpets were to sound the alarm of war; but before they sound one other fact must be made manifest, and that is that God associates his people with him. He requires them to ask what they want. As Jesus said, " Men ought always to pray, and not to faint." The adversaries of the Church were oppressing them, and hindering the work of God. We have seen that the souls of the martyrs under the altar were pleading, and now we have the saints on earth adding their prayers. An "angel stood at the altar, having a golden censer; and there was given unto him much incense, that he should offer it with the prayers of all saints upon the golden altar which was before the throne." After this "the angel took the censer, and filled it with fire of the altar, and cast it into the earth: and there were voices, and thunderings, and lightnings, and an earthquake," a token that God was moving speedily in answer to their prayers. This was but the prelude, but the sound of the moving armies of Jehovah preparing for the battle. The marshaling hosts were forming in line, and the very earth trembles beneath their tread. It is the brink of the storm that is soon to burst in all its fury. The gleam of the lightnings, and the distant roll of the thunders tell that the elements of destruction are moving on the devoted land.

"The first angel sounded" his trumpet blast, and at once "there followed hail and fire mingled with blood, and they were cast upon the earth: and the third part of trees were burnt up, and all green grass was burnt up." This is one of the first effects of war. The trees round about Jerusalem were destroyed for many miles, to build banks (as they were called) against the wall. Josephus tells us: "For all the trees that were about the city had been already cut down, for the erection of the former banks. Yet did the soldiers bring with them other materials from the distance of ninety furlongs" (a little more than eleven miles).

The Romans had an immense number of horses besides the flocks and herds necessary to feed so large an army. These would destroy the grass. This was a symbol of this first effect of war. But even this first chapter in the great drama was not without bloodshed and death, as indicated by the hail and fire mingled with blood. It also indicates that it comes from God. The Psalmist says: "Deliver my soul from the wicked, *which is thy sword.*" While the Romans were going according to the dictates of their own will, God was using them for the destruction of the foes of his people, and in answer to their prayers and the prayers of the martyrs.

When the second angel sounded, "a great mountain burning with fire was cast into the sea: and the third part of the sea became blood: and the third part of the creatures which were in the sea, and had life, died; and the third part of the ships were destroyed." This symbolized the effects of this war upon the sea. "At Joppa eighty-four hundred had been slain by Cestius and the city burned; but a number of fugitives had ensconced themselves in the ruins, and were living by piracy and brigandage. These Jews fled to their ships before the advance of the Roman soldiers. Next morning a storm burst on them, and after a frightful scene of despair forty-two hundred were drowned, and their corpses were washed upon the shore. Tarichenæ was a strongly fortified city on the shores of Lake Tiberias. It was taken by Titus, and six thousand Jews dyed with their blood the waters of that crystal sea." The burning mountain cast into the sea showed that there was no more hope of escape when God arose to judgment than there would be for ships to escape were a burning mountain literally hurled into the sea amid those ships.

"And the third angel sounded, and there fell a great star from heaven, burning as it were a lamp, and it fell upon a third part of the rivers, and upon the fountains of waters; and the name of the star is called Wormwood: and the third part of the waters became wormwood; and many men died of the waters, because they were made bitter." Bitter was their experience in coming to their death. This was to show that no part of the land was to escape. The hail and fire fell upon the earth, the burning mountain upon the sea, and the star on the rivers and fountains of water.

Now the "fourth angel sounded, and the third part of the sun was smitten, and the third part of the moon, and the third part of the stars; so as the third part of them was darkened, and the day shone not for a third part of it, and the night likewise." All nature was arrayed against these enemies of God and his people. In all these symbols a third part is affected, a definite for an indefinite number; and yet about one-third of the nation miserably perished in this war, so that the proportion was not far wrong.

This also corresponds precisely with Ezekiel's prediction of this same event, as recorded in the fifth chapter of his prophecy. The command comes to him to take a sharp knife, to take a barber's razor, and cause it to pass upon his head and upon his beard. Then he was to take this hair and divide it into three parts. A third part he was to burn in the fire in the midst of the city, when the days of the siege were fulfilled; a third part he was to smite about with a knife; and a third part to scatter in the wind. He was also to bind a few in number in his skirts. The revealing spirit then tells him: "A third part of thee shall die with the pestilence, and with famine shall they be consumed in the midst of thee: and a third part shall fall by the sword round about thee; and I will scatter a third part into all the winds, and I will draw out a sword after them." The same spirit that revealed this to Ezekiel revealed it to John, only under different symbols.

The whole land was deluged in blood. No place was safe, either on sea or land, and no nation ever suffered more bitterly. Jesus, speaking of this very time, says: "For then shall be great tribulation, such as was not since the beginning of the world to this time, no, nor ever shall be." When every feature of these symbols fits with accuracy the circumstances of this war—especially when Jesus said, "Verily I say unto you, this generation shall not pass, till all these things be fulfilled"—why should we labor to make them cover facts occurring hundreds of years subsequent and in countries far distant?

Here was a pause in the sounding of the trumpets for a startling announcement. John says: "And I beheld, and heard an angel flying through the midst of heaven, saying with a loud voice, Woe, woe, woe, to the inhabiters of the earth by reason of the other voices of the trumpet of the three angels, which are yet to sound!" Under these three woe-trumpets, as they have been called, they were to reach the culmination of this dreadful war. The scenes enacted—especially in Jerusalem—as the mighty conqueror struck the final blow were so terrific that heaven shuddered, and an angel was sent to prepare men for it by his dreadful cry of "Woe, woe, woe." But the Almighty arm must let the lifted thunder drop, though all earth should shudder at the effect of its fall.

"And the fifth angel sounded, and I saw a star fall from heaven unto the earth: and to him was given the key of the bottomless pit. . . . And there arose a smoke out of the pit, as the smoke of a great furnace; and the sun and the air were darkened by reason of the smoke of the pit. And there came out of the smoke locusts upon the earth: and unto them was given power, as the scorpions of the earth have power. And it was commanded them that they should not hurt the grass of the earth, neither any green thing, neither any tree; but only those men which have not the seal of God in their foreheads. And to them it was given that they should not kill them, but that they should be tormented five months: and their torment was as the torment of a scorpion, when he striketh a man. And in those days shall men seek death, and shall not find it; and shall desire to die, and death shall flee from them. And the shapes of the locusts were like unto horses prepared unto battle; and on their heads were as it were crowns like gold, and their faces were as the faces of men. And they had hair as the hair of women, and their teeth were as the teeth of lions. And they had breastplates, as it were breastplates of iron: and the sound of their wings was as the sound of chariots of many horses running to battle. And they had tails like unto scorpions, and there were stings in their tails: and their power was to hurt men five months. And they had a king over them, which is the angel of the bottomless pit, whose name in the Hebrew tongue is Abaddon, but in the Greek tongue hath his name Apollyon. One woe is past; and, behold, there come two woes more hereafter."

This star was an intelligent being, an angel. He comes to open the bottomless pit and turn loose upon the Jews this awful scourge. The fact that the locusts were commanded to hurt "only those men which have not the seal of God in their foreheads" connects this woe with the seals, and makes it all one. It forever crushes those wild, visionary interpretations that string these seals and trumpets along down the ages, locating some in one and some in another country. The unity of this book is wonderful, and yet no book ever written has suffered more dismemberment than it. These locusts are symbolical of the several parties in the heart of Jerusalem, that agreed in nothing else but in tormenting each other. They acted as demons from the pit. Language fails to picture their cruelty and villainy. Hear what Josephus says of them: "And here I cannot but speak my mind, and what the concern I am under dictates to me. I suppose that had the Romans made any longer delay in coming against these villains, that the city would either have been swallowed up by the ground opening under them, or been overflowed by water, or else been destroyed by such thunder as the country of Sodom perished by. For it had brought forth a generation of men much more atheistical than were those that suffered such punishment. For by their madness it was that all the people came to be destroyed."

"And in those days shall men seek death, and shall not find it; and shall desire to die, and death shall flee from them." Moses said of this very period: "And thy life shall hang in doubt before thee; and thou shalt fear day and night, and shalt have none assurance of thy life: in the morning thou shalt say, Would God it were even! and at even thou shalt say, Would God it were morning!" Jesus says: "There shall be great distress in the land, and wrath upon this people. . . . Upon the earth distress of nations, with perplexity; the sea and the waves roaring; men's hearts failing them for fear, and for looking after those things which are coming on the earth: for the powers of heaven shall be shaken."

The descriptions of the locusts are remarkable: "Their faces were as the faces of men. And they had hair as the hair of women, and their teeth were as the teeth of lions." One paragraph from Josephus fixes this symbol inevitably upon John and his followers during the siege: "For these Galileans had advanced this John, and made him very potent; who made them a suitable requital from the authority he had obtained by their means, for he permitted them to do all things that any of them desired. While their inclination to plunder was insatiable—as was their zeal in searching the homes of the rich, and for the murdering of the men and abusing of the women, it was sport to them—they also devoured what spoils they had taken, together with their blood, and indulged themselves in feminine wantonness, without any disturbance, till they were satiated therewith. While they decked their hair, and put on women's garments, and were besmeared over with ointments, that they might appear very comely, they had paints under their eyes and were guilty of such intolerable uncleanness that they invented unlawful pleasures and rolled themselves up and down the city as in a brothel house, and defiled it entirely with their impure actions. Nay, while their faces looked like the faces of women, they killed with their right hands; and when their gait was effeminate, they presently attacked men and became warriors, and drew their swords from under their finely dyed cloaks, and ran everybody through whom they met with. However, Simon waited for such as ran away from John, and was the more sanguinary of the two; and he who escaped the tyrant within the wall was destroyed by the other that day before the gates.''

No wonder they were likened to scorpions, and that they had power to hurt men. Five months is the normal life-period of the locusts; hence they have power to hurt men all the period of their life. While these destroying, tormenting agents seemed to be free, yet they were under the control of a superintending power; and that king was the angel of the bottomless pit, who was sent out under the direction of the Lamb. This angel's name—Abaddon or Apollyon—means "destroyer." Whether this angel was a spirit of good or of evil, he was nevertheless under the immediate direction of the Almighty. It was only as God ordered that he could act.

"One woe is past. . . . And the sixth angel sounded, and I heard a voice from the four horns of the golden altar which is before God, saying to the sixth angel which had the trumpet, Loose the four angels which are bound in the great river Euphrates. And the four angels were loosed, which were prepared for an hour, and a day, and a month, and a year, for to slay the third part of men. And the number of the army of the horsemen were two hundred thousand thousand: and I heard the number of them. And thus I saw the horses in the vision, and them that sat on them, having breastplates of fire, and of jacinth, and brimstone: and the heads of the horses were as the heads of lions; and out of their mouths issued fire and smoke and brimstone. By these three was the third part of men killed, by the fire, and by the smoke, and by the brimstone, which issued out of their mouths. For their power is in their mouth, and in their tails: for their tails were like unto serpents, and had heads, and with them they do hurt. And the rest of the men which were not killed by these plagues yet repented not of the works of their hands, that they should not worship devils, and idols of gold, and silver, and brass, and stone, and of wood; which neither can see, nor hear, nor walk: neither repented they of their murders, nor of their sorceries, nor of their fornication, nor of their thefts."

Some six hundred and eighty years before this time the Chaldeans, like a mighty scourge, had come from the banks of the Euphrates, taken Jerusalem, destroyed the temple, and carried Israel away into captivity. Now they are used as a symbol for the present destruction. From the four horns of the golden altar comes the voice to the sixth angel, commanding him to loose the four angels which are bound in the great river Euphrates. This command is the result of the prayers that have gone up from this golden altar. When atonement was made, each horn of the altar was sprinkled with blood. Through the blood of the Lamb these prayers have been offered, and they prevailed. The barrier, such as a great river, is removed, and these avenging powers represented by the four angels come unhindered to their work of destruction. The time—"an hour, and a day, and a month, and a year"—given them in which to "slay the third part of men" would indicate that the slaughter would not be alone at the final scene, when the city should fall into their hands; but from the time they encompassed the city their work should begin, and hour after hour, day by day, month by month, and year by year, through this fearful war the slaughter should go on. This was literally fulfilled. Long before the investing army reached the carcass, John and Simon and Eleazar, like dogs of war, were tearing and slaying their fellow-countrymen in a manner never known before in the history of war. We see the force of this symbol of the Chaldeans in the fact recorded by Josephus of the destruction of the temple: "However, one cannot but wonder at the accuracy of this period thereto relating. For the same month and day were now observed, as I said before, wherein the holy house was burned formerly by the Babylonians."

The number of the horses is given, and is amazing—"two hundred thousand thousand"—enough to eat up the "third part of the green grass." But these horses were symbolic, and every thing about them betokened their terrific power for destruction. Their riders were clad in "breastplates of fire, and of jacinth and brimstone," while they themselves had heads like lions, and out of their mouths issued fire and smoke and brimstone. "Their tails were like unto serpents, and had heads, and with them they do hurt." Of course this was not literal, but was intended to show the power for injury that God's avenging army had. Again we have that "third part of men killed."

"History tells us that fifteen strong cities of Galilee were carried by storm, and the masses of men, women, and children butchered; that about three millions of Jews, convened for their great annual passover, were crowded within the walls of Jerusalem when the Roman legions invested the city and shut them in; and that when the city fell scarcely so many thousand escaped—famine, pestilence, conflagration, their own sword, and the Roman sword, had combined their powers of torture and death to make this scene a climax of horrors." As has been said of these three millions, one million one hundred thousand perished.

For all these plagues, for all this suffering "the rest of the men which were not killed by these plagues yet repented not of the works of their hands," etc. In all the history of this period we hear not a note of repentance. Not a soul returns to God or calls upon him for mercy. But, throwing the reins of their mad passions upon the neck of lust for rapine and murder, they rush upon the thick basses of Jehovah's buckler as if they courted death. Men, bowing under the hand of famine, staggered from house to house, and robbed the inhabitants of their gold as greedily as if the fires of war were not burning all around them, and death was not the most common scene of every day's occurrence.

That they " neither repented of their murders, nor of their sorceries, nor of their fornication, nor of their thefts," hear what Josephus tells us just before the city fell: "But as for John, when he could no longer plunder the people, he betook himself to sacrilege, and melted down many of the sacred utensils, which had been given to the temple."

In the last sad scene, when pools of blood lay all over the marble floor of the temple, and torrents of blood in many places extinguished the fires, when the Roman soldiers themselves were weary of killing men, Josephus says: "The soldiers also came to the rest of the cloisters that were in the outer court of the temple; whither the women and children, and a mixed multitude of the people fled, in number about six thousand. But before Cæsar [Titus] had determined any thing about these people, or given the commanders any orders relating to them, the soldiers were in such a rage that they set that cloister on fire. By which means some of these were destroyed by throwing themselves down headlong; and some were burned in the cloisters themselves. Nor did any of them escape with their lives. *A false prophet* was the occasion of these people's destruction; who had made a public proclamation in the city that very day that God commanded them to get up upon the temple, and that there they should receive miraculous signs of deliverance. Now there was then a great number of false prophets suborned by the tyrants to impose upon the people." But this is enough to show the fulfillment of this part of this symbol.

CHAPTER X.

The Angel with the Little Book—The Temple and Altar Measured—The Two Witnesses—The Third Woe.

"AND I saw another mighty angel come down from heaven, clothed with a cloud: and a rainbow was upon his head, and his face was as it were the sun, and his feet as pillars of fire: and he had in his hand a little book open: and he set his right foot upon the sea, and his left foot on the earth, and cried with a loud voice, as when a lion roareth: and when he had cried, seven thunders uttered their voices. And when the seven thunders had uttered their voices, I was about to write: and I heard a voice from heaven saying unto me, Seal up those things which the seven thunders uttered, and write them not. And the angel which I saw stand upon the sea and upon the earth lifted up his hand to heaven, and sware by him that liveth forever and ever, who created heaven, and the things that therein are, and the earth, and the things that therein are, and the sea, and the things which are therein, that there should be time no longer: but in the days of the voice of the seventh angel, when he shall begin to sound, the mystery of God should be finished, as he hath declared to his servants the prophets. And the voice which I heard from heaven spake unto me again, and said, Go and take the little book which is open in the hand of the angel which standeth upon the sea and upon the earth. And I went unto the angel, and said unto him, Give me the little book. And he said unto me, Take it, and eat it up; and it shall make thy belly bitter, but it shall be in thy mouth sweet as honey. And I took the little book out of the angel's hand, and ate it up; and it was in my mouth sweet as honey: and as soon as I had eaten it, my belly was bitter. And he said unto me, Thou must prophesy again before many peoples, and nations, and tongues, and kings."

The first thing to be determined is: Who is this angel? We have no hesitancy in saying that it is Jesus himself. The description is almost identical with that of Jesus in the first chapter. The careful Bible reader need not be told that the term is more than once applied to Jesus in the Old Testament. The reader must not think that all the scenes portrayed in the preceding chapters have been enacted. Only the revelation of them has been made. Now the hour comes for their fulfillment. The seals have all been broken, the contents noted, and now the angel comes down to earth with the book open; and, setting his feet upon sea and land, he announces his presence by a loud cry that startles the seven thunders. These thunders syllabled some great fact, which John was about to record, but is commanded not to do so. The next verses reveal the reason. The angel, in the most solemn manner, swears that time shall be no longer. Not that time is to end and eternity begin, but the time for his judgments to begin was at hand. No more delay. The judgments uttered by these seven thunders will follow immediately, and they will be known in their fulfillment. So near is the cloud of wrath that the lightning's flash and thunder's peal are simultaneous.

But while the things that are to befall the Jews are at hand, yet there are other things of equal importance that lie in the future. Of these John must be apprised. Hence the voice "spake unto him again, and said, Go and take the little book which is open in the hand of the angel which standeth upon the sea and upon the earth." He went and asked for it. It was given with the command to take it and eat it up—that is, thoroughly digest its contents. He did so, and found that it was in his mouth sweet as honey, but in his belly it was bitter.

The other great persecuting power of the Chrisitan Church, pagan Rome, was to be destroyed, and the knowledge of this fact was sweet; yet the fearful calamities and the human suffering that were to befall them was bitter. It was glorious to have the yoke of their oppressor broken, but the suffering entailed upon even their enemies could not but pain the heart.

When the book was eaten, the angel announced to him that he must prophesy again before many peoples, etc.

Under Jewish law, when a criminal was executed, the witnesses, of which there must be at least two, were to strike the first blow. Here is the law: "At the mouth of two witnesses, or three witnesses, shall he that is worthy of death be put to death; but at the mouth of one witness he shall not be put to death. The hands of the witnesses shall be first upon him to put him to death." The Jewish nation was to die at the hands of God, but before the execution the witnesses are to be summoned.

The first announcement is: "There was given me a reed like unto a rod: and the angel stood, saying, Rise, and measure the temple of God, and the altar, and them that worship therein. But the court which is without the temple leave out, and measure it not; for it is given unto the Gentiles: and the holy city shall they tread under foot forty and two months." This measuring is for judgment. In Isaiah xxviii. 17, 18, we have the language: "Judgment will I lay to the line, and righteousness to the plummet: and the hail shall sweep away the refuge of lies, and the waters shall overflow the hiding-place. And your covenant with death shall be disannulled, and your agreement with hell shall not stand; when the overflowing scourge shall pass through, then ye shall be trodden down by it." Here God with his line and plummet measures them for the destruction that is to follow. So the temple, the altar, and the people that worship therein are measured for destruction; and, while the court of the Gentiles is excluded, the holy city is to be trodden under foot forty and two months.

There was never a time in the history of the Jew-

The Kingdom and Comings of Christ. 211

ish nation so terrible as that three and a half years (forty-two months) in which he took away the daily sacrifice, desecrated and profaned all the sacred vessels of the sanctuary. So this period is used symbolically to represent that. Used as a symbol, it was not necessary that the sufferings of this period should measure up to the exact time, though it is thought by some that this was the case. The language here is similar to that used by Jesus when speaking of the same thing: "And Jerusalem shall be trodden down of the Gentiles." The language used in this symbol fixes Jerusalem unmistakably as the place. It was called "holy city," and "the temple of God" was found nowhere else. Then the "court which is without the temple" given to the "Gentiles" is another strong pointer in this direction. Nowhere else is such a court found. The temple, altar, and people being measured for destruction, God summons his two witnesses.

"I will give power unto my two witnesses, and they shall prophesy a thousand two hundred and threescore days, clothed in sackcloth." Here is the three years and a half, lacking only fifteen days, spoken of before. Thus these witnesses are to stand by during the entire time of the execution. "These are the two olive-trees, and the two candlesticks standing before the God of the earth."

The question may be asked: "Who are these two witnesses?" They are only symbols of the "souls of them that were slain for the word of God, and for the testimony which they held," and of "all the saints" whose prayers were offered with the incense that rose from the golden altar which was before the throne — the *martyrs* and the *living saints* who were still suffering persecutions. These were men who had been converted to God through the agency of the Holy Spirit. Hence they are called in the symbol "the two olive-trees, and the two candlesticks standing before the God of the earth," referred to in Zechariah iv. The angel that talked to him asked him: "Knowest thou not what these be? And I said, No, my lord. Then he answered and spake unto me, saying, This is the word of the Lord unto Zerubbabel, saying, Not by might, nor by power, but by my Spirit, saith the Lord of hosts." It was, then, a religion wrought in the heart by the power of the Holy Spirit, through the preaching of the word. This is just the religion of Jesus, as taught in every part of the New Testament. Then we repeat that these two witnesses are symbols of the martyrs and saints of Jesus who stood firm for his faith. These faithful witnesses stood by their testimony while the executioners of God's judgments poured out the wrath of God upon this people whose hands were red with the blood of his saints.

"And if any man will hurt them, fire proceedeth out of their mouth, and devoureth their enemies: and if any man will hurt them, he must in this manner be killed."

The Kingdom and Comings of Christ. 213

Again we must say that this is not literal, but is only intended to show that God's fires of judgment then falling upon them was because the testimony of their mouth was condemning them. God was calling the world to listen to the testimony of these two witnesses, as he dealt the death-blow to these criminals.

"These have power to shut heaven, that it rain not in the days of their prophecy: and have power over waters to turn them to blood, and to smite the earth with all plagues, as often as they will."

Elijah prayed, and it rained not for the space of *three years and six months.* This miracle of shutting the heaven was wrought to convince wicked Ahab and idolatrous Israel of their sins. So these witnesses are sent for the purpose of convincing this wicked and adulterous generation of their sins. Moses turned water to blood, and smote the earth with plagues to convince Pharaoh and his people of their sins. So of these.

But, righteous as they are, this does not prevent the devil from killing them; for it is said: "And when they shall have finished their testimony, the beast that ascendeth out of the bottomless pit shall make war against them, and shall overcome them, and kill them. And their dead bodies shall lie in the street of the great city, which spiritually is called Sodom and Egypt, where also our Lord was crucified." God shields them until their testimony is finished. "They are immortal until their work is done;" then Satan—for this is the same "great red dragon, the old serpent called the devil and Satan," spoken of in the next chapter—overcomes them and kills them. The great indignity heaped upon them is indicated by the fact that their dead bodies are suffered to lie three days and a half unburied in the streets of the great city.

In some respects this is one of the most important verses in this vision, for it locates beyond a peradventure the *place* where these judgments take place. It is "the great city which spiritually is called Sodom and Egypt, *where also our Lord was crucified.*" Isaiah calls Jerusalem Sodom in the first chapter of his prophecy. It was a spiritual Sodom; and on account of the manner in which they hardened their hearts it is called Egypt; but, to settle the matter forever, it is called the place "where our Lord was crucified." No other place on earth can lay claim to this crowning act of iniquity but Jerusalem. It would seem that God, to forestall such wild and visionary interpretations as are given of this wonderful revelation, dropped for a moment the figurative, and used literal language. It would seem that Jesus was recalling his own expression, used while here on earth with reference to this wicked city. When certain Pharisees said to him, "Get thee out, and depart hence; for Herod will kill thee," he replied: "I must walk to-day, and to-morrow, and the day following: for it cannot be that a prophet perish *out* of Jerusalem. O Jerusalem, Jerusalem, which killest the prophets, and stonest them that are sent unto thee; how often would I have gathered thy children together, even as a hen doth gather her brood under her wings, *and ye would not!* Behold, your house is left unto you desolate."

Here Jesus declares that he must "walk to-day, and to-morrow, and the day following," intimating that in the midst of the fourth day he would perish under the hands of the citizens of Jerusalem. Here is the three days and a half to which this symbol, in part no doubt, refers. While the blood of her prophets and apostles was calling loudly for vengeance, the blood of Jesus came in for its share. When on his way to the cross the women bewailed and lamented him, he turned and said: "Daughters of Jerusalem, weep not for me, but weep for yourselves, and for your children. For, behold, the days are coming, in the which they shall say, Blessed are the barren, and the wombs that never bare, and the paps which never gave suck. Then shall they begin to say to the mountains, Fall on us; and to the hills, Cover us. For if they do these things in a green tree, what shall be done in the dry?" It does seem that every ray of prophecy on this subject turns in one burning focus upon this devoted city. And how men can apply these symbols to distant ages and different places is more than I can see.

"And they of the people and kindred and tongues and nations shall see their dead bodies three days and a half, and shall not suffer their dead bodies to be put in graves. And they that dwell upon the earth shall rejoice over them, and make merry, and shall send gifts one to another; because these two prophets tormented them that dwelt on the earth. And after three days and a half the Spirit of life from God entered into them, and they stood upon their feet; and great fear fell upon them which saw them."

Here is exultation over the fall of these saints. They felt when they had slain them as the rulers of the Jews felt when they succeeded in crucifying Jesus, and their joy was as short. It was the prayers of the souls of the dead martyrs and his persecuted saints that moved God to vengeance.

"And they heard a great voice from heaven saying unto them, Come up hither. And they ascended up to heaven in a cloud; and their enemies beheld them."

This is symbolical of the fact that these witnesses were called immediately before the king to testify as to the conduct of their foes. There is an allusion to these witnesses, and the judgment that is to fall upon those against whom they testify, in Hebrews x. 28–31: "He that despised Moses' law died without mercy under *two or three witnesses:* of how much sorer punishment, suppose ye, shall he be thought worthy, who hath trodden under foot the Son of God, and hath counted the blood of the covenant, wherewith he was sanctified, an unholy thing, and hath done despite unto the Spirit of grace? For we know him that hath said, Vengeance belongeth unto me, I will recompense,

The Kingdom and Comings of Christ. 217

saith the Lord. And again, The Lord shall judge his people. It is a fearful thing to fall into the hands of the living God." This is so plain that it needs no comment.

And now comes the final scene, the last blow: "And the same hour was there a great earthquake, and the tenth part of the city fell, and in the earthquake were slain of men seven thousand: and the remnant were affrighted, and gave glory to the God of heaven. The second woe is past, and, behold, the third woe cometh quickly." These were not literal shocks of an earthquake, but it represented the shock of the Roman army, who broke down the walls of the great city and slew right and left until they were weary of slaughter. Again we have a definite number to represent an indefinite, but the slain was up in the thousands. When the Roman soldiers broke into the city, the temple seemed to be the center of the great battle and the scenes of the greatest slaughter. As the altar and the temple and those that worship therein had been measured for destruction, so it was as Josephus says: " Now round about the altar lay dead bodies, heaped one upon another; as at the steps, going up to it, ran a great quantity of their blood; whither, also, the dead bodies that were slain above on the altar fell down."

Titus tried to save the temple, but it was set on fire. Josephus says: " While the holy house was on fire, every thing was plundered that came to hand; and ten thousand of those that were caught were slain. Nor was there a commiseration of any age, or any reverence of gravity; but children and old men, priests and profane persons, were all slain in the same manner, . . . yet was the misery itself more terrible than this disorder. For one would have thought that the very hill on which the temple stood was red hot, as full of fire was every part of it, that the blood was larger in quantity than the fire, and those that were slain more in number than those that slew them. For the ground did nowhere appear visible, for the dead bodies that lay on it; but the soldiers went over heaps of those bodies, as they ran upon such as fled from them."

This picture was not painted from imagination, for Josephus was at the time in the army of Titus, having been taken prisoner, and was an eye-witness of what he describes.

One angel alone stands before the throne who has not yet sounded his trumpet. One last act in the awful drama remains to be performed: "And the seventh angel sounded; and there were great voices in heaven, saying, The kingdoms of this world are become the kingdoms of our Lord, and of his Christ; and he shall reign forever and ever. And the four and twenty elders, which sat before God on their seats, fell upon their faces, and worshiped God, saying, We give thee thanks, O Lord God Almighty, which art, and wast, and art to come; because thou hast taken to thee thy great power, and hast reigned. And the nations were angry, and thy wrath is come, and the time of the dead, that they should be judged, and that thou shouldest give reward unto thy servants the prophets, and to the saints, and them that fear thy name, small and great; and shouldest destroy them which destroy the earth."

This completes the scene. The last grand blow is struck, that not only routs the armies of the enemy, but secures a complete victory. All is subdued under the sword of the rider upon the white horse, who took his place at the head of the column when the first seal was broken. When he took the little book out of the hand of him that sat on the throne, all heaven shouted: " Worthy is the Lamb that was slain to receive power, and riches, and wisdom, and strength, and honor, and glory, and blessing." Now as this conqueror returned from the war with all the standards of the enemy in possession, the mighty voices of heaven sound the pæans of praise, and say: "The kingdoms of this world are become the kingdoms of our Lord, and of his Christ; and he shall reign forever and ever."

There is no description of the final scene given. Only the result is announced: a complete victory. The nations were angry; but when this roused the anger of the Lamb, when the prayers of the souls of those under the altar, slain for his word and the testimony which they bare, and the prayers of his servants the prophets and the saints and them that feared his name, small and great, came up before him, mingled with a cloud of incense, then he arose to destroy them which destroyeth the earth. Jesus had said, when referring to this very fact: " There be some standing here, which shall not taste of death, till they see the Son of man coming in his kingdom." And again: " Verily, this generation shall not pass, till all these things be fulfilled." Now the first great persecuting power of the infant Church had been destroyed, and all nations were open to the gospel.

"And the temple of God was opened in heaven, and there were seen in his temple the ark of his testament; and there were lightnings, and voices, and thunderings, and an earthquake, and great hail.'

Paul in his Epistle to the Hebrews makes this plain. Now that the temple, with all its sacred implements of worship—even to the ark of the covenant on which rested the mercy-seat—had been destroyed, it was necessary to reveal to the Church the great fact that " Christ is not entered into the holy places made with hands, which are the figures of the true; but into heaven itself, now to appear in the presence of God for us."

Jesus said to the woman of Samaria: " Woman, believe me, the hour cometh, when ye shall neither in this mountain, *nor yet at Jerusalem*, worship the Father. . . . But the hour cometh, and now is, when the true worshipers shall worship the Father in spirit and in truth: for the Father seeketh such to worship him."

Now this thing was made manifest to all the kingdoms brought under the power of the Lamb. The ark, the true ark, was still safe, it was in heaven. Above it were still stretched the wings of the cherubim; but they were living creatures. The throne of God was the throne of grace, all sprinkled with the blood of the Lamb, who had the veil (his body) rent for the passage; and we "have a strong consolation, who have fled for refuge to lay hold upon the hope set before us: which hope we have as an anchor of the soul, both sure and steadfast, and which entereth into that within the veil; whither the forerunner is for us entered, even Jesus, made a high priest forever after the order of Melchisedec."

"And there were lightnings, and voices, and thunderings, and an earthquake, and great hail."

This doubtless was to give his people assurance that there was still a reserve of power, ready at any moment to be used for the destruction of their foes.

This closes the first main division of this book. We have not turned aside to combat the views of other men. It is true that we have occasionally alluded to some of these; that is all. There can be but one true interpretation of this book. We lay claim to one fact: we have been consistent in all our interpretations of it. We have presented nothing on our own *dictum*, but have in every instance given the proof of our views, substantiating them by proofs both from Scripture and history.

We have not tried in any instance, in interpreting a symbol, to explain all its parts, or, as some have expressed it, "to make it go on all fours." We might have entered more into detail, but our purpose was to give, as far as we were able, the purpose of the revealing spirit. We have made no display of ingenuity or of great learning; we are content if we have led the reader into a true understanding of the design and purposes of the book. The wild and visionary interpretations of it that reach along down the ages, even to our own time, have never served any good purpose; nor have men ever been able to agree upon any of these far-reaching theories.

CHAPTER XI.

The Second Great Persecuting Power, Pagan Rome—The Messiah Born—The Dragon—The Beast from the Sea—The Beast from the Earth—The Lamb on Mount Sion—The Fall of Babylon, or Rome.

WE come now to the overthrow of the second great persecuting power, pagan Rome. As a preface to the scenes of this part of Revelation we are taken back to the birth of the Messiah and to the effort made for his destruction; and, when this failed, to the effort to destroy the Christian Church by the devil.

"And there appeared a great wonder in heaven; a woman clothed with the sun, and the moon under her feet, and upon her head a crown of twelve stars: and she being with child cried, travailing in birth, and pain to be delivered."

This symbol is shown in heaven. The woman represents the Church. This is a figure quite common, especially in the prophecy of Isaiah. In the fifty-fourth chapter she is represented as a woman who is to have a very large increase of children, and she is commanded to get ready for them by enlarging her tent, and again in the sixty-second and sixty-sixth chapters. Perhaps Solomon alludes to the Church, as represented by a woman, when he says: "Who is she that looketh forth in the morning, fair as the moon, clear as the sun, and terrible as an army with banners."

This woman being clothed with the sun, with the moon under her feet, as to the exceeding beauty of her array, was the beloved of God, the Church for which Jesus gave his life, and her appearance was beyond any thing earthly. The crown of twelve stars represented that she was the Church of God. First there were twelve patriarchs, and next twelve apostles. In this symbol the Church is to give birth to the Messiah. When the time came for her delivery of the child, John says: "And there appeared another wonder in heaven; and behold a great red dragon, having seven heads and ten horns, and seven crowns upon his heads." There is no mistake about this being the devil, for in the ninth verse he is specially characterized as such, as we shall see. He is red, indicating the fact that he is a murderer and capable of bloody work. Dragon is another name for serpent, the guise under which he appeared to our first parents in the garden. His seven heads indicate his wisdom, and his horns and crowns that he is not alone in his work, but that kings and nations are at his command to work for him in persecuting the Church and slaying her children.

"And his tail drew the third part of the stars of heaven, and did cast them to the earth."

We have but little in the Scriptures to enlighten us as to the origin of the devil and his angels, but what we have shows us that they were once angels of light, and that "they kept not their first estate, but left their own habitation." No doubt they were led in their rebellion by this dragon, who is said to draw them with his tail—that is, they followed his leadership to their own ruin. Peter tells us they were "cast down to hell." But we must not forget that this is symbolic language, intended to represent to us the character who is engaged in this work of persecution.

"And the dragon stood before the woman which was ready to be delivered, for to devour her child as soon as it was born."

We know that the devil made the effort to destroy the young child Jesus when he was born, by instigating one of the kings under his control to do the bloody work. For "Herod sent forth, and slew all the children that were in Bethlehem, and in all the coasts thereof, from two years old and under."

"And she brought forth a man child, who was to rule all nations with a rod of iron: and her child was caught up unto God, and to his throne."

God warned Joseph in a dream to flee into Epypt, and thus was his life spared. It was as if God had caught him up out of harm's way. Not only so; he was taken to his throne. God anointed him King, thus setting him upon his throne. He was preserved for this throne. That this child was the Messiah is made plain by the expression, "He shall rule all nations with a rod of iron." Whatever that may mean, it is just what is said of the Messiah in the second Psalm, a Psalm that the apostles applied to Christ. There it is said to him: "Ask of me, and I shall give thee the heathen for thine inheritance, and the uttermost parts of the earth for thy possession. Thou shalt break them with a rod of iron." Here are the heathen and the uttermost parts of the earth given for a "possession," equivalent to "all nations" in this symbol.

"And the woman fled into the wilderness, where she hath a place prepared of God, that they should feed her there a thousand two hundred and threescore days."

This part of the symbol refers to the manner in which God provided for the protection of his people when they cried unto him, when under the hand of their oppressors in Egypt. He said to Moses: "I have surely seen the affliction of my people which are in Egypt, and have heard their cry by reason of their taskmasters; for I know their sorrows; and I am come down to deliver them out of the hand of the Egyptians." They were taken into the wilderness, where their enemies could not follow them, and yet in that wilderness they were fed forty years. Here the Church is to be protected in her persecution by the power of God for a space of about three and a half years. Whether this is a definite time, or the time of Israel's oppression under Antiochus Epiphanes, it does not matter. We have seen the folly of reckoning these days each as a year, no such custom in prophecy prevailing. God will see to it that his Church, as symbolized by the woman, shall be protected till the time of persecution and danger shall pass, be that time long or short.

"And there was war in heaven: Michael and his angels fought against the dragon; and the dragon fought and his angels, and prevailed not; neither was their place found any more in heaven. And the great dragon was cast out, that old serpent, called the Devil, and Satan, which deceiveth the whole world: he was cast out into the earth, and his angels were cast out with him."

This represents the desperate effort made by the devil and his angels for the destruction of Jesus Christ. Not content when Jesus was protected by the power of God in infancy, so soon as he enters upon his ministry he is met in the wilderness and sorely tempted of the devil. And again is another attack made in the garden of Gethsemane, when Jesus said to the chief priests when they came to arrest him: "But this is your hour, and the power of darkness." The dragon fought, and his angels, and prevailed not; Jesus stood firm, and overcame him and his army. He said to his disciples, "I beheld Satan as lightning fall from heaven," meaning by that that he was vanquished. They were cast out into the earth. There can be no mistake as to the identity of this dragon; he is the old serpent that tempted Eve, called the devil, which means the accuser of the brethren; and Satan, a *malicious hater* both of God and all the good. He works only for evil; but the Son of God was manifested that he might destroy the works of the devil.

"And I heard a loud voice saying in heaven, Now is come salvation, and strength, and the kingdom of our God, and the power of his Christ: for the accuser of our brethren is cast down, which accused them before our God day and night. And they overcame him by the blood of the Lamb, and by the word of their testimony; and they loved not their lives unto the death. Therefore rejoice, ye heavens, and ye that dwell in them. Woe to the inhabiters of the earth and of the sea! for the devil is come down unto you, having great wrath, because he knoweth that he hath but a short time."

The victory wrought in heaven over Satan and his angels wakes a note of praise that echoes loud and long; and to Christ and his blood is ascribed all the praise and virtue of this victory. The same martyrs, or those like them, that "loved not their lives to the death," are foremost in these ascriptions of praise; but while heaven rejoices because Satan has been cast out, yet earth is made sad by his taking up the fight among its inhabitants. While Christ by his death and resurrection has come off more than conqueror, yet his followers were to endure his temptations and feel the sting of his persecutions; for "when the dragon saw that he was cast unto the earth, he persecuted the woman which brought forth the man child. And to the woman were given two wings of a great eagle, that she might fly into the wilderness, into her place, where she is nourished for a time, and times, and half a time, from the face of the serpent. And the serpent cast out of his mouth water as a flood after the woman, that he might cause her to be carried away of the flood. And the earth helped the woman; and the earth opened her mouth, and swallowed up the flood which the dragon cast out of his mouth. And the dragon was wroth with the woman, and went to make war with the remnant of her seed, which keep the commandments of God, and have the testimony of Jesus Christ."

The victory of Christ over the devil is a symbol of the victory that his followers shall achieve in these fierce persecutions. This is shown by the two wings of a great eagle given her. God told Moses to say to Israel: "Ye have seen what I did unto the Egyptians, and how I bare you on eagles' wings, and brought you unto myself." God had helped Israel to get away from their oppressors, and had borne them to a place of safety. So this fact is used to assure his people persecuted by the dragon that he would bear them on eagles' wings to a place prepared for them. There they are to be nourished for a time, and times, and half a time from the face of the serpent—one mode of expression for three years and a half, the same prophetic time used some five times in this book of Revelation.

As the woman fled, the "serpent cast out of his mouth water as a flood after the woman, that he might cause her to be carried away of the flood." This is a symbol of the multiplied enemies that the devil raised up against the Christians at this time. So many were their enemies, and so persistent and wide-spread their persecutions, that it looked as if the struggling infant Church must be overwhelmed by them. "And the earth helped the woman; and the earth opened her mouth, and swallowed up the flood which the dragon cast out of his mouth." During the fierce persecutions of the Christians at Rome they took refuge in the catacombs beneath the city. We are told that often when the Christians were hotly pursued by their enemies they would disappear so suddenly, escaping into their subterranean retreats, known only to themselves, that the officers thought they had escaped by some magic. Thus the earth helped the woman. The hate of this dragon impelled him to make war with the remnant of her seed which kept the commandments of God and have the testimony of Jesus Christ.

This chapter must be looked upon as a sort of foreshadowing, in general, of the revelations that are to follow in detail. In other words, it is the preface to the coming revelations. Let us bear in mind in the outset that the revelation is dealing only with pagan Rome as it existed during this season of persecution. The symbols that begin in chapter xiii., and end in chapter xix., show how the war waged by the dragon against the remnant of the woman's seed is carried on, and what agencies are employed.

"And I stood upon the sand of the sea, and saw a beast rise up out of the sea, having seven heads,

The Kingdom and Comings of Christ. 231

and ten horns, and upon his horns ten crowns, and upon his heads the name of blasphemy. And the beast which I saw was like unto a leopard, and his feet were as the feet of a bear, and his mouth as the mouth of a lion: and the dragon gave him his power, and his seat, and great authority. And I saw one of his heads as it were wounded to death; and his deadly wound was healed: and all the world wondered after the beast. And they worshiped the dragon which gave power unto the beast: and they worshiped the beast, saying, Who is like unto the beast? who is able to make war with him? And there was given unto him a mouth speaking great things and blasphemies;. and power was given unto him to continue forty and two months. And he opened his mouth in blasphemy against God, to blaspheme his name, and his tabernacle, and them that dwell, in heaven. And it was given unto him to make war with the saints, and to overcome them: and power was given him over all kindreds, and tongues, and nations. And all that dwell upon the earth shall worship him, whose names are not written in the book of life of the Lamb slain from the foundation of the world. If any man have an ear, let him hear. He that leadeth into captivity shall go into captivity: he that killeth with the sword must be killed with the sword. Here is the patience and the faith of the saints."

This beast is a symbol of the *great Roman Empire*. The sea out of which the beast rose, as explained by the revealing angel, is "peoples, and multitudes, and nations, and tongues." This empire was formed out of the various countries and kingdoms of the civilized world. This is the empire under the Cæsars.

The seven heads are also explained by the angel. He says: "The seven heads are seven mountains on which the woman [Rome, the capital city] sitteth." It also refers to "seven kings," as we shall see when we reach the seventeenth chapter.

The ten horns "are ten kings," all of which will be explained and applied in due time.

Let it be distinctly understood that this is pagan Rome during the reign of the Cæsars, and that it does not go beyond it. John now sees the vision as a whole, as if the beast were possessed at one time of all these heads. But we shall see that when the symbol is explained at length, these heads rise one at a time. Every king, as represented by the seven heads, was a blasphemer. To each one was ascribed divine honors, and they demanded and received worship as a god.

The beast was like a leopard, with feet like a bear and mouth like a lion—three of the most terrible of wild beasts, as if the ferocity of all were combined in this one selected as a symbol of this great persecuting power. To this ferocious beast the dragon gave his power—selected him as his vicegerent, the instrument for tearing the Christians in the fury and ferocity of his power. And great authority for evil was given him.

The Kingdom and Comings of Christ. 233

This persecuting power becomes the prime minister of the devil.

One of the heads of the beast was wounded to death; and his deadly wound was healed: and all the world wondered after the beast.

This was the first head that appeared. When wounded to death, it was natural to expect to see the beast itself die. But it did not, because other heads came in its place.

It is well-known that the dynasty of Roman emperors was founded by Julius Cæsar. His power throughout the empire was supreme; but, when the old elements of liberty began to stir the heart of the people, Cæsar was slain. This first head received a wound unto death, and the people no doubt thought that the empire would fall with him; but it did not. There were other heads. Augustus was at once advanced to the head of government, and the empire survived; and all the world wondered after the beast. The dragon was still at the head of affairs, and if one prime minister fell, he at once advanced another to his place.

"And they [the people of the empire] worshiped the dragon which gave power unto the beast: and they worshiped the beast, saying, Who is like unto the beast? who is able to make war with him."

Devil-worship has been often practiced by the heathen, and we have no doubt but that these Romans did it. We know that they worshiped their standards and their emperors; and as they were put in power by the devil, and were the prime ministers of the devil, the worship of them was equivalent to the worship of the devil himself.

Gibbon says: "The deification of the emperor is the only instance in which they departed from their accustomed prudence and modesty." And again: "The imperious spirit of the first Cæsar too easily consented to assume during his life-time a place among the tutelar deities of Rome."

Of Caligula, Taylor says: "Finding no one dare to oppose his sanguinary caprice, he began to regard himself as something more than a mere mortal, and to claim divine honors; and finally he erected a temple to himself, and instituted a college of priests to superintend his own worship." If the people were so deceived as to believe him their god, no wonder they asked the questions: "Who is like unto the beast? who is able to make war with him?"

"And there was given unto him a mouth speaking great things and blasphemies; and power was given unto him to continue forty and two months. And he opened his mouth in blasphemies against God, to blaspheme his name, and his tabernacle, and them that dwell in heaven."

The dragon gave to him the power to speak great things and blasphemies. It is only necessary to study the power of Satan as it appears in the book of Job to see what he can do, and what he is permitted to do. But, as in the case of the devil in connection with Job, his power was limited, so this period of persecution was limited to the forty and two months so often referred to in this book. As we have said, this may have been the exact time, or it may be used as a definite for an indefinite period. But the persecutions referred to lasted just about if not exactly this time. No blasphemy is equal to that of arrogating the homage and worship due to God alone. This, as we have seen, these emperors did; and they blasphemed God's name, and his tabernacle, and them that dwell in heaven. Like the King of Babylon, they forced men to worship them, and thus blasphemed the worshipers of the one true God.

"And it was given unto him to make war with the saints, and to overcome them: and power was given him over all kindreds, and tongues, and nations. And all that dwell upon the earth shall worship him, whose names are not written in the book of life of the Lamb slain from the foundation of the world."

These Roman emperors had a world-wide sway, and they forced all nations to adopt their religion, in part at least. We give an instance from Rawlinson when writing of the Partheans and their submission to Rome: " He [Artabanus, their king] was also induced to throw a few grains of frankincense on the sacrificial fire which burned in front of the Roman standards and the *imperial image*, an act which was accepted at Rome as one of *submission and homage*." Thus they forced all nations to "worship him," but those whose names were in "the book of life of the Lamb" were excepted. No power could force them to worship the beast or his image. Many of then died a martyr's death during this period of three and a half years, when these deified emperors were trying to force the world to bow down in homage to them as God.

In the letter to the Church in Sardis, referring to this very time when "the devil shall cast some of you into prison, that ye may be tried," the promise is: "He that overcometh, the same shall be clothed in white raiment, and I will not blot out his *name out of the book of life.*"

Here, now, is an announcement that God wants all to understand, and he prefaces it with the words: "If any man have an ear, let him hear."

"He that leadeth into captivity shall go into captivity: he that killeth with the sword must be killed with the sword. Here is the patience and the faith of the saints."

God had his eye upon all the persecutions of his saints. He sees every hand that is lifted against them, and "he will requite a terrible retribution upon all persecutors in due time." Those who drag the Christians into captivity shall themselves be dragged into captivity. Those who kill the followers of Jesus with the sword shall themselves be killed with the sword. "Vengeance is mine, I will repay, saith the Lord;" and "it is a fearful thing to fall into the hands of the Lord." No saint

The Kingdom and Comings of Christ. 237

need raise his hand against his persecutors, but *patiently* endure, in full *faith* of the promise of God that he "will repay." "Here is the patience and the faith of the saints." When this beast had such great power, and the land was running red with the blood of innocent Christians; when Nero was filling his arena with them, and all Rome was enjoying their destruction; when the skins of wild beasts were wrapped around them, and they were worried to death by dogs; when inflammable materials were wrapped about them, and then set on fire to form walking torches to light the scene of an emperor's pleasure, many had their patience and their faith tried. And they must bear in mind what was written: *"He that overcometh shall not be hurt of the second death."*

Now another beast appears upon the scene.

"And I beheld another beast coming up out of the earth; and he had two horns like a lamb, and he spake as a dragon. And he exerciseth all the power of the first beast before him, and causeth the earth and them that dwell therein to worship the first beast, whose deadly wound was healed. And he doeth great wonders, so that he maketh fire come down from heaven on the earth in the sight of men, and deceiveth them that dwell on the earth by the means of those miracles which he had power to do in the sight of the beast; saying to them that dwell on the earth, that they should make an image to the beast, which had the wound by the sword, and did live. And he had power to give life unto the image of the beast, that the image of the beast should both speak, and cause that as many as would not worship the image of the beast should be killed. And he causeth all, both small and great, rich and poor, free and bond, to receive a mark in their right hand, or in their foreheads: and that no man might buy or sell, save he that had the mark, or the name of the beast, or the number of his name. Here is wisdom. Let him that hath understanding count the number of the beast: for it is the number of a man; and his number is six hundred threescore and six."

This second beast came up from the earth. He is not the creature of the nations, but has a different origin. Nor has he a fierce appearance as the first beast had. But this is only in appearance, for "he exerciseth all the power of the first beast before him," etc. He has two horns like a lamb. He is "a wolf in sheep's clothing." Who is this second beast? By all his characteristics, and the service he rendered the first beast, he is a symbol of the *pagan priesthood*. They were the creatures of the emperor's, as we have seen. You will remember that it is said of Caligula: "And finally he erected a temple to himself, and *instituted a college of priests to superintend his own worship*."

Very many commentators have seen papal Rome in this second beast. But this is impossible. Henry Cowles, on this point, says: "On the question whether this second beast can be papal

Rome, it should surely suffice to say that every feature of the description points us to the pagan priesthood; that this beast worked for the pagan emperor, as papal Rome certainly did not in the age of her first seven emperors, six hundred years before papal Rome became a well-defined system, and one thousand years before she became thoroughly a great persecuting power. Hence it is entirely inadmissable to find papal Rome in this second beast. As surely as this prophecy makes the first beast and the second contemporaneous and co-working, and as surely as history locates the persecuting activities of the Seven Heads of pagan Rome on the one hand and of papal Rome on the other one thousand years asunder, so surely do the stubborn facts of history rule out as absurd and impossible the theory that this second beast is papal Rome.''

In every thing this second beast is working for the first; and the powers ascribed to him are just such as a priest of the beast would perform. He maketh fire come down from heaven on earth in the sight of men. Fire fell upon the sheep of Job and burned them up. This was the work of the devil. These were his agents, and to them he gives this power.

The whole is a symbol of the power that these priests exercised over the people in bringing them to the worship of the emperors. Men were ostracised if they did not engage in this worship. No one was to sell to or buy from any one who had not the mark of the beast in his right hand or in his forehead.

"The ban of public sentiment fell on all who would not receive and wear this mark. They were ostracised from society, driven from the market-place, denied the right to any of the most common privileges of Roman citizens. Not only was the brand of opprobrium put on them, but the mark of Satan's vengeance."

God's people must know the name of the first beast whose image was set up for their worship. But there was great danger in revealing this name. Fierce enough were their persecutions already; and were the emperor's name announced, the fires would be kindled to a hotter flame. So it is communicated to them in numbers, and by a system with which the wise were familiar. "Let him that hath understanding count the number of the beast: for it is the number of a man; and his number is Six hundred threescore and six."

"The Hebrews and the Greeks used each their own alphabet for numerical purposes. In Hebrew the first letter is one; the second, two, etc.; the tenth, ten; but the eleventh is twenty; the nineteenth is one hundred; the twentieth, two hundred, etc. Hence each letter had a numerical power. In our passage the numerical power of the name is given to find the name itself. A preliminary question will be whether this name is to be spelled in Hebrew letters, with their numerical powers, or in Greek letters. It being manifestly

The Kingdom and Comings of Christ. 241

the intention of the writer to put his readers in the way to spell out the name, and yet not to give it so plainly as to expose himself or his brethren to persecuting vengeance; and, inasmuch as his readers (some of them being Jews) would have the advantage of the Roman magistrates in deciphering Hebrew letters, it becomes antecedently probable that he would use them—supposing this name to have been written in Hebrew characters with their known numerical power, and taking the name of Nero as it appears often in the Talmud, and in other Rabbinical writings,* we shall have as the numerical equivalent of these Hebrew letters in their order: 50+200+6+50; and 100+60 +200=666. This result must seem quite satisfactory, even though it rested on the mere fact that these seven Hebrew letters, by the sum of their numerical powers, give us precisely the well-known Hebrew name of Nero. But the proof that sustains the correctness of this solution is greatly strengthened by another remarkable fact. Let it be borne in mind that the received Greek text gives these three Greek letters (χ ξ ς), pronounced *chi, xi, vau;* and having in their order these numerical powers, 600+60+6=666. Now the fact is brought out and fully discussed by Ireneus, that in his day (A.D. 180) some manuscripts had a different reading for the middle character—viz., not ξ (χι), but ι (ιοτα). He insists, however, that the true reading is χι (ξ). Can the other reading be

*נריקמד

16

accounted for? It can, most readily. There was a second mode of spelling the name Nero in Hebrew—viz., by writing it not Neron, but Nero —*i. e.*, omitting the final (n). The numerical power of n is fifty. Strike off this final letter reduces the sum total of the number of his name from 666 to 616; and to write this amount in three Greek letters we must change the middle one as they stand in our text from (χι) to (ιοτα)—*i. e.*, from the letter which means 60 to the letter which means 10. Precisely this is the change which appears in the different reading of which Ireneus speaks. Hence it becomes substantially certain that the 'number of the beast' was understood by some at least before the age of Ireneus; certain also that they read in this number the name of Nero Cæsar; certain also that there being a second way of writing his name (*i. e.*, Nero rather than Neron), the change was made in the text which this other spelling of the name would require. This double coincidence is of the sort which could not occur by chance, and without a foundation in truth, one time in ten thousand. It amounts, therefore, practically to a demonstration." (H. Cowles.)

This settles the fact that the book was written during the reign of Nero, and that if he was the sixth head, or emperor, the seven heads represent pagan Rome, and nothing else; and that the early Christians so regarded it the testimony of Ireneus in the above quotation proves. He lived very near

The Kingdom and Comings of Christ. 243

the time in which the book was written, and those of his day spelled out the name of Nero with the "number of his name" as given in the book. This number has been forced to spell a great many names, but this answers to every feature of the symbol, and harmonizes with all other parts of the book. Therefore it must be the correct name. Now as the Church is assailed by such formidable foes, it is necessary to present the protector of the Church.

"And I looked, and, lo, a Lamb stood on the Mount Sion, and with him a hundred forty and four thousand, having his Father's name written in their foreheads. And I heard a voice from heaven, as the voice of many waters, and as the voice of a great thunder: and I heard the voice of harpers harping with their harps: and they sung as it were a new song before the throne, and before the four living creatures, and the elders: and no man could learn that song but the hundred and forty and four thousand which were redeemed from the earth. These are they which were not defiled with women; for they are virgins. These are they which follow the Lamb whithersoever he goeth. These were redeemed from among men, being the first-fruits unto God and to the Lamb. And in their mouth was found no guile: for they are without fault before the throne of God."

This Lamb of course is Jesus Christ, and the company with him are Jews," being the first-fruits unto God and to the Lamb;" and hence they are taken as samples of the whole. "If the first-fruit be holy the lump is also holy." The Lord is their shepherd; they follow him whithersoever he goeth. He is their protector, their friend, and they sound his praises. It is the song of victory.

"And I saw another angel fly in the midst of heaven, having the everlasting gospel to preach unto them that dwell on the earth, and to every nation, and kindred, and tongue, and people, saying with a loud voice, Fear God, and give glory to him; for the hour of his judgment is come: and worship him that made heaven, and earth, and the sea, and the fountains of water."

God never strikes without a warning, and without giving an opportunity to repent. The hour to strike down pagan Rome as a great persecuting power has come, and the angel proclaims the gospel, and calls upon men to fear God and give glory to him. This angel is merely a symbol of God's faithful ministers that were lifting up their voices to them that dwelt upon the earth—every nation, kindred, tongue, and people. The gospel, the everlasting gospel, was preached everywhere; and if men would not hear and heed it, it was their own fault, and they must perish in their sins.

"And there followed another angel, saying, Babylon is fallen, is fallen, that great city, because she made all nations drink of the wine of the wrath of her fornication."

The term Babylon here is used for Rome, as Sodom is used for Jerusalem. Fornication when

The Kingdom and Comings of Christ. 245

used as here means idolatry. Rome had forced her idolatry upon all the nations of the earth. She had made all nations drink of the wine of the wrath of her fornication; and now God was ready to punish her, and this angel is commissioned to declare her fall.

"And the third angel followed them, saying with a loud voice, If any man worship the beast and his image, and receive his mark in his forehead, or in his hand, the same shall drink of the wine of the wrath of God, which is poured out without mixture into the cup of his indignation; and he shall be tormented with fire and brimstone in the presence of the holy angels, and in the presence of the Lamb: and the smoke of their torment ascendeth up forever and ever: and they have no rest day nor night, who worship the beast and his image, and whosoever receiveth the mark of his name. Here is the patience of the saints: here are they that keep the commandments of God, and the faith of Jesus."

Here the line is clearly drawn. Babylon (Rome) had made all nations drink of the wine of her fornications, and to all such God would press the cup of his indignation, poured out without mixture; and, as in the case of the Jews, the smoke of their torment ascendeth up forever. "And they have no rest day nor night." This is a symbol to show that the overthrow of this great persecuting power is to be as a standing monument of God's wrath and indignation against sin. As God dealt with them so will he deal with like sinners in all times. Let God's saints patiently wait on God, who has said: "Vengeance is mine; I will repay." He knows when to strike, and just how hard. He may seem slow in his movements, especially to those suffering persecution and enduring trial, but let patience have her perfect work. God is not forgetful of his saints, nor unmindful of their rights.

"And I heard a voice from heaven saying unto me, Write, Blessed are the dead which die in the Lord from henceforth: yea, saith the Spirit, that they may rest from their labors; and their works do follow them."

Those who die in the Lord under these persecutions need not be troubled. God will remember them too. They shall rest from their labors; and, like the souls under the altar, God will hear their prayers, and they too shall be avenged of their adversaries.

"And I looked, and behold a white cloud, and upon the cloud one sat like unto the Son of man, having on his head a golden crown, and in his hand a sharp sickle. And another angel came out of the temple, crying with a loud voice to him that sat on the cloud, Thrust in thy sickle, and reap: for the time is come for thee to reap; for the harvest of the earth is ripe. And he that sat on the cloud thrust in his sickle on the earth; and the earth was reaped."

This was Jesus Christ, who had come for the

The Kingdom and Comings of Christ. 247

destruction of these persecutors of his people. The symbol of his appearing on a cloud is a familiar one. In Matthew Jesus, when speaking of the destruction of Jerusalem, said: "And they shall see the Son of man coming in the clouds of heaven with power and great glory." And again to Caiaphas: "Hereafter shall ye see the Son of man sitting on the right hand of power, and coming in the clouds of heaven."

Pagan Rome was ripe for punishment, and Jesus was to do the awful work. It is represented in the symbol as a field fully ripe for the harvest, and Jesus with a sharp sickle in his hand ready to reap. At the cry of the angel who came out of the temple, the Son of man thrusts in his sickle, and the earth is reaped. To make it doubly impressive, "another angel came out of the temple which is in heaven, he also having a sharp sickle. And another angel came out from the altar, which had power over fire; and cried with a loud cry to him that had the sharp sickle, saying, Thrust in thy sharp sickle, and gather the clusters of the vine of the earth; for her grapes are fully ripe. And the angel thrust in his sickle into the earth, and gathered the vine of the earth, and cast it into the great wine-press of the wrath of God. And the wine-press was trodden without the city, and blood came out of the wine-press, even unto the horse bridles, by the space of a thousand and six hundred furlongs."

As the symbol was doubled in Pharaoh's dream

—first the kine, and then the ears of corn—and as Joseph said unto him, "the dream was doubled unto Pharaoh twice; it is because the thing is established by God, and God will shortly bring it to pass;" so in this case the thing was doubled, first under the symbol of a harvest, and then of the vintage.

Isaiah, in speaking of the day of God's vengeance, represents Christ as coming from Edom with dyed garments from Bozrah, and the question is asked: "Wherefore art thou red in thine apparel, and thy garments like him that treadeth in the wine-fat?" And the answer comes: "I have trodden the wine-press alone; and of the people there was none with me: for I will tread them in mine anger, and trample them in my fury; and their blood shall be sprinkled upon my garments, and I will stain all my raiment."

The thousand and six hundred furlongs (200 miles) is approximately the length of Italy, the peninsular of which Rome is the great central city. The thought is that the land shall be deluged with blood, not that literally the blood should be to the horses' bridles. We must remember that this is a strong symbol, indicating that when the judgments of God should fall upon the land blood should flow from one end of the land to the other. "The historians who have written of the decline and fall of the old Roman empire have unconsciously written the fulfillment of these wonderful prophecies."

CHAPTER XII.

The Seven Golden Vials—Unclean Spirits Like Frogs—Preparation for the Great Battle—Judgment of the Great Whore, and Who She Is—The Joy over the Fall of Babylon—The King of Kings and His Armies—The Fowls Summoned to the Great Supper—The Beast and the False Prophet Cast into the Lake of Fire—The Dragon Cast into the Pit—The Millenium—The Judgment-day.

AS in the case of the destruction of Jerusalem, the first great persecuting power, the grand scene was first presented as a whole, and then, in after visions, the details are given under the seals and the trumpets; so in the destruction of pagan Rome, the second great persecuting power, the scene has been presented as a whole, and now comes this same scene in detail.

"And I saw another sign in heaven, great and marvelous, seven angels having the seven last plagues; for in them is filled up the wrath of God. And I saw as it were a sea of glass mingled with fire: and them that had gotten the victory over the beast, and over his image, and over his mark, and over the number of his name, stand on the sea of glass, having the harps of God. And they sing the song of Moses the servant of God, and the song of the Lamb, saying, Great and marvelous are thy works, Lord God Almighty; just and true are thy ways, thou King of saints. Who shall not fear thee, O Lord, and glorify thy name? for thou only art holy: for all nations shall come and worship before thee; for thy judgments are made manifest. And after that I looked, and, behold, the temple of the tabernacle of the testimony in heaven was opened: and the seven angels came out of the temple, having the seven plagues, clothed in pure and white linen, and having their breasts girded with golden girdles. And one of the four living creatures gave unto the seven angels seven golden vials full of the wrath of God, who liveth forever and ever. And the temple was filled with smoke from the glory of God, and from his power; and no man was able to enter into the temple, till the seven plagues of the seven angels were fulfilled."

Thus the whole scene is placed before the seer. The seven angels appear, having the seven last plagues; then the saints that had gotten the victory over the beast, standing on a sea of glass, with their harps, and they strike the prelude in anticipation of the grand victory to be accomplished when these seven angels shall pour out their vials upon the earth. They praise the righteousness of God in the acts he is about to perform. Then the temple doors are thrown open, and the seven angels come out, having the seven plagues, clothed in pure and white linen, and having their breasts girded with golden girdles. Then one of the four living creatures gives to these angels seven golden vials full of the wrath of God. All this is preparatory; and, as when God accepted the temple dedicated by Solomon, and filled it

The Kingdom and Comings of Christ. 251

with his glory, " so that the priests could not stand to minister because of the cloud: for the glory of the Lord had filled the house of the Lord," so as a manifestation of God's acknowledgment of the righteous act of his Son in preparing to pour out these vials of his wrath upon the earth.

"The temple was filled with smoke from the glory of God, and from his power; and no man was able to enter into the temple, till the seven plagues of the seven angels were fulfilled."

Every thing is now ready.

"And I heard a great voice out of the temple saying to the seven angels, Go your ways, and pour out the vials of the wrath of God upon the earth. And the first went, and poured out his vial upon the earth; and there fell a noisome and grievous sore upon the men which had the mark of the beast, and upon them which worshiped his image."

The effect of these vials is almost identical with the effect of the sounding of the seven trumpets at the destruction of Jerusalem. Wrath fell upon the *earth*, affecting only those men which had the mark of the beast, and upon them which worshiped his image.

"And the second angel poured out his vial upon the sea; and it became as the blood of a dead man: and every living soul died in the sea."

At the sound of the trumpet of the second angel a burning mountain was cast into the sea, making the third part of the sea blood, destroying the third part of the creatures in the sea that had life. Here the vial is poured into the sea, and the whole sea becomes as the blood of a dead man, and every living soul in the sea died. The judgments of God fell not only on the men on the land, but all who belonged to Rome that were upon the sea. No enemy of God and his children was to escape, whether on land or sea.

We need, in no age of the world, look for a literal changing of the sea into blood. But this is symbolical of the awful carnage that should sweep the sea as well as the land when God poured out the vials of his wrath upon these guilty, bloodthirsty idolaters. Their punishment might not have been so great had they worshiped their emperor and his image alone. But when they "caused that as many as would not worship the image of the beast should be killed; and caused all, both small and great, rich and poor, free and bond, to receive a mark in their right hand, or in their foreheads," then they deserved and received at the hands of a just and righteous God the full measure of punishment. Every soul stained with the blood of the saints must bleed and die, whether on land or sea.

"And the third angel poured out his vial upon the rivers and fountains of waters; and they became blood. And I heard the angel of the waters say, Thou art righteous, O Lord, which art, and wast, and shalt be, because thou hast judged thus. For they have shed the blood of saints and prophets, and thou hast given them blood to drink; for they are worthy. And I heard another out of the altar say, Even so, Lord God Almighty, true and righteous are thy judgments."

In the former vision the "star called Wormwood fell upon the third part of the rivers, and upon the fountains of waters," making them bitter. Here the angel pours his vial upon the rivers and fountains of water, and they become blood. The great law of retaliation comes in here: "With what measure ye mete, it shall be measured to you again." These had shed the blood of saints and prophets, and now they must drink blood. That this retribution is the work of God is announced by the voice heard from the altar, saying: "Even so, Lord God Almighty, true and righteous are thy judgments." It is at the altar that men pray. Here was seen the souls of the martyrs crying: "How long, O Lord, holy and true, doest thou not judge and avenge our blood on them that dwell on the earth." When these see the righteous judgment of God upon their adversaries, they acknowledge it.

"And the fourth angel poured out his vial upon the sun; and power was given unto him to scorch men with fire. And men were scorched with great heat, and blasphemed the name of God, which had power over these plagues: and they repented not to give him glory."

When the fourth angel sounded, "the third part of the sun was smitten," etc. So here the vial is poured upon the sun. This causes great suffering. As they are scorched by the intense heat of the sun they writhe in pain and blaspheme the God who has this power, instead of repenting.

"And the fifth angel poured out his vial upon the seat of the beast; and his kingdom was full of darkness; and they gnawed their tongues for pain, and blasphemed the God of heaven because of their pains and their sores, and repented not of their deeds."

Here the judgments fall upon the throne of the emperor, filling his kingdom with darkness. The head of this mighty empire, instead of saving his people from their punishments and calamities, is himself involved, and knows no way of escape or deliverance.

"And the sixth angel poured out his vial on the great river Euphrates; and the water thereof was dried up, that the way of the kings of the east might be prepared."

The Parthians, who lived beyond the Euphrates, were the first enemy that ever struck Rome a fatal blow. Gibbon tells us that "these armies, both of light and heavy cavalry, equally formidable by the impetuosity of their charge and the rapidity of their motions, threatened as an impending cloud the eastern provinces of the declining empire of Rome." The symbol of drying up the great river Euphrates that these kings of the East might cross easily and come against Rome is very expressive. As in the case of the destruction of Jerusalem,

The Kingdom and Comings of Christ. 255

every part of these symbols apply in the destruction of pagan Rome.

"And I saw three unclean spirits like frogs come out of the mouth of the dragon, and out of the mouth of the beast, and out of the mouth of the false prophet. For they are the spirits of devils, working miracles, which go forth unto the kings of the earth and the whole world, to gather them to the battle of that great day of God Almighty."

We have a most important pointer in this passage. The dragon and the first beast that came up out of the sea is mentioned by the same terms by which they were introduced to us: but the beast that came up out of the earth, "having two horns like a lamb, and who spake as a dragon," is called "the false prophet." As we have said, this beast was a symbol of the pagan priesthood—*false prophet*. The influence of these three—the devil, the deified emperor, and the priest of idolatry—combine in their work of prostituting the world to idolatry. As we have seen, they forced all the nations subdued by them to adopt their religion. The unclean spirits like frogs that came out of their mouths are symbols of that influence exerted over the kings of the earth to draw them into idolatry and into persecuting the saints, and thus leading them to their ruin, expressed by the "battle of that great day of God Almighty." "Behold, I come as a thief. Blessed is he that watcheth, and keepeth his garments, lest he walk naked, and they see his shame."

The great battle is about to be fought, and a warning voice is lifted to the saints. God is coming. His army is marshaling for the great charge. But his coming shall be all unexpected, like the coming of a thief. His watchful servants shall never be hurt. So all are warned.

"And he gathered them together into a place called in the Hebrew tongue Armageddon."

That is, the kings of the earth gathered at Armageddon — that is, the heights of Megiddo. "This was a place famed for battle and slaughter, where a host of Canaanites fell before Deborah and Barak; and where the good Josiah was mortally wounded in battle with Pharaoh Necho, a scene which became the more memorable because of the great mourning over the fall of Josiah to which Zechariah alludes. The significance here is essentially a place of immense slaughter. There the Almighty meets them in terrible retribution."

It is not that they are to meet actually on the heights of Megiddo, or Armageddon, but this field is a symbol of the place of slaughter. It was no one battle, but these kings and their armies were slaughtered all over the Roman empire. In madness and in fury army was dashed against army, and whole hecatombs of victims were piled in every direction, as Rome tottered to her final fall. The description of the final scene goes on.

"And the seventh angel poured out his vial into the air; and there came a great voice out of the temple of heaven, from the throne, saying, It is done. And there were voices, and thunders, and lightnings; and there was a great earthquake, such as was not since men were upon the earth, so mighty an earthquake, and so great."

The pouring out of this vial of the seventh angel reminds us of the seventh trumpet. The very artillery of heaven was turned loose. The voices of the mighty hosts of the sky are heard as they rush to the fray, while the solid earth trembles in the throes of an earthquake at the shock of battle. The mightiest empire ever erected on earth was going down on the red field, where the old serpent, the devil, and Satan, with kings of the earth, and all the angels of darkness, were arrayed on the one side; and Christ, followed by the armies of heaven, was on the other.

"And the great city was divided into three parts, and the cities of the nation fell: and great Babylon came in remembrance before God, to give unto her the cup of the wine of the fierceness of his wrath."

Babylon, or Rome, was divided. Internal discords tore this capital city of the nations into parts, thus destroying her own strength. "The cities of the nations," represented by the ten horns in the vision of the beast that came up out of the sea, fell. They were all on this Armageddon, and they must all share the same fate. But Rome is especially remembered, and the "cup of the wine of the fierceness of his wrath" is given to her. She suffers more than they all.

17

"And every island fled away, and the mountains were not found."

No hiding-places were left for the flying armies of this doomed nation, neither on sea or land.

"And there fell upon men a great hail out of heaven, every stone about the weight of a talent: and men blasphemed God because of the plague of the hail; for the plague thereof was exceeding great."

Not that there was a real hail, but this is symbolic of the fierce judgments of God that fell upon them on this great day of his wrath. The allusion is to the day when Joshua fought against the Canaanites, and "the Lord cast down great stones from heaven upon them." A Jewish talent was estimated at 114 pounds. Hailstones of such weight would fall like balls and bombs from a battery. The vial poured upon the air filled the very heavens with destruction. God's hand was against all these nations, with Rome, the spiritual Babylon, as the center.

We have seen that the revealing spirit in the case of Jerusalem dropped the symbolic sufficiently to let all know what city it was, when it told of the "two witnesses" whose dead bodies were exposed in the streets of the great city which spiritually is called Sodom and Egypt, *where also our Lord was crucified*. Nothing could be plainer than this. Isaiah in the first chapter of his prophecy calls Jerusalem Sodom, and here only of all the cities of earth was our Lord crucified. And now the same

The Kingdom and Comings of Christ. 259

revealing spirit, dealing with the second great persecuting power, points out with equal precision the city of Rome and her emperors, doing all but naming Nero as the one reigning at the time this book was written. The seventeenth chapter is invaluable in fixing the place of these predictions.

"And there came one of the seven angels which had the seven vials, and talked with me, saying unto me, Come hither; I will show unto thee the judgment of the great whore that sitteth upon many waters; with whom the kings of the earth have committed fornication, and the inhabitants of the earth have been made drunk with the wine of her fornication. So he carried me away in the spirit into the wilderness: and I saw a woman sit upon a scarlet-colored beast, full of names of blasphemy, having seven heads and ten horns. And the woman was arrayed in purple and scarlet color, and decked with gold and precious stones and pearls, having a golden cup in her hand full of abominations and filthiness of her fornication: and upon her forehead was a name written, MYSTERY, BABYLON THE GREAT, THE MOTHER OF HARLOTS AND ABOMINATIONS OF THE EARTH. And I saw the woman drunken with the blood of the saints, and with the blood of the martyrs of Jesus: and when I saw her, I wondered with great admiration. And the angel said unto me, Wherefore didst thou marvel? I will tell thee the mystery of the woman, and of the beast that carrieth her, which hath the seven heads and ten horns. The beast that thou sawest was, and is not; and shall ascend out of the bottomless pit, and go into perdition: and they that dwell on the earth shall wonder, whose names were not written in the book of life from the foundation of the world, when they behold the beast that was, and is not, and yet is."

One of the seven angels which had the seven vials came to show John the great mystery. None knew better than he, and John could not have had a better instructor. He promises to show him "the judgment of the great whore that sitteth upon many waters." The "many waters" is explained subsequently to be "peoples, and multitudes, and nations, and tongues." The Roman Empire was composed of many nations. She had taken into her folds nations in Europe, Asia, and Africa. Never in the history of the world were there so many nations acknowledging the same scepter as that held by the Cæsars at Rome; and never was there a more systematic, persistent, and successful effort made by any rulers to force their religion upon people subdued by them. They put their gods upon their victorious standards, and compelled worship wherever they went. These standards were characterized by Daniel and indorsed by Jesus as "the abomination of desolation;" so that it was truly said that "the kings of the earth had committed fornication with her, and the inhabitants of the earth had been made drunk with the wine of her fornication."

The Kingdom and Comings of Christ. 261

"'Fornication,' in the sense of the Old Testament prophets, is idolatry. This great harlot (Rome) had been intensely idolatrous; had wrought her religion into the very frame-work of her civil institutions and her fundamental law. In the period of her history here contemplated this abomination became even more open and outrageous than ever before, by the deification of her emperors and the demand set up that they should be worshiped as gods. In this fornication all the tributary kings of subject nations were involved. They were made drunk with the hot wine of her spiritual fornication." (H. Cowles.)

These nations made drunk persecuted the innocent Christians with all the folly and violence of men drunk with real wine.

The angel carried John away in spirit into the wilderness, where he saw a woman sit upon a scarlet-colored beast full of the names of blasphemy, having seven heads and ten horns. This is none other than the beast seen, in the early part of the vision, rise up out of the sea. Every point of the description, save it may be the color, answers to that given of the first beast. The dress and jewels of the woman show great wealth. Rome at this period was immensely wealthy, and her display of grandeur was marvelous.

The name written upon her forehead was wonderfully expressive, and it fully characterized Rome at this time.

The woman drunk with the blood of saints and

martyrs of Jesus refers to the bloody persecutions of that period. Who ever exceeded Nero in this bloody work—who lit the fires of his amphitheater with burning martyrs—who fired his own capital, and then laid the blame upon the Christians, that he might gloat over the inhuman cruelty inflicted upon them by his savage people?

When John saw her, he wondered with great admiration—not in an approving sense, but in wonder at her mighty power and bloodthirsty deeds. Here the angel proposes to tell him the mystery of the woman and the beast that carrieth her, which hath the seven heads and ten horns. At first it is enigmatical. "The beast that thou sawest was, and is not; and shall ascend out of the bottomless pit, and go into perdition." This is the empire under the Cæsars, as we have seen. When Julius Cæsar was slain, it was thought that his empire must perish; but Augustus seizes the scepter, and "it is." His ascending out of the pit refers to the fact presented in a former chapter where the dragon gave his power to the beast. He receives his power from the pit, as if he had come up out of it; but he is doomed, and shall "go into perdition."

"And here is the mind that hath wisdom. The seven heads are seven mountains, on which the woman sitteth."

There shall be a mystery about this no longer. My people shall know what this woman and beast are, for they both represent the same thing. The

The Kingdom and Comings of Christ. 263

seven heads have a twofold significance—the first locating the city; secondly, pointing out the succession of her kings.

"It need not disturb us that in the scenes of a vision, as in the scenes of a night-dream, there should be a slight and sudden change or shifting of some of the aspects, as here in verse 3 the woman sits on the beast and in verse 9 she sits on seven mountains. There is truth in both views, and they are by no means incongruous. Geographically she sat on the well-known seven hills of the great city Rome, but politically she sat on the seven-headed and ten-horned beast. These points are of prime importance to identify her in both these respects: her relation to *place*, and her relation to the great political powers of the world."

No other city of the world approaches this description. Every student of history knows that Rome was built on seven hills, and this was her well-known characteristic.

Now add to this the other fact, "And there are seven kings: five are fallen, and one is, and the other is not yet come; and when he cometh, he must continue a short space," and we have overwhelming evidence that Rome in the time of the Cæsars is meant, and no other city and no other time.

The seven heads had a twofold reference: First, the location of this persecuting power, pagan Rome; and second, the time—during the reign of the Cæsars; and further, that the vision was during the reign of Nero, whose name had already been given in the number 666. Five are fallen—viz., Julius Cæsar, Augustus, Tiberius, Caligula, Claudius. All these had fallen at the time when this vision was being shown, and this explanation of it was being given. Nero the Sixth was then on the throne. Galba followed him with a reign of only seven months, indeed "a short space."

"Thus with no forced construction, but in a most easy and obvious application of the revealing angel's words, we have the great facts of Roman history precisely indicated. An explanatory prophetic symbol, divinely given, ought to tally with history easily and with great precision and accuracy. It surely will if you bring it to the *right* history—*i. e.*, if you have the true application of the symbols of history. This history fits the angel's interpretation of these symbols perfectly. There can be no rational doubt, therefore, that this application of his symbols to history is the true one." (H. Cowles.)

The reader must remember that it is the *beast* that persecutes the Christians. There may have been no persecutions under the reign of Julius Cæsar, but he is used only as a part of the description of the beast by which he is identified. Nor are we told that the beast dies as soon as the seven heads by which he is identified fall; but the revealing angel goes on to say: "And the beast that was, and is not, even he is the eighth, and is of the seven, and goeth into perdition," showing that the empire continues after the fall of the seventh; and that the eighth is of the seven—that is, Otho, Vitellus, Vespasian, and others claimed to be Cæsars, though usurpers. Under them the *beast* still persecutes. But let the saints take courage. Imperial, persecuting Rome is fatally doomed, and must go into perdition.

"And the ten horns which thou sawest are ten kings, which have received no kingdom as yet; but receive power as kings one hour with the beast. These have one mind, and shall give their power and strength unto the beast. These shall make war with the Lamb, and the Lamb shall overcome them: for he is Lord of lords, and King of kings: and they that are with him are called, and chosen, and faithful."

Here we have the symbol of Rome as a persecuting power under the short reign of those who usurped the throne of the Cæsars. "One hour" is not a definite period, but is to represent the brief reign of these kings. Whether there were exactly ten—no more, no less—is not important to the symbol. It may be a definite for an indefinite number. They are the willing tools of the beast, giving their power and strength to him. With one mind they war with the Lamb; but—comforting thought— "the Lamb shall overcome them: for he is Lord of lords, and King of kings." The declaration is intended to strengthen the courage of the saints and make them endure hardness as good soldiers of Jesus Christ.

"And he saith unto me, The waters which thou sawest, where the whore sitteth, are peoples, and multitudes, and nations, and tongues."

This description answers precisely to Rome. She sat on numberless thrones of subject peoples. The conquered kings of a vast number of subjects were prisoners in her walls, and over these peoples and nations these ten kings were said to reign.

"And the ten horns which thou sawest upon the beast, these shall hate the whore, and shall make her desolate and naked, and shall eat her flesh, and burn her with fire. For God hath put in their hearts to fulfill his will, and to agree, and give their kingdom unto the beast, until the words of God shall be fulfilled."

Here is a symbol of the manner in which Rome shall be destroyed. These kings are to turn against her; Rome is to die by the hands of her own people. Civil war and discord were to destroy and make her desolate, to strip and make her naked, to devour her very substance, and set her on fire—all of which was done. God, who maketh the wrath of man to praise him, put it into the hearts of the people thus to destroy this destroyer of his people.

Does not history show us that the people of central Europe (Gauls, Germans, Goths, and others) and those of Asia (especially the Parthians) became the sword in God's hand for the destruction of Rome. They applied the torch to the mighty fabric of her power, and thus burned it with fire. Not only so, but Rome lost its place as the seat of empire, and it was transferred to Constantinople. And then the closing words of the angel would fix it unmistakably on Rome.

"And the woman which thou sawest is that great city, which reigneth over the kings of the earth."

She represents precisely pagan Rome. The language can apply to no other city of those times. And if it be pagan Rome, it strikes with resistless force against the theory held by so many that the woman is papal Rome. Every symbol so far applies naturally and easily to pagan Rome—time, place, kings, circumstances, and all—while papal Rome did not come into power for a thousand years after this book was written, and every symbol must be strained to represent it. I can see papal Rome nowhere in this book.

"And after these things I saw another angel come down from heaven, having great power; and the earth was lightened with his glory. And he cried mightily with a strong voice, saying, Babylon the great is fallen, is fallen, and is become the habitation of devils, and the hold of every foul spirit, and a cage of every unclean and hateful bird. For all nations have drunk of the wine of the wrath of her fornication, and the kings of the earth have committed fornication with her, and the merchants of the earth have waxed rich through the abundance of her delicacies."

This angel comes to make the announcement of

the fall of Rome, here called Babylon. We have seen that this was the name written upon the forehead of the woman upon the beast, and the revealing angel said: "And the woman which thou sawest is that great city, which reigneth over the kings of the earth." Pagan Rome falls under the power of God's judgments. Is it not wonderful that an infidel writer, in giving us the history of this very nation whose capital city was Rome, and the history of this very period, should select as the title of his book, " The Decline and Fall of the Roman Empire?" *Rome did fall*, and the cause of this fall is given. It "became the habitation of devils, and the hold of every foul spirit, and a cage of every unclean and hateful bird." It perished of its own corruption and rottenness. Perhaps no city of earth ever became more corrupt. Society was rotten to the very core, and this rottenness is symbolized by these devils, foul spirits, and hateful birds.

But this was not all: she had made all nations drink "of the wine of the wrath of her fornication," etc. The corrupting influence exerted upon all nations over which she reigned was another cause of her overthrow. She had forced other nations to commit idolatry, and made kings commit fornication (idolatry) with her.

"And I heard another voice from heaven, saying, Come out of her, my people, that ye be not partakers of her sins, and that ye receive not of her plagues. For her sins have reached unto heaven, and God hath remembered her iniquities. Reward her even as she rewarded you, and double unto her double according to her works: in the cup which she hath filled, fill to her double."

As in the case of Sodom and Gomorrah, God withheld his judgments until he had called righteous Lot and his family out, so arrangements are made for the rescue of his people in Rome. They are called to come out of her. Her sins had reached unto heaven, and the edict had gone forth to pour out the vials of his wrath upon her, doubling his judgments according to her deeds. She is to be recompensed according to her works.

"How much she hath glorified herself, and lived deliciously, so much torment and sorrow give her: for she saith in her heart, I sit a queen, and am no widow, and shall see no sorrow. Therefore shall her plagues come in one day, death, and mourning, and famine; and she shall be utterly burned with fire: for strong is the Lord God who judgeth her."

No city of earth had been so proud, no city more luxurious, and now her judgments are to be in proportion to her glory. And these judgments are to strike her just when she is pluming herself that she shall see no sorrow. Sudden and awful were the judgments of God upon this wicked city. "The Rome in the times of John was in fact blighted and scathed, tortured and smitten; her imperial power broken; her idolatrous influence crushed out; her persecuting terrors quenched in

God's own way, by judgments which might well make every ear tingle and every heart quail. A city called Rome is indeed standing now, nearly on the site of that Rome of old; but is it the same city—imperial now as then; mistress of the nations now as then; deifying her emperors, and compelling Christians to bow before her idolatrous military standards now as then; persecuting with fire and sword, with exile and torture, now as then? *Not at all.* This Rome and that have nothing in common but the name. The old Rome of the age of John, the Rome that sat on the seven-headed, ten-horned beast, has been politically dead for fifteen centuries."

"And the kings of the earth, who have committed fornication and lived deliciously with her, shall bewail her, and lament for her, when they shall see the smoke of her burning, standing afar off for the fear of her torment, saying, Alas, alas, that great city Babylon, that mighty city! for in one hour is thy judgment come. And the merchants of the earth shall weep and mourn over her; for no man buyeth their merchandise any more: the merchandise of gold, and silver, and precious stones, and of pearls, and fine linen, and purple, and silk, and scarlet, and all thyine wood, and all manner vessels of ivory, and all manner vessels of most precious wood, and of brass, and iron, and marble, and cinnamon, and odors, and ointments, and frankincense, and wine, and oil, and fine flour, and wheat, and beasts, and sheep, and horses, and chariots, and slaves, and souls of men."

The Kingdom and Comings of Christ. 271

This is a symbol of the effect that the fall of Rome will produce upon the kings and merchants of the earth that had been made rich by the abundance of her delicacies. They see all their trade swept away in her fall, and they lament and mourn.

"And the fruit that thy soul lusted after are departed from thee, and all things which were dainty and goodly are departed from thee, and thou shalt find them no more at all. The merchants of these things, which were made rich by her, shall stand afar off for the fear of her torment, weeping and wailing, and saying, Alas, alas, that great city, that was clothed in fine linen, and purple, and scarlet, and decked with gold, and precious stones, and pearls! For in one hour so great riches is come to naught."

Here the merchants, like the kings, weep and wail over the destruction of this great market of their merchandise.

"And every ship-master, and all the company in ships, and sailors, and as many as trade by sea, stood afar off, and cried when they saw the smoke of her burning, saying, What city is like unto this great city! And they cast dust on their heads, cried, weeping and wailing, saying, Alas, alas, that great city, wherein were made rich all that had ships in the sea by reason of her costliness! for in one hour is she made desolate."

Still another class, sailors and ship-masters, weep and wail because they see the destruction of the city that was the center of their trade. Thus the fall of this mighty city affected all classes of men.

"Rejoice over her, thou heaven, and ye holy apostles and prophets; for God hath avenged you on her."

Rome, the great persecuting power, goes down under the avenging hand of a righteous God in answer to the prayers of his saints, and heaven and all the good are called upon to rejoice, not so much at the fall of the wicked as at the deliverance of the righteous.

"And a mighty angel took up a stone like a great millstone, and cast it into the sea, saying, Thus with violence shall that great city Babylon be thrown down, and shall be found no more at all. And the voice of harpers, and musicians, and of pipers, and trumpeters, shall be heard no more at all in thee; and no craftsman, of whatsoever craft he be, shall be found any more in thee; and the sound of a millstone shall be heard no more at all in thee; and the light of a candle shall shine no more at all in thee; and the voice of the bridegroom and of the bride shall be heard no more at all in thee: for thy merchants were the great men of the earth; for by thy sorceries were all nations deceived. And in her was found the blood of prophets, and of saints, and of all that were slain upon the earth."

God would show how this mighty persecuting power was hurled down. The symbol is that of a mighty angel casting a stone like a great mill-

The Kingdom and Comings of Christ. 273

stone into the sea, pronouncing its doom as it falls; picturing the utter desolation by hushing all sounds and shutting out all sights, and concluding with the reason of this utter overthrow. She had deceived all nations with her sorceries, led all into idolatry and persecution. The blood of prophets and all that were slain upon the earth was found in her.

"After these things I heard a great voice of much people in heaven, saying, Alleluia; Salvation, and glory, and honor, and power, unto the Lord our God: for true and righteous are his judgments; for he hath judged the great whore, which did corrupt the earth with her fornication, and hath avenged the blood of his servants at her hand. And again they said, Alleluia. And her smoke rose up forever and ever."

Heaven rejoices at the righteous judgments of God in overthrowing this mighty persecuting city, the great whore, which, as we have seen, is none other than pagan Rome. She had corrupted the the earth with her fornication (idolatry), and had shed profusely the blood of his saints, and for this God had avenged their blood; and as she went down under his power it sent a thrill of joy all through heaven that voiced itself in the shout, "'Alleluia" (praise of Jah—*i. e.*, Jehovah the Lord), " and her smoke rose up forever and ever." The fact of this righteous judgment upon this great persecuting power was to be known throughout all generations. It is a standing monument of God's
18

wrath upon the corruptions of idolatry and the persecutions of his saints—as if a column of smoke ascending forever in the sight of men would remind them of the destruction and torment of those lying under the wrath of God.

"And the four and twenty elders and the four beasts [living creatures] fell down and worshiped God that sat on the throne, saying, Amen; Alleluia."

These prominent personages that appear all through these visions, as in deep sympathy with the work of the Lamb and the interests of his saints, join in the chorus, "Alleluia," that swells throughout heaven. By their falling down and worshiping God that sat on the throne they show that it was God who had executed these judgments and wrought this deliverance.

"And a voice came out of the throne, saying, Praise our God, all ye his servants, and ye that fear him, both small and great. And I heard as it were the voice of a great multitude, and as the voice of many waters, and as the voice of mighty thunderings, saying, Alleluia: for the Lord God omnipotent reigneth."

It is not said who uttered this voice; but it came out of the throne, and it was a command for all, both small and great, to join in the song of praise; and in response it came like the voice of a great multitude, like the roar of the sea, and the echo of mighty thunderings—all syllabled in that pæon of praise and of victory, "Alleluia." Jehovah had taken the reins of government into his hands, and it was enough to make heaven and earth glad. The joy was universal, and they shout:

"Let us be glad and rejoice, and give honor to him: for the marriage of the Lamb is come, and his wife hath made herself ready. And to her was granted that she should be arrayed in fine linen, clean and white: for the fine linen is the righteousness of saints. And he saith unto me, Write, Blessed are they which are called unto the marriage supper of the Lamb. And he said unto me, These are the true sayings of God."

Now that the two great persecuting powers, Jerusalem and Rome, had been swept out of the way, there was nothing to hinder the spread of the gospel. Jesus the Lamb was ready to be united to his people, and to go forth hand in hand with them to people the world with his saints. The bride, in the beauty of holiness, was to show to the world the loveliness of the religion of Jesus. And blessed are they which are called unto the marriage supper of the Lamb. Glorious privilege! exalted honor! All this is a symbol of the prosperity of the Church of Jesus Christ after the removal of these great hindering causes.

"And I fell at his feet to worship him. And he said unto me, See thou do it not: I am thy fellow-servant, and of thy brethren that have the testimony of Jesus: worship God: for the testimony of Jesus is the spirit of prophecy."

So glorious was the appearance of this revealing

angel that John mistook him for the Lord himself, and fell at his feet to worship him, and is forbidden on the ground that he is a fellow-servant of his; and that God only is worthy of adoration, as all the prophets who had testified of Jesus had shown.

"And I saw heaven opened, and behold a white horse; and he that sat upon him was called Faithful and True, and in righteousness he doth judge and make war. His eyes were as a flame of fire, and on his head were many crowns; and he had a name written, that no man knew, but he himself. And he was clothed with a vesture dipped in blood: and his name is called the Word of God. And the armies which were in heaven followed him upon white horses, clothed in fine linen, white and clean. And out of his mouth goeth a sharp sword, that with it he should smite the nations; and he shall rule them with a rod of iron: and he treadeth the wine-press of the fierceness and wrath of Almighty God. And he had on his vesture and on his thigh a name written, KING OF KINGS, AND LORD OF LORDS."

The chief actor in the scene now appears, riding on a white horse out of opened heaven. He is the commander of the armies that follow. His name is given—Faithful and True—and the war in which he is engaged is a righteous war. He did not strike till he had weighed well the offense against his people and the justice of his cause. His eyes were as a flame of fire: he could see into the depths of iniquity; he knew all. On his head were many crowns; his resources were unbounded; under his command were all the allies and powers necessary to the accomplishment of his purpose. He himself was the " Wonderful," the deep significance of whose name no man knew but he himself. And he was clothed with a vesture dipped in blood. Those who look upon Christ as only a God of mercy are fearfully mistaken. "Justice and judgment are the habitation of his throne." Paul asks the question: " Is God unrighteous who *taketh vengeance?* (I speak as a man) God forbid: for then how shall God judge the world?" No fact is more clearly stated in the Scriptures than that he will take vengeance upon his enemies. As we have seen, when the prophet Isaiah predicted his coming to judge Jerusalem, he cried out: " Who is this that cometh from Edom with dyed garments from Bozrah? this that is glorious in his apparel, traveling in the greatness of his strength?" And is answered: "I that speak in righteousness, mighty to save." The question is then asked to bring out the fact: " Wherefore art thou red in thine apparel, and thy garments like him that treadeth in the wine-fat?" The answer is given: "I have trodden the winepress alone; and of the people there was none with me: for I will tread them in mine anger, and trample them in my fury; and their blood shall be sprinkled upon my garments, and I will stain all my raiment. For the day of vengeance is in mine heart, and the year of my redeemed is come. And I looked, and there was none to help; and I wondered that there was none to uphold: therefore mine own arm brought salvation unto me; and my fury, it upheld me. And I will tread down the people in mine anger, and make them drunk in my fury, and I will bring down their strength to the earth." So in this case the same mighty champion is seen mounted on a white horse, with his vesture dipped in blood. He is again treading down his enemies. Every title applied to him here shows us clearly that this conquerer is Christ—Faithful and True, the Word of God, and King of kings, and Lord of lords. No other is entitled to these names. But he goes forth not alone. The armies which were in heaven follow him upon white horses like his, the symbol of victory. They are clothed in fine linen, white and clean. The revealing angel tells us that the "fine linen is the righteousness of the saints." They are in full harmony and sympathy with their leader.

"And out of his mouth goeth a sharp sword." Jesus is to conquer with his word. His commands are obeyed to the letter. Every power of the universe is at his command. He speaks, and armies move; earthquakes rend the solid earth, and lightnings leap from the batteries of the sky. He has no golden scepter for his foes now. Their rebellion has reached a point where the cup of their iniquity is full, and he rules now with a rod of iron. He lifts his hand to smite and destroy all these nations that are drunk with the wine of Rome's fornication. King's and lords have to submit to his power, by virtue of the victory he has achieved, for he is King of kings and Lord of lords. As he and his armies go forth to the final battle against the multiplied nations that war against him, John says:

"And I saw an angel standing in the sun; and he cried with a loud voice, saying to all the fowls that fly in the midst of heaven, Come and gather yourselves together unto the supper of the great God; that ye may eat the flesh of kings, and the flesh of captains, and the flesh of mighty men, and the flesh of horses, and of them that sit on them, and the flesh of all men, both free and bond, both small and great."

This angel is seen standing in the sun—that is, in the east as the sun rises. His voice rings out through the vast concave of heaven, summoning every bird of prey to the battle-field, for a feast such as they have never enjoyed.

"The slain of the Lord shall be many, and they shall eat to the full."

This is symbolical of the great slaughter that should take place at the fall of Rome. When the day of battle shall close, and mountain and plain shall be strewn thick with the bodies of the slain—of kings, captains, mighty men, horses, and soldiers—free, bond, small, and great, then these fowls that fly in the midst of heaven are to partake of this "supper of the great God."

No attempt is made to describe the battle scene,

but John sees the hosts gathering, and witnesses the final act.

"And I saw the beast, and the kings of the earth, and their armies, gathered together to make war against him that sat on the horse, and against his army. And the beast was taken, and with him the false prophet that wrought miracles before him, with which he deceived them that had received the mark of the beast, and them that worshiped his image. These both were cast alive into a lake of fire burning with brimstone. And the remnant were slain with the sword of him that sat upon the horse, which sword proceeded out of his mouth; and all the fowls were filled with their flesh."

There was one mighty shock as these multiplied nations hurled themselves against him that sat on the horse and against his army. The leaders—the beast, pagan Rome, the false prophet, and the pagan priesthood—were seized and cast alive into a lake of fire burning with brimstone. This is a symbol of the complete overthrow of this great persecuting power. The victory is complete and final. The remnant were slain, and their bodies given to the fowls that in the early morning had been invited to the supper of the great God.

One fact in this symbol should be specially noted. The beast seen coming up out of the sea, with the seven heads and ten horns, which we have seen answers in every feature to pagan Rome and the false prophet, synonymous with the beast that came up out of the earth, are both here—here at the same time and place; so one cannot represent pagan Rome and the other papal Rome, that as a persecuting power followed a thousand years after. Everywhere in this vision they are cotemporary, the latter always subordinate to the former, and exercising his power in seducing kings, nations, tongues, and peoples to worship the beast and his image. Both were cast at the same time into the burning lake, the prison house of the lost, first prepared for the devil and his angels. They did the devil's work, and they must share the devil's hell; for, you remember, "the dragon gave him his power, and his seat, and great authority." (H. Cowles.)

The beast and the false prophet have been taken and cast into the lake of fire burning with brimstone. Shall the archenemy, the instigator of all the wickedness and crime, escape? No. Hear what John says of him:

"And I saw an angel come down from heaven, having the key of the bottomless pit and a great chain in his hand. And he laid hold on the dragon, that old serpent, which is the Devil, and Satan, and bound him a thousand years, and cast him into the bottomless pit, and shut him up, and set a seal upon him, that he should deceive the nations no more, till the thousand years should be fulfilled: and after that he must be loosed a little season.".

This is not literal, but, like all else in this book, is symbolical. The devil has had great power. He stood before the woman to devour her child as soon as it was born, and when this child is divinely preserved he persecutes the woman, gives his power and his seat to the ferocious beast that comes up out of the sea, who in turn marshals all the kings and peoples against the followers of Christ, to crush out the saints from the earth. His emissaries have been overthrown, and now the power of this archenemy must be curtailed as far as the Church of God is concerned. An angel came down from heaven, signifying that his authority was from God, and he lays hold upon the devil and casts him into the bottomless pit, and shuts him up, and sets a seal upon him, that he should deceive the nations no more till the thousand years should be fulfilled.

The thousand years is a definite period given to indicate an indefinite. Not that he was to be bound for just ten centuries—no more, no less—but this is a round number, used frequently in the Scriptures to indicate a long period. This is graciously realized, as far as God's people are concerned. Jesus said: "I saw Satan as lightning fall from heaven." What power has he over one who abides in Christ, one who walks faithfully in the highway of holiness? Over this the unclean shall not pass. "No lion shall be there, nor any ravenous beast shall go up thereon, it shall not be found there; but the redeemed shall walk there: and the ransomed of the Lord shall return, and come to Zion with songs and everlasting joy upon their heads: they shall obtain joy and gladness,

The Kingdom and Comings of Christ. 283

and sorrow and sighing shall flee away." Then, as far as the true followers of Christ are concerned, the devil is bound. Christ in this grand battle broke his power, and put his Church where it could move on to the salvation of the world.

"And I saw thrones, and they sat upon them, and judgment was given unto them: and I saw the souls of them that were beheaded for the witness of Jesus, and for the word of God, and which had not worshiped the beast, neither his image, neither had received his mark upon their foreheads, or in their hands; and they lived and reigned with Christ a thousand years. But the rest of the dead lived not again until the thousand years were finished. This is the first resurrection. Blessed and holy is he that hath part in the first resurrection: on such the second death hath no power, but they shall be priests of God and of Christ, and shall reign with him a thousand years."

Who are they that sit upon the thrones? Evidently the souls of the martyrs which have played so important a part in moving by their pleadings and prayers their Lord to avenge them of their enemies. They were first seen under the altar, crying, "How long, O Lord?" Now the time of their exaltation has come. The two great persecuting powers have been overthrown and Satan bound, and now their Lord and King fulfills the promise he made: "To him that overcometh will I grant to sit with me in my throne, even as I also overcame, and am set down with my Father in his throne." These martyrs now occupy the most exalted position. This is a symbol of their having overcome. They were faithful to the death, held on to their integrity until Christ in answer to their prayers had overthrown all their foes and bound the very devil himself. They were faithful witnesses for Jesus and the word of God, loving not their lives unto the death, and Christ is true to his promise: "Be thou faithful unto death, and I will give thee a crown of life." With crowns upon their heads, and seated upon thrones in the presence of all, they are to reign with Christ for a thousand years.

"But the rest of the dead lived not again until the thousand years were finished. This is the first resurrection."

This is not a literal resurrection, nor is it a resurrection of the body. This whole book, and especially this part of it, is full of symbols. See "the great chain," "the old serpent," the "seal," the "thrones," the "second death," the "camp of the saints," etc. So this resurrection is symbolical. The passing from sorrow to joy is often in the Old Testament Scriptures represented by a resurrection. Ezekiel xxxvii. represents Israel as dead and scattered as dry bones in a valley, but by the breath of God they have a resurrection. This was not literal, but symbolical. Other cases might be cited, but this is enough to establish the fact.

In the New Testament we have the same figure. Ephesians v. 14: "Awake thou that sleepest, and

The Kingdom and Comings of Christ. 285

arise from the dead, and Christ shall give thee light." And again in Ephesians ii. 1: "And you hath he quickened, who were dead in trespasses and sins." In Romans xi. 15, Paul, in speaking of the salvation of the Jews, says: "What shall the receiving of them be, but life from the dead?"

Now this first resurrection was only the passage of these martyrs from the death of sorrow to the life of joy. Their prayers were fully answered. Jesus had returned from his conquest against their foes in complete triumph, and they are lifted to thrones and are to have a joy peculiar to themselves in seeing the cause for which they died triumphing as never before. They shall partake of the joy of their Lord. The rest of the dead know nothing of this joy. It is peculiar to those who "were beheaded for the witness of Jesus and for the word of God."

That the thousand years here is a definite number used for an indefinite period we can easily determine by marking its use elsewhere in the Scriptures. In the second commandment (Ex. xx. 6) it is said: "And showing mercy unto thousands of them that love me, and keep my commandments." Thousands means not unto thousands of people, but unto the thousandth generation—that is, forever; for in the preceding verse it is said: "Unto the third and fourth generation of them that hate me." Moses repeats the thought in Deuteronomy vii. 9: "Know therefore that the Lord thy God, he is God, the faithful God, which keepeth covenant and mercy with them that love him and keep his commandments to a thousand generations." He does not mean just a thousand—no more, no less—but it is a definite number, and a large one, to express the boundlessness of God's mercy to them that keep his commandments. The expression of David (Ps. l. 10), "The cattle upon a thousand hills," is of a like character. And again (Ps. xc. 4): "For a thousand years in thy sight are but as yesterday when it is past." Again (Ps. xci. 7): "A thousand shall fall at thy side, and ten thousand at thy right hand." This, in fact, is a favorite number to express a large and indefinite number.

Strange as it may appear, the passage under consideration is the only one in all the Bible in which there is any allusion to the millennium; and yet no fact has fixed itself more strongly upon the mind of the Church than that there is to be a millennium, and nothing about which there is so much indefiniteness. Some think that it will be before Christ's second coming; some, after. Some think it will be merely a time of great prosperity in the Church, when the powers of darkness will give way to mighty displays of God's glory in the salvation of sinners; others, that the world has been divided in its duration to seven thousand years; that the first six thousand, now nearly at an end, will be succeeded by a Sabbatic thousand, when the Church shall have rest from her enemies, and great glory shall be vouchsafed to it; and many others. Ask these men for their reasons for their beliefs, and they can give no good and satisfactory scriptural reasons. Like that other error, that Gabriel shall sound the last trumpet, for which there is not a shadow of proof from the Scriptures, men have always talked of a millennium; therefore there must be one. Now if we examine this single passage in the light of the symbolic character of this entire book, we shall find that it refers alone to the martyrs of Jesus, whose joy at the overthrow of the two great persecuting powers—Jerusalem and pagan Rome, the powers that beheaded them—and the binding of Satan, who instigated these persecutions, is to thrill them for an indefinite period. God gives them this peculiar pleasure because of their faithfulness. Other dead, not of the martyrs, enter not into this joy. "This is the first resurrection. Blessed and holy is he that hath part in the first resurrection: on such the second death hath no power, but they shall be priests of God and of Christ, and shall reign with him a thousand years." Theirs was a hard death. In it they exemplified the power of the religion of Jesus. They proved their confidence in the promises of God of another and better life; and that faith in Christ was the very thing that could give them this life. Thus honoring God, God honors them by revealing to the Church and to the world that he was "not unrighteous to forget their work." It is written:

"If we suffer, we shall also reign with him." And again: "And if children, then heirs; heirs of God, and joint heirs with Christ; if so be that *we suffer with him*, that we may be also glorified together." Peter says (1 Pet. iv. 13): "But rejoice, inasmuch as ye are partakers of Christ's sufferings; that, when his glory shall be revealed, ye may be glad also with exceeding joy."

The martyr saints are to be honored. God makes them his ministers, symbolized by being made priests of God and of Christ. They also sit upon the thrones spoken of, and reign with him a thousand years. This is all of it.

"And when the thousand years are expired, Satan shall be loosed out of his prison, and shall go out to deceive the nations which are in the four quarters of the earth, Gog and Magog, to gather them together to battle: the number of whom is as the sands of the sea. And they went up on the breadth of the earth, and compassed the camp of the saints about, and the beloved city: and fire came down from God out of heaven, and devoured them. And the devil that deceived them was cast into the lake of fire and brimstone, where the beast and the false prophet are, and shall be tormented day and night forever and ever."

This symbol would indicate that after this long period of rest and rejoicing at the overthrow of the powers of darkness there is yet to be one more blow from the hand of God. The devil had only been shut up in the bottomless pit for a period. The seal upon that pit was after a time to be broken, and he loosed out of his prison. It would seem that the object of this loosing is to put him in a position to be hurled into the lake of fire and brimstone. God knows that all he needs is an opportunity to show his hand.

As the time for the final coming of Christ to judge the quick and dead draws near Satan is loosed. At once he sets to work to deceive the nations which are in the four quarters of the earth. Once more he gathers them together to try and recover his lost fortunes.

John seizes upon an Old Testament picture, where the greatest army ever gathered together for battle is mentioned (Ezek. xxxviii., xxxix.), Gog and Magog. These multiplied thousands come up, and are wholly overthrown. And to give an idea of their countless numbers and their utter overthrow, the prophet tells us that the wood of their weapons—shields, bucklers, bows, arrows, hand staves, and spears—will serve the people for firewood for seven years, and that all Israel shall be seven months in burying the dead of their army. They compassed the camp of the saints about, and the beloved city; but before they had time to strike a blow fire came down from God out of heaven, and devoured them; and the devil that deceived them was cast into the lake of fire and brimstone. This ends forever the power of the devil upon earth, and the next symbol is that which presents to us the resurrection and the great judgment-day.

"And I saw a great white throne, and him that sat on it, from whose face the earth and the heaven fled away; and there was found no place for them. And I saw the dead, small and great, stand before God; and the books were opened: and another book was opened, which is the book of life: and the dead were judged out of those things which were written in the books, according to their works. And the sea gave up the dead which were in it; and death and hell delivered up the dead which were in them: and they were judged every man according to their works. And death and hell were cast into the lake of fire. This is the second death. And whosoever was not found written in the book of life was cast into the lake of fire."

It is clearly taught in the scriptures that there shall be a "resurrection of the just and of the unjust." Jesus said: "Marvel not at this: for the hour is coming, in the which all that are in the graves shall hear his voice, and shall come forth; they that have done good, unto the resurrection of life; and they that have done evil, unto the resurrection of damnation."

It is also taught that there shall be a day of judgment following this resurrection, and that Jesus is to be the judge. Paul says: "God hath appointed a day, in the which he will judge the world in righteousness by that man whom he hath ordained." And again: "We must all stand before the judgment-seat of Christ."

The symbol here used shows that all the dead, small and great, shall stand before God. Even the sea shall give up the dead which are in it, and death and hell (hades, the place of the departed) shall make a full deliverance on that day; and, when emptied, shall, as no longer of any use, be cast into the lake of fire. The books are opened: the utmost accuracy is to be observed; each individual is to be examined, and then the book of life is to be appealed to to see if his name is found there; if not, that settles the matter, and he is cast into the lake of fire. This casting into the lake of fire is the second death. It is a final and eternal separation from God and the good.

In the beginning of these revelations, in addressing the Church at Sardis, Jesus promises that "he that overcometh, the same shall be clothed in white raiment; and I will not blot out his name out of the book of life, but I will confess his name before my Father, and before his angels."

CHAPTER XIII.

The New Heaven and the New Earth—The New Jerusalem—The General Invitation.

IN our approach to these closing chapters of Revelation we must not forget that this is a book of symbols, and that these chapters are symbolic as well as the rest. If we adhere strictly to this, we will find them a most beautiful and striking representation of the Church of Jesus Christ on earth, when he had overthrown her foes and fully established the plan upon which he purposed to bring the world under his scepter.

"And I saw a new heaven and a new earth: for the first heaven and the first earth were passed away; and there was no more sea."

Isaiah had foretold of this time, and the revealing angel applies this prophecy in these symbols. When speaking of the Church of the Messiah that should embrace the Gentiles, he says: "For, behold, I create new heavens and a new earth: and the former shall not be remembered, nor come into mind. But be ye glad and rejoice forever in that which I create; for, behold, I create Jerusalem a rejoicing, and her people a joy. And I will rejoice in Jerusalem, and joy in my people: and the voice of weeping shall be no more heard in her, nor the voice of crying." This is the new heaven and earth seen in the vision of John. The Mosaic state of the Church had passed away, and the Christian state had been established.

"And there was no more sea." The sea represents nations. "The waters which thou sawest, where the whore sitteth, are peoples, and multitudes, and nations, and tongues." (Rev. xvii. 15.) Under the first arrangement God had his Church in a nation—the nation of the Jews—but now the Church is universal, members are taken from all nations; and yet God has no nation he calls his own, his peculiar people. As Christ said, " My kingdom is not of this world." Members of his Church can be found among all people; nor is it necessary for them to forswear allegiance to their earthly rulers to become members of his kingdom. On the other hand, all are exhorted to be subject to their earthly rulers. His is not a national Church.

"And I John saw the holy city, new Jerusalem, coming down from God out of heaven, prepared as a bride adorned for her husband."

This new Jerusalem is a symbol of the Church. Paul, speaking of it, says: " For it is written, that Abraham had two sons, the one by a bondmaid, the other by a free woman. But he who was of the bondwoman was born after the flesh: but he of the free woman was by promise. Which things are an allegory: for these are the two covnants; the one from the Mount Sinai, which gendereth to bondage, which is Agar. For this Agar is Mount Sinai in Arabia, and answereth to Jerusalem which now is, and is in bondage with her children. But Jerusalem which is above is free, which is the mother of us all." (Gal. iv. 22–26.) And again: " But ye are come unto Mount Sion, and unto the city of the living God, the heavenly Jerusalem." (Heb. xii. 22.)

" Prepared as a bride adorned for her husband." John the Baptist speaks of the Church as the bride and Jesus as the bridegroom. (John iii. 29.) Paul says: " I have espoused you to one husband, that I may present you as a chaste virgin to Christ." The Church must be clothed in "the beauty of holiness." Christ is coming to take his bride to his Father's house, and she must keep herself unspotted from the world, loving her Lord with all her heart.

"And I heard a great voice out of heaven saying, Behold, the tabernacle of God is with men, and he will dwell with them, and they shall be his people, and God himself shall be with them, and be their God. And God shall wipe away all tears from their eyes; and there shall be no more death, neither sorrow, nor crying, neither shall there be any more pain: for the former things are passed away. And he that sat upon the throne said, Behold, I make all things new. And he said unto me, Write: for these words are true and faithful. And he said unto me, It is done. I am Alpha and Omega, the beginning and the end. I will give unto him that is athirst of the fountain of the water of life freely."

The Kingdom and Comings of Christ. 295

The new Jerusalem is not taken from earth up to heaven, but it cometh down from God out of heaven. It is to be here on earth for a time. The temple has been thrown down; Jerusalem has been destroyed. And now God sets up his tabernacle among men. "The tabernacle of David which had fallen" he had again set up, "that the residue of men might seek after the Lord, and all the Gentiles, upon whom my name is called, saith the Lord, who doeth all these things." (Acts xv. 17.) God promises to dwell among his people and make them his. The Gentiles are now to be his people. "And it shall come to pass, that in the place where it was said unto them, Ye are not my people; there shall they be called the children of the living God."

"And God shall wipe away all tears from their eyes." This is a symbol of the fact that the religion of Jesus is to be a solace for all the woes of earth. Isaiah, in speaking of just this period, says: "And the Lord God will wipe away tears from off all faces." (Isa. xxv. 8.)

"And there shall be no more death, neither sorrow, nor crying, neither shall there be any more pain: for the former things are passed away." Taking this in its symbolic sense, we find that death is now spoken of as *sleep*, because Jesus has given promise of a resurrection.

"I would not have you to be ignorant, brethren, concerning them which are *asleep*, that ye sorrow not, even as others which have no hope." The hope of living again takes away the sorrow and lifts us above pain—the sorrow and pain without hope.

"And he that sat upon the throne said, Behold, I make all things new. And he said unto me, Write: for these words are true and faithful."

This is a moral creation, not a physical. Isaiah foretold this. "For the Lord God shall call his servants by another name: that he who blesseth himself in the earth shall bless himself in the God of truth; and he that sweareth in the earth shall swear by the God of truth; because the former troubles are forgotten, and because they are hid from mine eyes. For, behold, I create new heavens and a new earth: and the former shall not be remembered, nor come into mind. But be ye glad and rejoice forever in that which I create: for, behold, I create Jerusalem a rejoicing, and her people a joy. And I will rejoice in Jerusalem, and joy in my people: and the voice of weeping shall be no more heard in her, nor the voice of crying." (Isa. lxv. 15–19.) Here the new name, "Christian," given to his people is spoken of. God shall be their God, and they shall be his people. As the bride, they shall take his name, "Christian."

The New Jerusalem is also spoken of as the joy of the Lord. All things are new. Paul says: "If any man be in Christ, he is a new creature: old things are passed away; behold, all things are become new." (2 Cor. v. 17.) "For in Christ Jesus neither circumcision availeth any thing, nor uncircumcision, *but a new creature.*" (Gal. vi. 15.)

"And he said unto me, It is done. I am Alpha and Omega, the beginning and the end. I will give unto him that is athirst of the fountain of the water of life freely. He that overcometh shall inherit all things; and I will be his God, and he shall be my son."

In the same grand prophecy of Isaiah we have the invitation: " Ho, every one that thirsteth, come ye to the waters." And Jesus exclaimed: " If any man thirst, let him come unto me, and drink." And he promised to give to the woman of Samaria water of which if she drank she should never thirst.

" Shall inherit all things." Paul tells us: "All things are yours, . . . and ye are Christ's; and Christ is God's." " Having nothing, yet possessing all things."

" I will be his God." We become the children of God. By the spirit which makes us new creatures in Christ we are enabled to cry Abba, Father. " The Spirit itself beareth witness with our spirit, that we are the children of God: and if children, then heirs; heirs of God, and joint heirs with Christ." Thus we as the sons of God inherit all things. How very plain it is that this beautiful symbol refers to the Church of Jesus Christ as it now exists!

" But the fearful, and unbelieving, and the abominable, and murderers, and whoremongers, and sorcerers, and idolaters, and all liars, shall have their part in the lake which burneth with fire and brimstone: which is the second death."

Here are pointed out those who are excluded from the blessings of the New Jerusalem. They shall follow the beast, the false prophet, and the dragon into the lake burning with fire and brimstone. Fearful fate! From this second death there is no resurrection. When the seal of the second death is set upon the soul, hope dies, and the soul is damned forever.

"And there came unto me one of the seven angels which had the seven vials full of the seven last plagues, and talked with me, saying, Come hither, I will show thee the bride, the Lamb's wife."

This angel comes now to show to John more in detail the glorious city, the New Jerusalem. The Church, as we have seen, is the Lamb's wife. So the revelation now to be made is with reference to the Church of Jesus Christ; and let us bear in mind that it is the Church on earth, not in heaven.

"And he carried me away in the spirit to a great and high mountain, and showed me that great city, the holy Jerusalem, descending out of heaven from God, having the glory of God: and her light was like unto a stone most precious, even like a jasper stone, clear as crystal; and had a wall great and high, and had twelve gates, and at the gates twelve angels, and names written thereon, which are the names of the twelve tribes of the children of Israel: on the east three gates; on the north three gates; on the south three gates; and on the west three gates. And the wall of the city had twelve foundations, and in them the names of the twelve apostles of the Lamb."

As the first or material Jerusalem was built upon a high mountain, so this symbolic city is upon a great and high mountain. In a subsequent part of this description it is said, "for the Lord God giveth them light." God is the light of his Church; and the light is glorious, compared here to the light of a precious stone clear as crystal. The wall is a symbol of God's protecting care. It is said: "In that day [the very time of which we speak] shall this song be sung in the land of Judah; We have a strong city; salvation will God appoint for walls and bulwarks. Open ye the gates, that the righteous nation which keepeth the truth may enter in." (Isa. xxvi. 1, 2.) And again: "Violence shall no more be heard in thy land, wasting nor destruction within thy borders; but thou shalt call thy walls Salvation, and thy gates Praise. The sun shall be no more thy light by day; neither for brightness shall the moon give light unto thee: but the Lord shall be unto thee an everlasting light, and thy God thy glory." (Isa. lx. 18, 19.)

This last expression is the very language of the symbol, "having the glory of God." Both the prophecy and the symbol refer to the same thing, and nothing is plainer than that Isaiah is speaking of the Christian state of the Church in all the latter part of his prophecy. Jesus himself at Nazareth, when he read this part of Isaiah, said: "This day is this scripture fulfilled in your hearing."

"And had twelve gates," three on each side. These gates are for the admission of those who desire to become citizens of this city. They may come from any quarter or from any nation, and will be admitted, for "in him shall all nations be blessed." The twelve angels represent the twelve apostles. They were sent of God for this purpose. Jesus said: "Whosoever sins ye remit, they are remitted unto them; and whosoever sins ye retain, they are retained;" "and whatsoever thou shalt bind on earth shall be bound in heaven; and whatsoever thou shalt loose on earth shall be loosed in heaven."

Jesus commits the management of the affairs of his Church to the apostles when he ascends on high, and these are typical of his true ministers in all ages. They stand at the gates to admit those who come to Christ. The Christians are also still known as the true Israel of God: "Know ye therefore that they which are of faith, the same are the children of Abraham." The Christian Church is still the children of Israel.

"And the wall of the city had twelve foundations, and in them the names of the twelve apostles of the Lamb."

Paul, when writing to the Ephesians, who were Gentiles, says: "Now therefore ye are no more strangers and foreigners, but fellow-citizens with the saints, and of the household of God; and are built upon the foundation of the apostles and prophets, Jesus Christ himself being the chief corner-stone." "And he that talked with me had a golden reed to measure the city, and the gates thereof, and the wall thereof. And the city lieth foursquare, and the length is as large as the breadth: and he measured the city with the reed, twelve thousand furlongs (fifteen hundred miles). The length and the breadth and the height of it are equal. And he measured the wall thereof, a hundred and forty and four cubits, according to the measure of a man, that is, of the angel."

This symbol of the city is taken from the Holy of Holies of the temple, which was a perfect cube. "The length and the breadth and the height of it were equal."

"And the building of the wall of it was of jasper: and the city was pure gold, like unto clear glass. And the foundations of the wall of the city were garnished with all manner of precious stones. The first foundation was jasper; the second, sapphire; the third, a chalcedony; the fourth, an emerald; the fifth, sardonyx; the sixth, sardius; the seventh, chrysolite; the eighth, beryl; the ninth, a topaz; the tenth, a chrysoprasus; the eleventh, a jacinth; the twelfth, an amethyst. And the twelve gates were twelve pearls; every several gate was of one pearl: and the street of the city was pure gold, as if it were transparent glass."

That no one might misinterpret this symbol, John constantly refers to the figures used by Isaiah in describing the Church. Isaiah says: "O thou afflicted, tossed with tempest, and not comforted, behold, I will lay thy stones with fair colors, and lay thy foundation with sapphires. And I will make thy windows of agates, and thy gates of carbuncles, and all thy borders of pleasant stones."

The riches of the world are laid under tribute to give expression to the glory and beauty of the Church of Jesus Christ.

"And I saw no temple therein: for the Lord God Almighty and the Lamb are the temple of it. And the city had no need of the sun, neither of the moon, to shine in it: for the glory of God did lighten it, and the Lamb is the light thereof."

Under this new arrangement, there are no fixed places where alone God can be worshiped, as was the case in Jerusalem; but as Jesus said to the woman of Samaria: "Woman, believe me, the hour cometh, when ye shall neither in this mountain, nor yet at Jerusalem, worship the Father. . . . But the hour cometh, and now is, when the true worshipers shall worship the Father in spirit and in truth: for the Father seeketh such to worship him. God is a spirit: and they that worship him must worship him in spirit and in truth."

John saw no temple, for there was none. Wherever men might be, they could worship God; for he is a Spirit, and is equally present everywhere. When Jesus sent his disciples into all the world, he said: "Lo, I am with you alway, even unto the end of the world." This mighty Holy of Holies is accessible to all. "Jesus said: I am the light of the world: he that followeth me shall not walk in darkness, but shall have the light of life." "In him was life, and the life was the light of men." "That was the true light which lighteneth every man that cometh into the world." "And the nations of them which are saved shall walk in the light of it: and the kings of the earth do bring their glory and honor into it. And the gates of it shall not be shut at all by day; for there shall be no night there. And they shall bring the glory and honor of the nations into it.

Jesus is the Sun of righteousness, whose healing wings are spread over all the earth. Isaiah says: "And the Gentiles shall come to thy light, and kings to the brightness of thy rising." (Isa. lx. 3.) And again: "I will also give thee for a light to the Gentiles, that thou mayest be my salvation unto the end of the earth." (Isa. xlix. 6.) And again: "Who are these that fly as a cloud, and as the doves to their windows? Surely the isles shall wait for me, and the ships of Tarshish first, to bring thy sons from far, their silver and their gold with them, unto the name of the Lord thy God, and to the Holy One of Israel, because he hath glorified thee. And the sons of strangers shall build up thy walls, and their kings shall minister unto thee: for in my wrath I smote thee, but in my favor have I had mercy on thee. Therefore thy gates shall be open continually; they shall not be shut day nor night; that men may bring unto thee the forces of the Gentiles, and that their kings may be brought." (Isa. lx. 8–11.) This passage is a clear explanation of this symbol.

"And there shall in nowise enter into it any thing that defileth, neither whatsoever worketh abomination, or maketh a lie: but they which are written in the Lamb's book of life."

God's children must be pure and holy, for without holiness no man shall see the Lord. Men without spiritual life may unite with the visible Church, but only those who have been regenerated by the Holy Ghost shall be numbered among the true followers of God. Paul says: "The foundation of God standeth sure, having this seal, The Lord knoweth them that are his. And, Let every one that nameth the name of Christ depart from iniquity." (2 Tim. ii. 19.) Only those born of the Spirit have their names "written in the Lamb's book of life."

"And he showed me a pure river of water of life, clear as crystal, proceeding out of the throne of God and of the Lamb. In the midst of the street of it, and on either side of the river, was there the tree of life, which bare twelve manner of fruits, and yielded her fruit every month: and the leaves of the tree were for the healing of the nations."

This river of life proceeds from the throne of God and of the Lamb. God only through Jesus Christ can give life to dead souls. There is none other name under heaven given among men whereby they can be saved. God and God only is the author of salvation. The tree of life is to furnish food to the saints, and the leaves are for the healing of the nations. This cannot be a description of heaven, for there is no need of healing there. Man lost his right to life by the transgression, and Jesus restores him to his lost inheritance. "You hath he quickened [made alive], who were dead in trespasses and sins." The blessed gospel of Jesus Christ, like the leaves of the tree of life, is for the healing of the nations.

"And there shall be no more curse: but the throne of God and of the Lamb shall be in it; and his servants shall serve him: and they shall see his face; and his name shall be in their foreheads. And there shall be no night there; and they need no candle, neither light of the sun; for the Lord God giveth them light: and they shall reign forever and ever."

The manifest presence of God and the Lamb in his Church shall be a guaranty from every curse. His people need fear nothing.

"Christ hath redeemed us from the curse of the law, being made a curse for us: for it is written, Cursed is every one that hangeth on a tree: that the blessing of Abraham might come on the Gentiles through Jesus Christ; that we might receive the promise of the Spirit through faith." (Gal. iii. 13, 14.)

"For the law of the Spirit of life in Christ Jesus hath made me free from the law of sin and death. For what the law could not do, in that it was weak through the flesh, God [did by] sending his own Son in the likeness of sinful flesh, and for sin, condemned sin in the flesh." (Rom. viii. 2, 3.)

No other sacrifice is needed to put away the curse, hence no more need of a temple, of typical sacrifices. The work has been done, "and there shall be no more curse."

"And his servants shall serve him." The grand work of spreading the gospel to the ends of the earth is committed to the hands of his servants. "And they shall see his face." Jesus has promised to be with his servants "even to the end of the world." His presence is always manifest to his faithful servants.

"And his name shall be in their foreheads." When one is baptized with water, the name of the "Father, Son, and Holy Ghost" is written upon the forehead. This is the outward sign of the inward baptism of the Holy Spirit, whereby we know ourselves as the children of God. Jesus is present with us in the person of the Holy Spirit, by which God's name is written on our foreheads. The work of Jesus performed by his servants is to be a continual service.

"And there shall be no night there." This is a symbol of the continued work of the Church.

"And they need no candle, neither light of the sun." It is "not by might, nor by power, but by my Spirit, saith the Lord of hosts." The work of salvation is accomplished through no earthly agency. Men are born of the spirit, and this promise of the divine presence and help is to extend to the end, for "they [the servants of God] shall reign forever and ever."

This closes the vision, and the angel closes by saying: "These sayings are faithful and true: and the Lord God of the holy prophets sent his angel to show unto his servants the things which must shortly be done. Behold, I come quickly: blessed is he that keepeth the sayings of the prophecy of this book."

These are the final remarks of the revealing angel, and he tells John plainly that he has shown his servants the things which must *shortly be done*, not things that are to transpire from one to two thousand years after. *Shortly* meant the same in the days of John that it means now, and the things that had been revealed would shortly be done. For instance, the destruction of Jerusalem took place in the year 67, just after the Revelation was written, and the destruction of Rome followed in about three years. When the Revelation began, the very first utterance is: "The Revelation of Jesus Christ, which God gave unto him, to show unto his servants *things which must shortly come to pass.*"

"Behold, I come quickly." This second coming of Christ to judge the two guilty nations, and to destroy them, was near at hand; and that his servants might know of it, and be ready when the signs pointed out should appear, to fly to a place of safety, Jesus Christ sent his angel to show unto them the things that must shortly be done. The warning note is sounded at the beginning, and when the grand panorama had passed in review, he again calls out to them: "Behold, I come quickly: blessed is he that keepeth the sayings of the prophecy of this book." In other words, take warning, and be ready when he shall come.

"And I John saw these things, and heard them. And when I had heard and seen, I fell down to worship before the feet of the angel which showed me these things. Then saith he unto me, See thou do it not: for I am thy fellow-servant, and of thy brethren the prophets, and of them which keep the sayings of this book: worship God."

No doubt John, deeply impressed with the appearance of the angel and the wonderful revelations he had made, mistook him for the Son of man, and fell at his feet to worship. But he is informed that he is but a fellow-servant of his, and not to be worshiped.

"And he saith unto me, Seal not the sayings of the prophecy of this book: for the time is at hand."

The things foretold in the prophecy of this book were so near at hand that John is commanded to leave it open; in other words, not to seal them. When Daniel prophesied, the revealing spirit told him to "shut thou up the vision; for it shall be for many days." (Dan. viii. 26.) And again: "Shut up the words, and seal the book, even to the time of the end." Why was he to seal his book? Because the time was long. There was not to be an immediate fulfillment—"it shall be for many days." But the time of the visions of John were at hand.

This clearly sets aside all those systems of interpretation of this book that spread the visions over centuries, even down to the present time. The Churches scarcely had time to read and to hear read the sayings of the prophecy of his book before the rider upon the white horse drew his sword and sounded the charge. John was to write the book, and send it at once to the seven Churches; and "blessed is he that readeth, and they that hear the words of this prophecy, and keep those things which are written therein: for the time is at hand." (Rev. i. 3.) So short was the time that there was no time for change of relations.

"He that is unjust, let him be unjust still: and he which is filthy, let him be filthy still: and he that is righteous, let him be righteous still: and he that is holy, let him be holy still. And, behold, I come quickly; and my reward is with me, to give every man according as his work shall be."

The revelation was not given that men might change their relation to God, for all had had the gospel preached unto them. It was given that his people might prepare for the coming calamities and seek a place of safety; which, as we have learned, they did, fleeing to Pella when Jerusalem was overthrown. They were also warned to come out of the devoted city of Rome when the judgments of Almighty God were about to fall upon it.

"I am Alpha and Omega, the beginning and the end, the first and the last."

Jesus would have his people know that he is the same that appeared in such splendor to John at the beginning. There he says: "I am Alpha and Omega, the beginning and the ending, saith the Lord, which is, and which was, and which is to come, the Almighty." (Rev. i. 8.)

"Blessed are they that do his commandments, that they may have right to the tree of life, and may enter in through the gates into the city. For without are dogs, and sorcerers, and whoremongers, and murderers, and idolaters, and whosoever loveth and maketh a lie."

The calamities that are coming are not intended for his people, those that keep his commandments. They are to still have a place in his Church, still to eat of the tree of life. He had promised in the beginning: "To him that overcometh will I give to eat of the tree of life, which is in the midst of the paradise of God." (Rev. ii. 7.)

He repeats the promises. They shall also have a place in the New Jerusalem, among the pure and holy; while without are dogs, and sorcerers, and all other abominable and unholy people.

"I Jesus have sent mine angel to testify unto you these things in the Churches. I am the root and the offspring of David, and the bright and morning star."

By this expression Jesus himself unites this revelation into one grand whole. It begins with letters to the Churches, and now he declares that he had "sent his angel to testify unto you these things in the Churches." This Jesus is the blessed Messiah of Jews and Christians. He is the "root and the offspring of David, and the bright and morning star." As dwellers in the New Jerusalem, or as members of his Church, they are now to go forth to work for the salvation of the world.

"And the Spirit and the bride say, Come. And let him that heareth say, Come. And let him that is athirst come. And whosoever will, let him take the water of life freely."

The Church, now freed from the incubus of the two great persecuting powers, is to offer life and salvation to every creature. The Spirit and the bride (the Spirit and the Church) give a cordial invitation, and cry, "Come." Any that hear are included, especially he that is athirst, and whosoever will can come to this river of life that flows out of the throne of God and of the Lamb. Blessed invitation! It is as wide as the world. It is the gospel of the Son of God.

"For I testify unto every man that heareth the words of the prophecy of this book, If any man shall add unto these things, God shall add unto him the plagues that are written in this book: and if any man shall take away from the words of the book of this prophecy, God shall take away his part out of the book of life, and out of the holy city, and from the things which are written in this book."

So much was dependent upon this revelation—especially the safety of his people in the midst of the awful calamities that were to befall the nations, and they were so intimately involved that the threats of this verse are spoken against him who shall alter in any particular the things that are written therein. It was a message from Jesus to his people, who were soon to witness such calamities as earth had never seen, and they must know just how and when to act. Either precipitancy or delay would be fatal. Hence the frequent warning: "He that hath an ear let him hear what the Spirit saith to the Churches."

"He which testifieth these things saith, Surely I come quickly: Amen. Even so, come, Lord Jesus. The grace of our Lord Jesus Christ be with you all. Amen."

Here again the warning of the speedy coming of Christ is given; and John, it would seem, adds, "Even so, come, Lord Jesus;" and then pronounces the benediction: "The grace of our Lord Jesus Christ be with you all. Amen."

CHAPTER XIV.

The Folly of Modern Adventism—Christ to Remain in Heaven to the Judgment—Mistakes of Modern Adventists.

THE idea that Jesus Christ will ever come in the flesh again to earth and reign for a thousand years, or for any period of time, is utterly fallacious and unworthy of our Saviour. Besides, the teachings of the Scriptures go solidly against it. And yet in almost every period of the world's history from the ascension of Christ to the present men have been expecting and predicting it. Even in the days of the Apostle Paul men were looking for the coming of Christ, and were troubling the Church with their views; and some of them did not scruple to write a letter in the name of Paul, setting forth their peculiar views, as we learn from an expression in Paul's Second Epistle to the Thessalonians (ii. 1, 2), in which he says: "Now we beseech you, brethren, by the coming of our Lord Jesus Christ, and by our gathering together unto him, that ye be not soon shaken in mind, or be troubled, neither by spirit, nor by word, *nor by letter as from us*, as that the day of Christ is at hand."

These men claimed to have a revelation from the Spirit on this subject. They preached it and, as we have said, forged a letter in the name of Paul, in which they made him to substantiate their

(313)

views. From that time to the present men have been urging these views upon the Church. They claim that Christ will come, that the righteous dead will be raised, and those that are looking for his coming will be gathered together unto him; that he will set up his throne somewhere, perhaps at Jerusalem, and will reign here on earth for a thousand years. This we say is utterly unworthy of Christ, and has not a particle of support from the Scripture.

Just before the death of Christ he said to his disciples: "It is expedient for you that I go away: for if I go not away, the Comforter will not come unto you; but if I depart, I will send him unto you."

While Jesus was here in the flesh his presence was restricted to a favored few. But few could see him; but few could hear him. It took time for him to go from place to place. His Church after his death was not to be confined to the narrow limits of Palestine, but it was to take in the world: "All nations shall serve him." Hence it was expedient that he go away; for upon his going depended the coming of the Spirit, whose presence was not to be limited by time or space. He was simply omnipresent, and of never-waning, never-wearying energy. He could be in every land and deal with every heart at once; and as the Christians were to be co-workers with Christ, the increase of the Church would only augment the power of the Spirit for the accomplishment of good.

The Kingdom and Comings of Christ. 315

We gather from this last conversation of Jesus with his disciples that his presence in heaven as an advocate with the Father was necessary, if not indispensable, to the presence of the Spirit upon earth. If he went not away, the Spirit would not come. And is not the presence of Jesus in heaven to-day as indispensable to the presence of the Spirit upon earth as at any time in the history of the world?

What folly to wish for Jesus in the flesh here on the earth! How many multiplied millions would never see him! And then, in comparison with the constant, *abiding* presence of the Spirit, how unsatisfactory it would be for the most favored one to catch a sight of him now and then, and hear but a word or two from his lips while crowded from his presence by the surging multitudes that would press upon him by night and by day! O it is a thousand times better for us to have Jesus praying for us in heaven than to have him reigning here on earth, even under the most favorable circumstances. But the Scriptures are very explicit on the fact that Christ's place is in heaven, and will be to the end of time. Peter, in preaching to the Jews, tells them that it had been predicted of Jesus that "the heavens must receive [him] until the time of the restitution of all things."

· We are taught that when Christ comes it will be to judge the world. In the First Epistle to the Thessalonians Paul tells us that "the Lord himself shall descend from heaven with a shout, with the voice of the archangel, and with the trump of God: and the dead in Christ shall rise first; then we which are alive and remain shall be caught up together with them in the clouds, to meet the Lord in the air: and so shall we ever be with the Lord." (1 Thess. iv. 16, 17.) Dead and living saints are to be caught up to meet the Lord in the clouds, and with him in heaven (not on earth) we are to live forever. "I go to prepare a place for you," said Jesus, "that where I am ye may be also."

This unscriptural doctrine of the coming of Christ to reign on earth has been a source of trouble wherever and whenever preached; and every age has produced men who have talked of and taught it, and simple-minded people have ever been found to believe it. Time and time again have men worked on the prophecies to prove when the Lord would come. Mistakes and disappointments never dampen their zeal, nor do they teach them wisdom. They set a time, and prove it to a fraction; and yet when the Lord fails to come at the time they have fixed, they set right to work to recast their calculations and to fix another time.

The close of the year 1000 was fixed as the time. Let us read what a writer says of it:

THE LAST DAY OF THE YEAR 1000.

It was believed in the middle ages that the world would come to an end at the expiration of one thousand years of the Christian era. This expectation in Christian countries was universal. The year 1,000 was a period of suspense, terror, and awe. The histories of this dark period give vivid accounts and incidents of the state of the people under the influence of this awful ap-

The Kingdom and Comings of Christ. 317

prehension. A writer in *Sunday at Home* reproduces the picture with much distinctness, and relates an incident of the manner that the hours were numbered on the supposed final night of the year, which might aptly suggest a dramatic subject for a poet:

When the last day of the year 1000 dawned, the madness had attained its height. All work of whatever kind was suspended. The market-places were deserted. The shops were shut. The tables were not spread for meals. The very household fires remained unlighted. Men, when they met in the streets, scarcely saw or spoke to one another. Their eyes had a wild stare in them, as though they expected every moment some terrible manifestation to take place.

Silence prevailed everywhere, except in the Churches, which were already thronged with eager devotees, who prostrated themselves before the shrines of their favorite saints, imploring their protection during the fearful scenes which they supposed were about to be displayed.

As the day wore on the number of those who sought admission grew greater and greater, until every corner of the sacred edifices, large as these were, was densely crowded, and it became impossible to find room for more. But the multitude outside still strove and clamored for admission, filling the porches and door-ways and climbing up the buttresses to find a refuge on the roofs which they could not obtain inside.

A strange and solemn commentary on the text which binds men to watch because "they know not whether the master of the house will come at even, or at midnight, or at the cock-crowing, or in the morning," was presented by the multitudes which filled the churches that night.

Watch in very truth they did. Not an eye was closed throughout that lengthened vigil; not a knee but was bent in humblest supplication; not a voice but joined the penitential chant, or put up a fervent entreaty for help and protection.

There were no clocks in those days, but the flight of the hours was marked by great waxen tapers, with metal balls attached at intervals to them. These fell, one after another, as the flames reached the strings by which they were secured, into a brazen basin beneath, with a clang which resounded through the church.

At the recurrence of each of these warning sounds the awe

of the vast assembly seemed to deepen and intensify, as each in terrible suspense supposed that between him and the outburst of divine wrath only the briefest interval now remained.

At last the night, long as it was, began to draw to an end. The chill which precedes daylight pervaded the air, and in the eastern sky the first pale gleam of morning began to show itself. The light grew stronger in the heavens, and the flame of the candles paled before it; and at last the rays of the risen sun streamed through the windows on the white and anxious faces of the watchers. The night had passed away. A new day, a new year, a new century had begun. The text that says that "no man knoweth the day nor the hour" had a new meaning.

Then in our own day we have had some experience in this line. About the year 1840 William Miller announced that Christ would come and set up his throne upon earth in October, 1843. He said that at this time the world would be burned up and cleansed by fire for the abode of the risen righteous.

These were the points made by Mr. Miller in working out his problem: "1. The little horn of Daniel viii. is the Roman papal power. 2. The 'daily sacrifice' which the little horn 'took away' (chap. viii. 11-13) was the pagan worship of idols in old Rome. 3. The papal power abolished this pagan idolatry in A.D. 508 or A.D. 538. 4. The 'sanctuary' which was 'cleansed' (chap. viii. 14) is this entire world, and its cleansing is to be by fire in 1843. Now, to find the exact time of this great conflagration and cleansing he called in the aid of chapter ix. 23-25."

We will not follow out all his reasoning and figuring, for its failure is the proof of its fallacy. He, with all others of his kind, takes the unscriptural,

The Kingdom and Comings of Christ. 319

untenable ground that a day stands for a year in prophecy.

The spirit in which these dupes of a delusion take their frequent disappointments, were it not so sad, would be amusing. Let me in conclusion give a single quotation from one of them who is rallying his brethren for one more waiting. In speaking of the "little book" given by the angel to John to be eaten by him, after quoting the passage, he says: "These are the directions given to the Church for their further movements, after their first disappointment; and, my brethren of the advent faith, I would not chide you; for you have eaten of this little book for the past forty years with a keen relish; ay, you have endured the bitter, too, which has followed, like heroes. If I could chide you, it would be in this: that you now refuse to eat more. The bitter has been *so bitter* (yet the sweet was truly as sweet as honey) and has been *so exhausting* (apparently) that many, very many, have decided that it is best *for the body* that we should eat no more. Truly the result of every morsel since taking the book from the angel has been bitterness. But, my brethren, if we are the people of God, there is just one step more for us to take, and only one. Hear it right from the lips of the same angel that told John to take the book from the hand of the first angel: '*And he said unto me, Thou must prophesy again* [What, again? Yes, again] before many peoples, and nations, and tongues, and kings.'"

Then, after making calculations, the author winds up by fixing on 1889 as the year, and says: "Why shall we not expect the Lord in 1889? The writer, while he lays claim to no worldly wisdom, and makes no pretensions as to being a prophet, yet has no doubt that the year 1889 will bring the event mentioned in the last verse of Daniel's prophecy, and means and expects to be ready."

So we see that no amount of disappointment can dampen the ardor or cloud the faith of these false interpreters of prophecy. Having accepted as true that Christ is to reign in the flesh on earth, nothing else will do them.

The doctrine, as taught by the "Second Adventists," that Christ is to reign in the flesh here on earth is entirely outside the Scripture. Peter tells us plainly that the "heavens must receive him until the times of restitution of all things." All who hold this doctrine disparage faith by their longing desire to see Christ come and inaugurate a system of work here on earth that shall be superior to that now in operation. But this will never be. When Christ shall come again—which he surely will—it will be "with a shout, with the voice of the archangel, and with the trump of God: and the dead in Christ shall rise first: then we which are alive and remain shall be caught up together with them in the clouds, to meet the Lord in the air: and so shall we ever be with the Lord [not on earth, but in heaven]. Amen."

www.ingramcontent.com/pod-product-compliance
Lightning Source LLC
Chambersburg PA
CBHW030016240426

43672CB00007B/974